outofprint   1250
                      DI

THE SUGARMILL

The
SUGARMILL

The Socioeconomic Complex
of Sugar in Cuba
1760-1860

MANUEL MORENO FRAGINALS

Translated by Cedric Belfrage

MONTHLY REVIEW PRESS / NEW YORK AND LONDON

Library of Congress Cataloging in Publication Data
Moreno Fraginals, Manuel.
  The sugarmill.
  Translation of El ingenio.
  Includes bibliographical references.
    1. Sugar trade—Cuba—History. 2. Sugar—Manufacture and refining—
Cuba—History. 3. Sugar machinery.
I. Title.
HD9114.C89M613   338.4'7'664122097291   73–90074
ISBN 0–85345–319–5

Originally published as *El Ingenio: el complejo económico social
cubano del azúcar,* by the Comision Nacional Cubana de la UNESCO,
copyright © 1964 by Manuel Moreno Fraginals.

First Printing

Monthly Review Press
62 West 14th Street, New York, N.Y. 10011
21 Theobalds Road, London, WC1X 8SL, England

Manufactured in the United States of America

To Raúl Cepero Bonilla, absent yet present:
these things we talked about for so many years

CONTENTS

Preface   9

Part 1: The Road to the Plantation

    From Trapiche to Sugarmill   15
    Factors of Growth   17
    The Sugarmill as Intellectual Adventure   30
    Large-Scale Manufacture in 1800   33
    The First Dance of the Millions   41

Part 2: The Crisis of the Superstructure

    Sugar Institutions   47
    Church and Sugarmill   51
    The Ideological Transformation   59

Part 3: Expansion and Transformation

    Sugar Opens Up the Island   65
    Along the Sugar Road   70
    The Death of the Forest   73

Part 4: A Technico-Economic Parenthesis

    Internal Data for the Sugarmill   81

Part 5: The Work

    Hands for Sale   131
    Life in the Mill   142

Notes   155

Index   179

PREFACE

A few introductory words to help the reader understand the aims, content, and methods of this book. I propose to analyze the main aspects of the historical development of Cuban sugar. I am concerned with sugar as the foundation of the semi-plantation economy established in the island for nearly two centuries; that is, as a basic element in Cuba's economic structure. And I propose to place this within the framework of the global production complex.

Sugar developed along with a series of social, political, religious, and other external phenomena that have generally been treated autonomously, without causal relation to the production structure. I aim, on the contrary, to follow the trails which start with sugar and surface in the founding of a university chair, in a decree on tithes, in a characteristic style of town mansion, or in the dire effects of deforestation and soil erosion. I undertook this investigation with the conviction that without an exhaustive study of the sugar economy, there is no possibility of interpreting Cuban history.

I began my studies of sugar some twenty years ago, and my first publication on the subject dates from that period: a modest article in the student vein entitled *Del esclavo al obrero asalariado* (From slave to wage-worker). Thus I started to compile the documentation I am now using. Later, teachers at the Colegio de México—and especially Silvio Zavala, whom I can never thank enough for what he did for me—taught me the techniques of historical research and of the handling of sources that I have continued to use. I have not, however, stuck to the canons of historical methodology in writing this book. For certain personal reasons I have used an unorthodox method.

For more than a decade I worked for big industrial concerns, Cuban and foreign, making economic investigations and sometimes personally directing sales, promotion, administration, or publicity departments. In the course of this work I studied such diverse things as buying and selling real estate, administering a lottery, setting up a chain of radio stations, certain Caribbean soft-drink markets, and the complexities of the Venezuelan beer business. *Practical* economic activity—and I stress the word *practical*—compelled me to learn more and more about the methodology of industrial and market research, and left me familiar with it. This had a dual effect upon me personally: I acquired a new profession and the ability to handle previously unknown tools, and at the same time had a valuable living experience. Direct contact with high bourgeois strata acquainted me from the inside with the cold bowels of the money world. I came to know—by traveling it—the tortuous road of perpetual cost reduction, of distribution, of warehousing and sales problems, of labor conflicts, and of the desperate effort to keep abreast of market trends.

My survival as an economic technician depended on the accuracy of my calculations. I spent ten years in a world which has always been barred to theoreticians, and which can only be assimilated by personal experience. The Revolution separated me from that world, setting me to tasks that were large in human content if small in importance. But living under the Revolution—a process something like daily decantation into a new bottle—has enabled me to write this book differently from the way I would have done it earlier. Returning to the study of history (which I never completely left), I blocked out the job as if I were embarking on a modern industrial investigation. My first goal would be to discover the precise flow of production of the typical sugarmill in each period after 1760 (the first year with solid data), and the minutiae of its problems of labor force, costs, production, volume and profitability of investment, supply, financing, warehousing, distribution, and markets. On this base I would build the first historical tabulation of the chief indices applicable to a sugarmill: cane cut per man, production per man, production per area sown, production per amount of cane cut and fuel used, production per peso invested in each sector, etc. I was confident that if I could bring these factors to the surface in various critical periods of our sugar-producing life (1760, 1792, 1814, 1832, 1848, 1857, 1868, 1884, and 1895), I would have torn off the dark curtain that covers Cuban history.

This task had to be complemented by another no less difficult one: to reconstruct Cuban sugar statistics—including those for molasses, *aguardiente,** and rum—from 1760 to 1963. Using Cuban statistics necessitated familiarity with world sugar statistics in order to fix Cuba's relative year-by-year position among consuming and exporting countries. Finally, I had to trace two centuries of sugar prices in the major markets, bearing in mind transportation problems and costs in each period and fiscal legislation in each country, to arrive at an exact understanding of competitive conditions in these markets.

Here, then, is the first volume of the project, covering some aspects of the process between 1760 and 1860. The politico-commercial aspects of this period, along with others up to the first U.S. intervention, appear in Volume 2. The third volume deals exclusively with the republican period. My historical explorations have been made possible by the individual and institutional help I have received under the revolutionary government. The analysis of the industry's technical evolution, for example, required sources which were once extremely hard to

* *Aguardiente* is the term used for strong liquor in general (from *agua ardiente,* burning water) or for liquor distilled from a specific agricultural product, in this case sugarcane. (Trans.)

come by in our libraries. As a result of the revolutionary process, many private bibliographical collections of rare value came into the possession of the Biblioteca Nacional, which quickly put them at the disposal of investigators. After carefully comparing the three great sugar bibliographies now in existence, I can say that in this area the resources of the Biblioteca Nacional are on a par with those of the Library of Congress in Washington or the British Museum. Furthermore—and this is most important—sugarmill ledgers, harvest and grinding reports, etc., from the end of the eighteenth century have become available, enabling me to study material to which my predecessors had no access.

Through bibliographical sources and manuscripts I have been able to reconstruct the world of the old eighteenth-century trapiches—the early mills—with their maximum production of 12,000 arrobas. In this Noel Deerr's great work, *History of Sugar*, was a splendid technological guide. But it was not enough to learn the theory; I needed to live the problem I was studying. I began this phase of the study, made possible by the extraordinary help of the Universidad Central at Las Villas, in 1960. The professors of the School of Agricultural and Livestock Sciences know how much this book owes to them. Thanks to constant consultations and the invaluable contribution of the university *compañeros,* I was able to verify the techniques of the past. The laboratory for the experiments was a surprising one: the raspadura (low-grade sugar) factories of Las Villas, which maintain essentially the same production processes as of old. Workers in these factories will remember the daily visit of the professor who spent long hours sampling syrups, checking procedures against data obtained from old books, taking measurements, photographing production apparatus (they still use open kettles from the old ruined sugarmills), and analyzing finished products. In Quemado Hilario, with an ox-propelled grinding mill and clay molds made for it in Camagüey, I produced a sugar clarified with guaiacum-tree sap and purged with applications of clay, which yielded two fifths of white, two of yellow, and one of *cucurucho* (tips). I still recall with some emotion how after the first failures I learned the correct technique thanks to a "sugarmaster," aged ninety-six, who had been a kettle-minder in a small mill at the end of the Ten Years War.

Bit by bit I brought back to life the forgotten

world of the primitive factories; and I was startled to note how the sugar terminology of the eighteenth century, which I thought to have been irretrievably lost, survived among these groups of workers. Hearing from old lips the sugar-usage of the words *bombón, sable, fondaje, canoa, coco,* I had a personal interview with the past. Advised by men of real knowledge in the field, personally studying modern sugar technology, taking advanced agricultural and industrial courses, I gradually mastered difficulties which at first had seemed insuperable.

Thus through practical experience and technological analysis; by scanning hundreds of technical books, harvest reports, and ledgers; by patiently examining the thousands of files in the Junta de Fomento collection; and—most important—through the constant help of data supplied by so many *compañeros,* I have put together this small contribution to Cuban historiography. Since my sources have often been as unconventional as my methods, it is natural that I should have reached other than conventional conclusions. For this I claim no personal merit; it is the logical result of traveling virgin territory where new panoramas come into view.

Without false modesty I present my work as a simple, incomplete one which will surely be excelled by sugar historians with more knowledge and better techniques. I have approached it without concern for polemics and without pretensions to a new and definitive interpretation of Cuban history. This is simply what I have been able to do up to now, and I have done it honestly, giving it the best that I have. I have sought to do an analytical, compact job of research because I think the Revolution needs basic studies firmly rooted in documentary sources. Thus far I have gone. I plead forgiveness if at times I put too much emotion into my sentences. I am not ashamed of it: passion is the noblest ingredient of history.

ACKNOWLEDGMENTS

In my book on José Antonio Saco I stated that any work of investigation is in the last analysis a work of collaboration. I have much more reason to say this now since, in its research aspect, this book which bears my name alone is a collective job. It is very hard to name all those who in one way or another contributed ideas and concrete data, offered suggestions, and helped me establish contact with the distant and ever living world of the past. However, there are some whom it would be unjust to omit.

I will always be grateful for the institutional help afforded me by the Universidad Central in Las Villas, and for the warmth which its rector, Silvio de la Torre Grovas, always accorded to my efforts. Equally, I want to put on record the invaluable daily collaboration of *compañeros* professors Emilio Planas, Sergio Mayea, Rafael Guerra, Arnoldo Guardarrama, Omar Díaz de Arce, José Saínz Triana, and Fernando Matiñán.

Many persons in Havana collaborated intimately in these sugar researches. I took full advantage of the work done by the Institute of Ethnology and Folklore. Among other things, they gave me the data about the sugarmills of 1826 shown on Vives' map. I worked with them on a collective investigation of life in the slaves' barracoon. I also had access to the splendid sugar chronology which they are preparing. The group of investigators there, under the direction of Argeliers León and Isaac Barreal, is a fine example of what can be achieved when work is systematized and scientifically disciplined.

I have mentioned a small part of the services given me by the Biblioteca Nacional. Acknowledgments are due to the director, María Teresa Freyre, to the sub-director, María Iglesias, and to *compañero* Israel Echeverría. My gratitude also to the *compañeros* of the Colección Cubana: Amalia Rodríguez, Amelia Plascencia, Zoila Lapique, Eudoxia Lage, Juana Zurbarán, María Luisa Antuña, Teresita Batista, and Feliciana Menocal.

In the Archivo Nacional I obtained invaluable help, including the compilation of Cuban sugar patents made by *compañera* Violeta Serrano under the direction of Dr. Julio Le Riverend Brusone.

Among specialized libraries I should mention those of the Empresa Consolidada del Azúcar, directed by Roberto Guardiola, and of the Asociación de Técnicos Azucareros, where I was personally attended to by *compañero* Ariel Cañete.

The big British firm Fawcett, Preston & Co. sent me all the documentation it had on Cuba, including data on the first steam engine successfully used in a Cuban sugarmill.

I must omit many other *compañeros,* but wish to make special mention of four. First, José Luciano

Franco, that young investigator who has spent half a century studying our history. Working across from me for two years, he kept passing to me—along with his cigarettes—any mention of sugar he came upon; he lent me books and answered more than one request a day for information. The help of Juan Pérez de la Riva was so unstinting that I don't know if some parts of this book are his or mine. Virgilio Perera did a complete revision of the manuscript, corrected calculations, and introduced facts and observations. Finally, I want to speak of the prodigious memory of my father, for many years a sugarmill administrator and technician in the international sugar business. To him I owe not only much technical data, but also traditions handed down by word of mouth that were already old when he—a born folklorist—collected them in his childhood.

To all of them, and to the many I have not mentioned, many thanks.

—Manuel Moreno Fraginals

Havana, January 1964

1
THE ROAD TO THE PLANTATION
(1763–1802)

. . . for the time when the wealth of the island will multiply and it will have five or six hundred thousand Africans within its shores. I speak now for that future time . . .

—*Francisco de Arango y Parreño*

FROM TRAPICHE TO SUGARMILL*

The name the English gave to the Antilles was specific: "Sugar Islands"—a geographical label with an economic, mercantile flavor as distinct as it was apt; for while these islands produced much other merchandise, such as coffee, cacao, and indigo, it was sugar that gave them their definitive character. Yet Cuba, despite being the largest of the islands, remained outside the plantation economy until the middle of the eighteenth century. Nor was this—as historian Francisco de Arango y Parreño erroneously stated, and all historians later repeated—because the island was backward in developing sugar. It was simply that sugar was then but one factor in its economic life, and thus not decisive in its destiny.

When the English took Havana in 1762 they found nearly one hundred sugarmills in that province alone, with a total production approaching 500,000 arrobas.[1] ** These mills belonged to Cuba's small but aggressive oligarchy which, displaced from tobacco by the Factoría, the royal trading agency, found in sugar a new road to economic power. They were the result of indigenous efforts in the island and had been established in contempt of colonial laws. Since they constituted an extra-legal world, officially they did not produce sugar: Arango y Parreño, basing himself on documents of the Real Compañía de La Habana, could thus state that our maximum sugar

exports before 1763 amounted to only 20,000 arrobas —roughly 1,300 boxes—carried by two or three ships a year.[2] In this, as in much else, Arango consciously lied. All Cuban history of the end of the eighteenth and beginning of the nineteenth centuries was invented by him to serve class interests.

The Havana oligarchy jumped all obstacles to start their sugarmills, and by mid-century they had broadened their activity in response to an ever expanding market with prices running extremely high. The production process posed few problems from a technical standpoint. Hardly any machinery existed in the mills except the grinding apparatus worked by animal power. In fact, the only real problem was labor. The number of slaves decided the volume of production and the yield was measured in arrobas per Negro. The growth of sugar manufacturing was determined by the ability to employ labor on a grand scale. In other words, *sugar development depended on the slave trade.* The installed capacity of the nearly one hundred mills operating in 1761 allowed for an extraordinary growth of production simply by adding more hands.

With the English occupation, the plantation concept of the British Antillean colonies—which, as we have seen, was nothing so exotic for our oligarchy—took root in our island. Creole society was ready for the sugar adventure. The Englishman freed the Creole from the yoke of the Cádiz merchants, did away with the extra-legal situation which had raised production costs and impeded mercantile operations and plantation development, and restored ancient municipal privileges. Thus

---

* The trapiche was both the early cane-grinding machine and the mill itself. Here we have generally used "trapiche" to describe the mill and "grinding mill" to describe the machine. (Trans.)

** An arroba is a Cuban weight of 25.36 pounds. (Trans.)

15

Cuban sugar producers look back on that moment as an aurora borealis of liberty[3]—especially with regard to the slave trade, which was a fundamental necessity. For the first time the Creole oligarchy negotiated directly with the English slaver. In former days slaves brought by the Real Compañia Inglesa were sold through Spanish merchants or such usurious and rapacious middlemen as Richard O'Farrill, Cornelio Coppinger, Villanueva Pico, and Daniel Goy. Under English domination the Liverpool merchant brought his Negroes from his Jamaica depots for direct sale in Havana. The Cuban *hacendado* was doubly favored because saturation of the English Antilles had lowered the price of slaves, now for sale not merely cheap but subsidized. Under existing conditions it took several years of clearing ground, sowing cane, and erecting brick-kilns, buildings, and a grinding mill to develop a sugarmill. Since the British occupation only lasted eleven months, and since after that Cuban production rose unprecedentedly, this growth must have originated with the introduction of slaves.

One understands why Arango calls this year "a happy time." The happiness of the *hacendados* was the tragedy of the toiling classes. As an indication of what was to follow years later, the barbarities of slavery broke out again in a colony which until then, as the English said themselves, had been the most humane in the Antilles.[4] And documents tell us how blacks and mulattoes—slaves or freedmen—fled in terror from the conquered city to which the invader brought his murderous work regime and his master-race prejudices. Even many years later official steps had to be taken to get back "the smart niggers who made themselves scarce during the war with the English." We also find in this period the disappearance of the last Cuban sugarmill belonging to a mulatto family: Rosenda de Neyra's Nuestra Señora de la Candelaria.[5]

The owners of the sugarmills of 1761 have the same surnames as those who plastered themselves with noble titles over the next fifty years: Herrera, Garro, Santa Cruz, Montalvo, Cárdenas, Peñalver, O'Farrill, Armenteros, Arango. They formed one family in the feudal sense of the word, carefully forging links with each other, economically calculating each marriage so that accumulated fortunes would not be dispersed and hereditary offices would remain within the original nucleus. They had in their

hands the Cabildo* and control of the local Church. And to this complex of power—decisive in itself for the extra-legal economic development we have noted—must be added favorable objective conditions.

To make the island a great sugar producer four objective conditions were necessary. First, fertile lands close to seaports. Second, forests yielding high-quality lumber for the grinding mills, carts, and buildings, and enough firewood for the boilers. Third, abundant cattle to feed the slaves and haul the grinding mills and carts. Fourth, work implements. The Havana oligarchy had lands covered with rich forests, and although the cutting of these was limited by royal ordinances, it was already almost a tradition to disobey the laws. There was also substantial cattle-raising, partly stimulated by the growth of sugar production in the Sugar Islands. It is odd to note how Cuban historians have insisted on the abundance of cattle in this period and the contraband trade in hides, but have omitted to mention that this contraband was based on the sugar of the Antilles.[6] For over a century oxen and cured meat moved from our southern coast to Jamaica and Haiti, where they hauled grinding mills and fed slaves. Until 1730 cured meat was a basic export from the island. Here, then, it was simply a question of Cuban producers consuming themselves what they had formerly exported.

Nor was the fourth objective condition—work implements—any problem. These, lacking mechanical complexity, were made in Havana or easily imported. We must bear in mind that Havana was a large fortified city with plenty of artisans, an important foundry, and the first shipyard in the Americas. In a place where warships and cannons were made, the construction of wooden grinding mills, kettles, and skimming pans was easy. One of the main causes of the Havana shipyards' decline was precisely the continuing exodus of qualified labor from the city to the sugarmills.

All this clearly and logically explains the Cuban sugar boom of the second half of the eighteenth century, which idealist historians have tried to attribute to the "rediscovery of the island by the English," the "benevolent despotism of Charles III's policies," "good government," or the "ideas of the

---

* The Cabildo was the administrative council of a town or province—in this case Havana. (Trans.)

period." To assess the role of the English in this process one must consider that in eleven months they introduced as many blacks as would normally have entered in twelve or fifteen years. This labor force could not have been immediately absorbed if the production capacity had not already been in existence; thus the real importance of the English was in enormously accelerating an inevitable historical process. Introducing five to ten thousand slaves, putting all installed capacity into production, forging strong economic links and opening up large credits that had to be respected after the evacuation, the English broke the productive equilibrium of the island in a single year.

What happened in our history after that is known to all Cubans, only it has always been explained upside down. The Havana sugarmills, with their new slaves, were able to boost annual production to perhaps a million arrobas. In the second half of the eighteenth century the average price of this sugar was over 14 reales and often more than 20.[7] We must conclude that we are dealing with a subjugating force of many millions of reales, which explains, in cold cash, the "magnanimous government" of Charles III.

FACTORS OF GROWTH

The labor force

Between 1763 and 1792 all the factors braking Cuban sugar development were eliminated and the island was transformed into the top world producer. Sugarmill towers broke into our fields and became part of the scenery. The renovating tidal wave shook up the little trapiches and the sugar invasion began, cutting down virgin forests and covering those fertile lands most accessible to seaports. The integrating process of large-scale manufacture was born.

It must be emphasized that the tremendous advance of sugar in the eighteenth century's second half went hand in hand with extremely high prices, which were maintained for over sixty years. In 1748 sugar was quoted at 18 and 12 reales in the port of Havana, in 1760 at 16 and 12.* With very slight

variations these averages were sustained until the French Revolution when the market, distorted by the ruin of Haiti, rose to fabulous highs of 40 and 36—to return to the normal level of 16 and 13½ at the end of the century. Only in the years 1787–1790 was there a minor fall to a low of 12 and 9½, a price still extraordinarily profitable but bewailed by *hacendados* as meaning "imminent ruin."

Under the stimulus of high prices, Creole sugarmen extended production and invaded the world market, where capitalism reigned, causing a commercial expansion which in turn helped to do away with the old production structure. In all this there is an intricate economic complex which has not been properly studied and which differs from that of other colonies. Step by step we have been able to arrive at an elementary analysis. England was first of all European countries in capitalist development. Its specific characteristics enabled it to evolve rapidly, giving definitive "big plantation" form to the sugar-production process that Spain had initiated in the Antilles. France followed suit almost immediately. Thus sugar received and gave a strong thrust in the development of capital: it was essentially a big motor that accelerated English industrial growth, complementing and increasing it. The English fleet found its most productive employment in the triangular trade. Many English inventors and manufacturers depended substantially on sugar and the slave trade. And the Sugar Islands were important to the fast growth of England's thirteen American colonies.[8]

In Cuba the process worked in reverse. Here the development was not imposed by the metropolis, but was born of the effort of the colony itself. Of course, it was not spontaneous, but was the result of an economic current communicated to Cubans in their contacts with the other Antilles. Sugar, along with other contraband products, had a revitalizing influence. Thus the direct relations between English and Cubans during the occupation of Havana brought the previously gestating process to a head. When the Creole oligarchs were thrown into a world

* Until around 1860 sugar prices were quoted in this form. The first figure indicates the price of an arroba of purged white sugar, the second refers to brown sugar. When pressure on refiners necessitated almost exclusive production of second-grade

sugar, the quotation was made in reverse; that is, the first number referred to brown and the second to white. In any case, no confusion is possible since the larger figure always refers to white.

To interpret these figures correctly it should be borne in mind that 10 and 8 were considered very profitable prices.

market where capitalist forms of production prevailed, and where the need to find foreign outlets for merchandise took primacy over all else, the work system which had been developing in primitive form suffered a profound change. The relatively patriarchal type of slavery, maintained as long as production was limited by the special conditions of the period, was replaced by intensive exploitation of the Negro. Now it was no longer a matter of extracting a certain quantity of useful products from him, but of producing surplus value for its own sake.[9]

With the opening of the door of the world market, an ever increasing output—and its corollary, ever lengthening work days—became an inherent necessity for Cuban producers. Volume and work-intensity rose, to the detriment of small producers; bigger and bigger production units came into being in a growth that was not organic but conglomerative. The usual way of classifying this new type of relationship is to identify it with wage-labor "cooperation." But Marx has clearly shown how in modern colonies the application of cooperation rests on a regime of despotism and servitude which is almost always a slave regime.[10] In this it differs from the capitalist form, which from the outset presupposes the existence of free wage-workers who sell their labor to capital. We are dealing with a quantitative change in an agricultural industry, where the relatively large labor force revolutionizes the objective conditions of the work process, although the system as such does not change. Its form is that of a production mechanism whose parts are human beings. The operation retains its manual character, depending on the strength, skill, speed, and assurance of the individual worker in handling his implement.

Thus what is characteristic in the transformation we see in Cuba, with the extravagant growth of this cooperation, is its quantitativeness. Just as there is no change in the work regime, there is no technical mutation. Growth is on the basis of more canefields, more woodcutting, more kettles, more molds, more carts, more oxen; but all this without altering previous patterns, apart from submitting the Negro to an ever more bestial way of life, reducing his useful years to an incredible extent. A new world is created which adds to the barbarism of slavery the civilized torments of overwork.[11] This characteristic method of extending sugar production in turn has repercussions on the whole colonial society and, as it develops, absorbs a large part of the energy once given to other activities.

Intensive and extensive exploitation of the Negro made him a costly raw material and required an urgent and expanding process of replacement. To the slaves needed for starting and expanding the factories must be added those daily devoured by the work. Sugar and Negroes grew alongside one another: this was the great contradiction undermining Cuba's whole system of production. Two essential premises of the capitalist system were present in the new sugar enterprises: the production and circulation of commodities. But the fundamental base was lacking: the wage-worker. Thus we have the slave system, but slavery for the production of commodities destined for the world market. It differed from the capitalist production system not only in the form in which killing work hours were imposed, but also in the impossibility of constantly revolutionizing production methods, an inherent part of capitalism.

From the end of the sixteenth century we find sugarmills in the Spanish Antilles with a work force of one hundred slaves and a production capacity of 10,000 arrobas (115 tons) per harvest and grinding season—that is, a yield of 100 arrobas per Negro, which was the Cuban average maintained up to the beginning of the nineteenth century. Here is the most palpable and definitive proof of the impossibility of technologizing production on the basis of slave labor—a fact made tragically clear by Cuban sugar enterprises. Thus there arose a type of economic entrepreneur who was characterized by his employment of slaves and his wealth based on slavery, but who fully realized that slavery was at the same time the great brake, the chain shackling him to the past and preventing the leap into full capitalism. A castrated, impotent semi-bourgeois, with merchandise and market like the revolutionary bourgeois who intellectually inspired him, but self-contradictorily forced to chain himself to the past in order to survive. Their subconscious frustration made these men who tried to use up in one great effort all that the future could not offer them.

Slavery was defeated in all the mainland areas possessing indigenous populations who sold their work for a pittance. In Mexico, the Real Compañía Inglesa's agents recognized early in the eighteenth century the impossibility of doing important business—for there the pauperized mass of the free population competed below the cost of maintaining a slave.[12] But in Cuba and other depopulated Caribbean islands, black slaves were the cheapest and quickest solution to the sugar production process. During the eighteenth century our burgeoning sugarocracy tried to obtain them in two ways: from established English slavers, or through slave-trading concerns created by the sugar producers themselves. In the first case they made direct use of existing channels—for instance, Baker & Dawson—or acted indirectly, as in the contracts of Coppinger and Uriarte. In the second case the *hacendados'* direct slave-trading projects failed for many years: they lacked the refined techniques at which the English and Danes were so adept. Projects multiplied, however, under the spur of double profits from slaves and sugar, and such respectable slaving companies were born as that sponsored in 1778 by the Marquis de Cárdenas de Monte-Hermoso, the Counts de Gibacoa, Lagunillas, and Vallellano, and representatives of the Belén and San Francisco monasteries.[13] But slaving was a complicated business and twenty years passed before the first successful Cuban expedition—on September 18, 1798, when a cargo of 123 blacks brought directly from Senegal by Luis Beltrán Gonet arrived at Havana. That was a day of festivities and rejoicing at the Real Consulado,* whose council foregathered to congratulate the triumphant entrepreneur.[14] At last the national slave trade, destined in the end to devour its own parents, had taken shape.

How many blacks were brought to Cuba in the eighteenth century we do not know. For sugar production alone, excluding those used for other purposes, it is easy to calculate that the average between 1765 and 1790 was about two thousand slaves a year. This figure does not coincide with official estimates: just as the sugar statistics are fraudulent, so are those of the slave trade. As an indication of the trade's profitability, we have the Real Compañía de La Habana, whose first deal garnered from the transaction alone—that is, without risking any money or contributing any work—a profit of 133,371 pesos, equivalent to 10 percent of the contract. And this profit was considered "the

most contemptible that could be imagined in an American deal of this sort." [15]

Independent of the activity of official, authorized slave traders like Cornelio Coppinger, Villanueva Pico, Daniel Goy, Uriarte, etc., there was a regular trade in slaves with the big English dealers through their agents. The presence of these agents in Cuba, even when their activity was totally prohibited, is a proven fact. Agustín Cramer was one of these who combined his engineer's profession with the more lucrative trade in blacks. Philip Allwood—representative of Baker & Dawson, the pride of Liverpool—was trading massively with our *hacendados* well before the official agreement between that firm and the Crown. Yet despite all this official or unofficial activity, the number of blacks brought to Cuba fell short of the urgent needs of sugar development. In its explosive awakening the sugarocracy was dominated by avarice and boundless ambition to become wealthy. In the decade of 1780 *hacendados* and speculators made disreputable scenes with the arrival of each slave ship, to a point where an agreement—contained in a proclamation made by Capitán General Ezpeleta on November 10, 1786—had to be made between the big oligarchs and the governor. It was thus hoped to avoid the "confusion and disorder" manifested at sales, and above all to put the black merchandise in the hands of the richest citizens, who could put "cash down." [16]

From then on intellectual spokesmen for the nascent sugarocracy identified the colony's felicity with the introduction of blacks. This is the first thought appearing in the first known writings of Arango. Sugar-slaver pressure was so strong as to break all legal bonds, and just as it had destroyed the monopoly of Cádiz and Seville in the 1760s, it now removed the brakes from the black traffic. Between January 28, 1789, and April 12, 1798, eleven royal cedulas, orders, and decrees were issued freeing and giving momentum to the great Spanish-Cuban slave trade.[17]

Although the slave was the key to the solution of the sugar-labor problem, the wage-worker also played an important role in this stage of rapid growth: he participated actively in production in the last decades of the eighteenth century, and this would be repeated again after 1850. In its dramatic upsurge the sugarmill absorbed all the small peasantry raising tobacco and minor crops, the shipyard

---

* See pp. 47–51 for a discussion of this institution. (Trans.)

and foundry workers, and innumerable other small artisans. It is on record how the growing white populations of Güines, Santiago, and Bejucal were either drawn into the sugarmills by the high wages or forced into them by the destructive violence of the sugar producers. Tree felling and ground clearing, construction of buildings, brick-kiln tasks, all the technical direction, and even much of the cane cutting and carting were the work of free laborers who functioned alongside slaves. Always—even in the periods of greatest slave-barbarism—piece-work contracts were made with free laborers. This coexistence of two different work regimes within the same production unit predictably created complex problems in human relations, but it could never be altogether eliminated: the prodigious expansion of the sugarmills meant a large and constant labor shortage.

On the foundation of slavery there grew a deformed industry whose "yield point," in its marginal cost curve, was a unit of three hundred slaves. Yet until the first twenty years of the nineteenth century, it could not achieve that number. The average number of serviceable slaves per mill in the last decade of the eighteenth century was below eighty—hence the enormous importance of the wage-worker. And this despite the emergence in that period of the first production "monsters," such as La Ninfa mill, which had 350 slaves acquired by Francisco de Arango y Parreño and Intendente Pablo José Valiente through the filching of public moneys.

The land

Sugar expansion produced a growing need for new lands and a standard method of occupying them. The first requirement was sites for new mills; second, places to which old ones could be moved; and third, ways to enlarge the remainder. The establishment of new mills was the logical result of the rise in production, taking advantage of rising prices as the market grew and competition fell. For the same reason, the owners of mills on "exhausted soil" sought new land. In this sense the old-time mill was a nomadic entity. Intensive and uncontrolled cultivation reduced soil fertility, causing an annual fall in cane production. With but one variety of cane (Creole) being sown, and with primitive methods transforming only 2–3 percent of processed cane

(industrial yield) into sugar, it was necessary to cultivate only exceptionally fertile land. Furthermore, until the end of the eighteenth century, and to a great extent up until the middle of the nineteenth, the mills used firewood as basic fuel, and each boiler had its own furnace. This whole irrational system led to the abandonment of land—sometimes because of low productivity, sometimes because, although it still yielded well in cane, deforestation had lengthened the distance from the firewood supply and the long hauls swelled production costs. In the worst cases both factors were present—impoverishment of the soil and razing of forests. Until the end of the eighteenth century the maximum life of a mill was estimated at forty years. If we add to this the disappearance of the old trapiche as it gave way to really important factories, we see that the problem was not merely one of more land for more mills, but also one of more land for each mill.

We have already shown how the new sugar producers based their calculations on four factors: forest, cattle, savanna, seaport. The Havana area fully filled these physical requirements. The island's narrowness there put every mill near an embarkation point—north or south—reducing the long, costly, and difficult transport to the sea. The lack of large-scale sugar development and the old forestal laws had preserved enough timber for buildings and fuel. Enough cattle was already raised to feed a city that ate meat daily, leaving plenty to haul trapiches and carts. Socioeconomic factors were equally favorable. Havana was the port favored by all colonial legislation, the area of greatest demographic development in the island, and the commercial center par excellence. The city had a high concentration of capital and a wide influence. Previous tobacco cultivation had traced roads into the countryside and created rural nuclei. It was the logical area for the first expansion of sugar.

The initial phases of expansion are hard to follow in detail. First, we have to estimate the average land area occupied by each mill. Contemporary writings include under the heading "sugarmills" both diminutive ones with five to ten slaves and others with one hundred or more. On the basis of reasonably reliable figures, we can calculate that a cane area of some 320 caballerías* was cut in the last normal harvest before

* A caballería was a Cuban measure equal to 13.4 hectares or 33.16 acres. (Trans.)

20

the English seized Havana. In 1792 the total amount of land occupied by Havana sugarmills exceeded 5,000 caballerías.* Thus the average area for each mill was from 10 to 12 caballerías in 1762 and about 22 in 1792. In the process of expanding its productive capacity, the sugarmill had doubled its occupation of land.[18]

This physical occupation of barely populated lands produced a formidable social problem and an abrupt break in the system of land-ownership legislation. The self-granted land grants, entailed estates, and positions gained through use of municipal governing powers made the Havana oligarchy a class of landlords without peasants, masters without servants, semi-proprietors of forests they were legally forbidden to cut. With a feudal superstructure inherited from Spain, they lacked feudal relations of production. Seigniors retaining only the agrarian base of European seigniory, they had no vassals to exploit and to provide them with surplus value in the form of feudal land rents. The feudal trappings of a non-feudal economic reality have led our historians into the most curious errors.[19]

It is symptomatic that prior to the sovereignty of sugar these oligarchs measured their possessions by the "flat league." We still read in 1792 of the Count de Casa-Montalvo as lord of fifty leagues of land—that is, 5,500 caballerías. This does not mean that these men were therefore *latifundistas*. The word latifundio had no meaning in an underpopulated colony where land ownership was a mere statutory right entered in the books, carrying with it no special social status determined by the produce of the soil. Property is only the external aspect of the latifundio. Socioeconomic attributes are necessary for its real existence: the land as means of production and social nucleus. In sum, the latifundio is not a quantitative concept—the amount of land owned—but one of economic relations. There can be no latifundio in sparsely populated colonies, especially when the underpopulation is in no way a consequence of the land system. The sugar industry, with its violent occupation and populating of lands, established the conditions which transformed juridical power into economic relations, producing the tragic dimension

of the latifundio. This began when the irrepressible advance of the sugarmills gave rise on a large scale to the conflicts tobacco had initiated years earlier. Thus the sugarmill, with its continuous appetite for land, transformed the ancient land rights of the Indies into effective juridico-bourgeois relations at the service of sugar-producing forces.

The system of capitalist production itself created the appropriate form of property in land: "It first creates for itself the form required by subordinating agriculture to capital. It thus transforms feudal landed property, clan property, small-peasant property in mark communes—no matter how divergent their juristic forms may be—into the economic form corresponding to the requirements of this mode of production." [20] This process, noted by Marx, was sometimes less visible in the European countries than in Cuba, where in only twenty years of sugar expansion the whole juridical system based completely on feudal-type grants, forestal laws, and entailed estates was liquidated. The accelerated legal process can be followed step by step in the voluminous file on "natural tobacco lands," started by the Real Consulado in 1796 under the aegis of the Laws of the Indies and ending in 1830 with quotations from Adam Smith.[21]

Small tobacco planters were the first to feel the brutal impact of sugar expansion. Their lands were the logical ones for immediate occupation: fertile, naturally irrigated, sufficiently cleared to be ready for immediate cane planting, and with enough nearby forests to keep the furnaces blazing. They were well situated, with ready-made roads to seaports—for tobacco too was an export product. And lastly, they were in the only populated areas which could provide wage-workers for the mills. Thus sugar would root its extended dominion in ground formerly dedicated to tobacco.

The Havana oligarchy of the second half of the eighteenth century, to whom the Factoría had closed all avenues of economic expansion via tobacco, had a resentful and scornful attitude toward that plant. Arango mentions tobacco as a business engaged in by his grandfather, who also had sugarmills. For him tobacco planters were miserable *pejugaleros* (outservants), and he prided himself on the fact that his rich compatriots neither owed their fortunes to tobacco, nor crossed the threshold of the Factoría.[22] The Marquis de Cárdenas de Monte-Hermoso speaks

* The "Havana zone" at the time extended westward to Bahía Honda.

disparagingly of tobacco planting as a pursuit of the lower orders.[23] This leaves no doubt that tobacco was an important economic mainstay of a large number of free peasants whose roots were in the soil.

In the thinly populated Cuban countryside tobacco growers were a type of peasant almost impossible to reduce to submission. Evicted from one place, they usually had a nearby fertile spot to move to, and the landlord's proprietorial rights lacked effectiveness when no coercive force existed to back them up. The municipal hierarchy did its utmost to convert these people into serfs, and in the mid-eighteenth century we find a proposal by various councilmen, including Martín Calvo de la Puerta, for the expulsion of tobacco growers from areas suitable for pasture—thus leaving them without land—except when their work was being done for a landlord.

But the Crown was interested in the high profits of tobacco and protected the growers' rights to raise it in natural tobacco lands. There then began the process of controlling the tobacco business, which was repeated on five occasions: in 1701, when the royal commissioners started to buy tobacco; in 1711, when the Factoría was established; in 1724, when the first direct contracts were made with the tobacco growers; in 1740, when the Real Compañía de Comercio was founded; and in 1760, when the Real Factoría became the exclusive buyer.

We find the Real Factoría facing from the outset the same knotty problem of a labor force that we observed in the sugarmill. There was no other solution but to protect the tobacco growers' right to their land against the cattle-sugar interests of the oligarchy. Later it was necessary to grant new lands, offer subsidies, and become a reliable buyer in order to encourage the small producer on whom the tobacco crop necessarily depended. Thus the much-maligned Factoría not only curtailed the oligarchic powers of the gentlemen of the Cabildo, but laid the foundations for the small, free rural class that was slowly populating the Havana countryside. This of course dealt a terrible blow to the business of the rich *hacendados*—hence Arango's hatred of the Factoría—and prevented the formation of an economic upper class based on tobacco. These policies created a nucleus of some ten thousand small farmers who in one harvest alone delivered 340,984 arrobas of tobacco. Since these policies had no basis in existing law, only in interpretations of the Real Cédula of

1659 * and in the Factoría's coercive powers, the tobacco growers kept their lands with no specific titles. The oligarchic beneficiaries of self-granted grants interpreted the physical possession as real proprietorship, which cut into their rights without giving them rents or indirect benefits—hence the sugar producers' hatred and scorn for this small peasant class. And thus the expulsion of the tobacco growers from their land had a triple significance for the sugarocracy: it was a solution to the problem of land needed for the expansion of sugar; it restored property rights which they saw as having been usurped; and it liquidated a peasant class which, forced into the sugarmills, helped solve the labor problem. If we add to all this the political objective of liquidating the Factoría and taking over the tobacco business, we can understand the bloodthirsty fury with which the nascent sugarocracy seized tobacco lands.

Until the end of the eighteenth century, and especially after the collapse of Haitian sugar, the plunder of the tobacco lands proceeded through the valleys of Jaruco to San Felipe and Santiago, through Managua and Calabazar, achieving its height of shamelessness in Güines. San Julián de los Güines grew up around a group of peasant families who had settled there in the last third of the eighteenth century. With its fertile soil and natural irrigation by the Río Mayabeque, Güines became the most important agricultural center of the Havana area. The Havana-Güines road, created by tobacco and lumber production, was a basic artery for internal traffic. The Factoría found in Güines the best tobacco-growing soil and it quickly became the number one zone for producing all types of tobacco. But it was also the best soil for sugar, and green canefields began to stipple the area.

The decisive penetration of Güines by Havana sugar enterprises began around 1784. At that time only four small trapiches existed there, belonging to Sebastián de la Cruz, Santiago Garro, Juan de Alonso Rodríguez, and Mauricio Landrón.[24] While these were of little importance in the muscular world of sugar, the same was not true for the owners of plantations under construction—Juan Tomás de Sola, Luis Peñalver, and Miguel de Armenteros. The price

* A Real Cédula is a letters patent, certificate, or other order issued by the King. (Trans.)

of Güines land grew daily, and with it the pressure on tobacco growers. The crucial year was 1792. The Haitian disaster produced the most prodigious increase in sugar prices in history, and, inspired by visions of astronomic profits, the Havana oligarchy assumed governmental prerogatives and threw restraint to the winds in the plunder of tobacco lands. The Factoría had an established practice of burning so-called spoiled tobacco. Using corrupt officials to take advantage of this, Havana sugarmen put thousands of arrobas to flame and ruined the small Güines tobacco planters. It was no coincidence that both sugar prices and tobacco burnings reached their peak in that same year.[25] Arango, the Havana oligarchy's intellectual spokesman and the great apologist for these depredations, tried to paint them in patriotic colors. He writes of a José de Coca who, "disgusted by the burnings, set fire with his own hand, in a single morning, to the eleven best tobacco fields in the area." [26] Arango's text suggests that de Coca, brought to the verge of despair by the Factoría, burned up in a morning the fruit of his own toil—a view which has been solemnly echoed by historians up to our times. But what happened was something else: The eleven best tobacco fields burned by de Coca were not his but belonged to the tobacco growers. On the smoking ruins of these fields and sheds, cane was sown and a mill erected: Nuestra Señora de las Mercedes. Its proprietor: José de Coca.

Naturally none of this could have occurred without total official support and effective control by the public authorities. The support was enlisted by bribery. In the last decade of the eighteenth century, the two key administrators sent from Spain were the most rapacious the colony ever knew: Luis de Las Casas, Governor, and José Pablo Valiente, the Intendente, or administrator of the Treasury. The Havana oligarchy's bribe to the former was a sugar estate located in Güines itself, which with contempt for minimal decorum was christened Friendship.[27] A frontman named Joaquín de Aristarain was put in as make-believe "owner," mocking the law. Since one sugar estate was not much, Las Casas built another, likewise in Güines, this time using his nephew, the Count de O'Reilly, as "owner" of record. It was called Alejandría, and was among the largest in the area. Contemporary documents feel no need for fig leaves and describe Las Casas's activity as a sugar baron—buying kettles, reserving the best slaves in

each cargo for himself, and daily inspecting his grinding mill, being constructed under the French technician La Faye.[28] Meanwhile Valiente, an associate of the Count de Mopox y Jaruco in the disreputable traffic in flour, partnered Arango in ownership of the world's largest sugar estate of the period, La Ninfa.[29] Given such unity of interest, we can understand why the sugar barons—who have been the intellectual creators of our written history—speak of these two men as model administrators. And we should realize that by merging the functions of government and sugar production they hastened Cuba's transition to capitalism, and felt obliged to make such radical changes in the colonial superstructure that they have logically and justly passed into history as great reformers. For all its brutality, the awakening of sugar was a step forward.

The tobacco growers, reduced to impotency, sought refuge on ever more remote lands, but the sugar tide pursued them relentlessly. A handful remained on the periphery of Güines until 1798, but tobacco production had fallen to such a point that Virginia leaf was being imported to cover Havana's needs. Compelled for sheer survival to protect the tobacco growers, the Factoría issued a decree that all purchases of tobacco lands must be made through it. The Real Consulado, dominated by the sugarocracy, protested indignantly. For the first time, definite bourgeois arguments appear in our legal literature. They contend that "an offense is being committed against Property Rights which neither the Intendente nor the Capitán General may infringe." On March 15, 1798, at the instance of the Factoría, the Capitán General was instructed by royal order to prevent hacendados from violating the tobacco growers' rights. Later the Real Consulado would call this decree "a fatal blow to the big landowners of the island." [30]

The most startling of all documents left us by the eighteenth-century sugarocracy, Nicolás Calvo's report to the Real Consulado, was provoked by the problem of land-plunder at the end of the century. Calvo relates how, crossing the Mayabeque plain, his French technician Julian Lardière jumped from the trap in which they were riding and cried: "This is the soil, this is the place where nature has assembled everything for sowing cane and making sugar." Then he tells how he envisioned the whole Güines tobacco zone covered with irrigated canefields, with water-powered grinding mills at brief intervals and the wide plain occupied by three hundred sugarmills. All this to make the proposal "that tobacco growers sell out to sugarmill masters and quit the valley. Let them go to new lands which the King will grant them, and thus will be achieved happiness for the farmers, a well-populated Island, and wealth for the Royal treasury." The report was so cynical that the Governor declined to approve its publication.[31]

Also of this period—and also generated by sugar—is the exaltation of Vuelta Abajo tobacco as the world's best. This thesis was propounded in terms of new lands and old lands: the latter produced "a stunted tobacco with little or unpleasant fragrance and of no substance," while the former yielded a "handsome, balsamic, and fragrant" crop: "The whole world is now asking for Vuelta Abajo tobacco." This was a mere excuse for pushing tobacco westward, since Vuelta Abajo did not then mean the same thing geographically as it does now. Planting tobacco in Vuelta Abajo simply meant moving beyond Artemisa, the western limit of the red-soil belt deemed peerless for sugar. In short, tobacco was to be put beyond the possible area of sugar expansion—it was a mere coincidence that Vuelta Abajo turned out to be really good tobacco land. As usual, it was Arango who summed up for the sugarocracy the tobacco planter's transformation into a sugar worker. He presents the transition from tobacco to sugar as idyllic: "There was no assumption that freedom of traffic would thus come to the poor man's hovel offering new and safer occupations, or that he would be forced to abandon tobacco planting . . ."[32] He blames the Factoría for producing the disaster by basing its agricultural policy on small peasants instead of relying on big landowners. Finally, he propounds the sugar producer's solution: put tobacco at the service of sugar—"Let it go directly abroad in exchange for Negroes, sugarmill equipment, and other freely traded requirements."

After making such statements, Arango foresees his opponents' answers, ending his report with the admission: "I already seem to hear the vague charge against me of being a man of Havana and a *hacendado,* using this—as has been attempted with others—to try to throw suspicion on my views." But his views were in fact suspicious, and as for the suggestion that he was a Havana *hacendado,* there was nothing vague about it: it was the correct and precise hallmark of an economic class. The reply to Arango came from Rafael Gómez Robaud, one of the few colonial officials not under the sugarmen's thumb. He made such irrefutable observations as these:

The Güines district, where all the tobacco used to be grown, has been converted since 1797 into sugar and coffee plantations, established on lands which were obtained almost by force from poor farmers. The powerful men of Havana take whatever they want and have the tobacco plantations destroyed, ruining the cultivation of the fine Güines leaf. Backed by the Capitán General and the Intendente, they help bring about this desolation and make good business out of it.[33]

In fact, an elementary economic phenomenon was in operation. Since both crops were unable to survive in the same zone, the more productive one ousted the one bringing in smaller profits. At the same time, expropriation of the land from the masses laid the foundation for the capitalist system of production. By the beginning of the nineteenth century the problem of tobacco lands was finally settled, although it was to return sporadically for many years as the sugar tide swept on. Between 1800 and 1830 the situation was given juridical form, and from then on we have voluminous files of cases which in practice were resolved by force. When the sugarocracy was at the peak of its power it offered the final legal argument: "The struggle between tobacco growers and *hacendados* arose from the latter's need to defend themselves against abuses committed by the peasants."[34]

The ousting of the tobacco growers was merely an episode—although one of great social importance—in the transformation of Cuba's land system. Seen in full perspective, the conflict was a three-cornered one: sugar–tobacco–cattle. Coffee became important as a cyclical force offering great alternatives, and obedient to the same interests as sugar. Tobacco naturally offered more drama because its growers constituted an incipient peasant class, defenseless and without resources, confronting the power of the governing oligarchy. On the other hand, the cattle ranches belonged for the most part to the same oligarchy that developed the sugarmills. These landlords merely continued and accelerated the process of land division begun at the beginning of the century—the "demolition of the haciendas," as it was juridically termed at the time.

Hacienda demolitions were a means of fabulous

capital accumulation. Speculation in land reached extreme limits. Toward the end of the eighteenth century, in the highly depopulated area of Matanzas, a caballería of land sold for more than 500 pesos, compared with less than 80 a few years earlier. In Güines prices rose from 100 to 2,000 pesos in less than fifteen years. Within thirty years the "league" standard of land measurement was replaced by the caballería, in a caballería to league ratio of 1:108. The change of terminology reveals the deep change in the real-estate business. Many businessmen with capital but no land, eager to get into the sugar-producing adventure either on their own account or through loans, hurled charges of "latifundista!" at the land-owning oligarchy, while the oligarchy added profitable land speculation to its bountiful sugar business. When only the landlord had a place to establish sugarmills, property achieved its authentic latifundio status. Static rights entered in books became dynamic rights.

Financing

Until the mid-eighteenth century, the sugarmill was an agricultural institution with an initial capitalization dominated by the value of canelands, reserves of standing wood-fuel, oxen and their pastures, food plots for slave and employee maintenance, and typically agricultural implements. It consisted of a small animal-powered mill, three to five kettles to boil down the cane juice, an average of thirty to forty slaves, and from three to five caballerías of maintenance plots, timber, and pastureland. It was in fact a small center for processing an agricultural product, the sowing, care, cutting, and transportation of which occupied a high percentage of the labor force. The other tasks consisted of producing maintenance crops, woodcutting, and cattle-tending. If we bear in mind the seasonal nature of the work—only five months per year, resting on Sundays and holy days—we see that this was no industry in the modern sense of the word. The language of the period is precise in calling sugar producers "farmers." Often the whole estate was called a "trapiche," identifying the production process with the one and only machine it possessed, which at that was usually hauled by bullocks—the water-powered mill was an exception—and which depended on the work in the fields. Another basic aspect of the agricultural

character of the sugar factories of 1761 was that they were self-sufficient units. The workers, slave and free, ate corn, tubers, and meat produced on the farm itself. They lived in estate shacks, cultivated their own food plots (*conucos*) in an elementary form of agricultural exploitation, and learned to make the manioc cakes that served as their bread.

Such was the general setup of the Havana area's 89 sugarmills in 1759. The expansion process, in motion long before the English occupation, raised that number to 93 in 1760, 98 in 1761, and 106 after the occupation in 1764. After that we have no hard figures until 1792, when we find 237 estates in active operation.[35] From 1761 to 1792 production rose from 370,826 arrobas to about 1.2 million, or about 4,300 tons to 13,800 tons. These figures show the rise in average production capacity as well as in the number of units, but there is one aspect of great interest. Classifying the units by their production capacity, we find sixty-four small, thirty medium-sized, and four large. The large ones had about one hundred slaves and produced over 10,000 arrobas per harvest. (They were Gabriel Peñalver's Jesus, María y José, Juan O'Farrill's Santo Cristo de la Veracruz, Ignacio Peñalver's Nuestra Señora de Loreto, and María Teresa Chacón's San Miguel del Rosario.) The outstanding feature of the growth is the proliferation of mills—over one hundred new ones—and the expansion of small and medium-sized ones. But the big ones did not grow bigger. Apparently 100 slaves and 10,000 arrobas was the greatest capacity aspired to, and when that figure was reached capital was invested in a new unit.

What factors held back the capacity of the individual sugarmill until the end of the eighteenth century? We have seen that mills grew on the basis of more Negroes and not of a transformation of production techniques. Yet quantitative growth inevitably produced qualitative changes. The increasing and ever more intensive exploitation of Negroes led to conflicts which required a rigid system of discipline. Their shacks were not conducive to security in personnel management, and the *conucos* assigned them for growing their food ceased to be productive. It became necessary to build concentration areas, presaging the barracoons of the nineteenth century. The elimination of the *conucos* affected the economy of the sugarmills: they lost their self-sufficiency and became consumers of cured meat and codfish, both of

25

which were export-trade products. The work speed-up increased the number of accidents and reduced the workers' physical reserves; the quack who was adequate before could no longer cope with the mounting sick list, and the estate had to install a shack-hospital, "buy" a nurse, and arrange for a doctor on a retainer basis. The containers previously hewn out of cedar or *jobo* from nearby forests now required a proficient carpentering job, or the *hacendado* had to buy ready-made pieces for them in the Havana market. The wooden trapiche would not stand up to the intensified rhythm, and iron rollers, shafts, and frames also had to be bought in Havana. The transportation of sugar became more complicated and the animal-powered system proved inadequate.

These and many other factors slowed the introduction of big factories. To understand the process, we must think of sugar not as a product but as an economic complex. Production could not be stepped up unless all the structures impeding its normal development were modified at the same time. For this reason the initial growth was based on small units responding to old conditions. Up until 1792, the normal thing for the top sugarmen to do was to develop not one production giant but four or five medium or large mills: the Count de Casa-Montalvo and the Marquis del Real Socorro ended up with nine and ten respectively. Very small estates—trapiches with five or six slaves—died a natural death or confined themselves to producing raspadura, which was not for export but was for the poorest social groups.

What was significant about this kind of growth was that it required minimal credit. Since high prices and demand remained constant, the sugar producers were favorably placed *vis-à-vis* the merchants. The only credit problem was the blacks, and, as we have seen, this could be solved. The second half of the eighteenth century in Cuba was further characterized by a large volume of currency, due to military spending and to the sugar business itself. *Macuquina* money—an old gimmick of colonial economies, hard to convert into free-exchange *divisas* but imposed on Cuba—was steadily reinvested. As its name suggests, it was a debased currency with a big gap between its real and its nominal value. To take it out of Cuba one had to convert it into hard currency, paying the difference, plus a 9 percent tax, to the Crown. Such being the case, and with Havana industry offering

broad perspectives for development, the merchant preferred to do business in this money rather than exchange or export it. Meanwhile Vera Cruz merchants traded freely with Havana and took advantage of the exchange differential to make large purchases in our port, using hard currency and profiting from the depreciation reflected in prices. This financial juggling gave the *hacendado* more currency with which to do business, maintained the speculations of the merchants, and kept sugar exports booming. Since *macuquina* money was a blessing to these circles, it was forged on an impressive scale. In 1779 the counterfeit, and in 1781 the genuine, *macuquina* was called in. There was a 40 percent difference between the real and nominal values.[36]

As for military appropriations, a good part of them was used to set up the sugarmills. La Cabaña thus turned out to be the costliest fortress ever built on earth. Skill was developed early in the art of "borrowing" official funds for private businesses, especially sugar: in the first years of the seventeenth century, Juan Maldonado el Mozo, son of Havana's governor, dipped into the public till to build his sugar estate, and the Mozo tradition continued to flourish in Cuban sugar until 1959.[37]

The Anglo-Spanish war of 1779 gave a new kind of push to the island's economy. Havana was filled with soldiers, and sugar—as it was invariably to do down through the centuries—drew life from death. In a very few years 35 million pesos entered Cuba, filling the void left by the calling-in of *macuquina* money, causing spectacular inflation, enriching merchants and *hacendados,* and creating in turn new funds for investment. Arango describes this in his *Discurso sobre la agricultura.* But the most important aspect of the war—which Arango knew but does not mention —was not the 35 million but the opening of the new United States market. We have noted how the Sugar Islands supported the economy of the thirteen colonies. United States independence brusquely cut off trade relations between the new republic and the English Antilles, and Cuba, because of its type of production and geographical situation, became a substitute for Barbados. A new market was opened up both for the United States and for Cuba. Cuba offered a solution to the fearsome crisis facing those Americans who had supplied the Sugar Islands with estate implements, Negroes, cloth for outfitting slaves, crating planks, barrel staves, hoops and nails, and countless other products. A further impulse for close mercantile relations came from the United States' important distilling industry: for a century Massachusetts had been manufacturing the "finest West Indian rum" which sold lavishly in England and which the Empire bestowed on its soldiers as an obligatory ration.[38] And so the United States businessman came to roost in Havana.

Their products piled up or production paralyzed after the few years of market upheaval caused by the severance of relations with the Sugar Islands, United States manufacturers and shrewd slave-dealers channeled Negroes and implements into Cuba at low prices, extending generous credit and accepting sugar and molasses in payment. The potency of this trade was enough to break the Spanish monopoly, as the English occupation had shattered the privileges of Cádiz and Seville. In free trade, as in many other areas, Spanish laws were drafted *a posteriori* to recognize an unalterable *de facto* situation. The illegality of the operations prevents us from exactly measuring this United States influence in the first years of the great sugar boom, but there is no doubt that, beginning in the 1780s, enormous United States investment and loan capital was poured into the sugarmills. The Real Consulado itself recognized this activity, which the Laws of the Indies flatly prohibited. A report of 1796 casually mentions United States businessmen trading "both in large and small quantities at warehouses and shops they have opened for the purpose . . ."[39]

Around 1786–1788 a slight drop in prices marked the only small depression of the second half of the eighteenth century. This was a normal economic adjustment process, inevitable at the end of a war. In an uncontrolled economy with primitive work forms and legal status, competing in a market dominated by the capitalist system of production, normal contradictions sharpen and recurrent crises are intensified. Great international commotions, especially wars, throw a market seriously off balance. The excess of currency during a war leads to heavy speculation and a logical inflation process. Such commercial speculations reach plunderous proportions in the first months of peace, raising and sometimes depressing prices beyond normal limits. Cuba experienced this for the first time in the 1780s with the end of the war in the thirteen colonies. The consequences became increasingly painful as capitalism advanced—a fact first brought home in 1857 and then again in 1920.

From the outset sugar was to march over the same perilous road: high prices, prodigious expansion of the industry with the money of the investing and avidly reinvesting merchant, more and more currency in circulation, faster and faster turnover of capital, an inflationary spiral—a complex of phenomena which was dubbed "fat cows" in Cuba's vivid vernacular. Then the crash of prices, crisis for the producer who had not capitalized his investment, ruin for mills built under exceptional market conditions and unviable in the slump, withdrawal of investment and finance capital and a reduction of currency. But this—the period of "lean cows" in our vernacular—does not ruin the moneylending merchant with accumulated capital to weather the crisis, for when the price curve returns to normal he has in his hands substantial properties which he has seized for debt. Thus yesterday's moneylending merchant—today's banker—always emerges the winner: he is the man defined by Arango as the one with "money and warehouses."

The 1786–1788 recession only affected small producers who depended on the Spanish merchant, or investors with minimal capital. For weighty political reasons Arango, however, tried to picture it as a serious general crisis. He left a description which, while only applicable at the time to a small economic sector, was to provide a lively future portrait of a whole producing class: "When we saw we were alone and made up our accounts, we realized that only a tenth part remained to us of what we had poured in. The rest had vanished abroad in payment for trifles; and the worst of it was that most of what little remained had been used to develop haciendas that did not pay their way."[40]

The 1790s were decisive in the transformation of Cuba into a sugar plantation. For our burgeoning sugarocracy, Haiti was a symbol and a goal. When the Havana *Gaceta* published that French colony's fantastic production figures in 1791, Arango fearlessly predicted that with adequate financing for slaves Cuba could double them in three years. He dreamed of the plantation and used the word in its correct economic sense. He envisaged an island with a half-million working slave population. He would live long enough to see it and be sorry.

Haiti's revolution speeded the process in Cuba. For a few white moralists of the period, the Haitian events were the frightful denouement of a perverse system. Various clergymen saw them as a curse sent by God. But Cuba's sugarocracy was jubilant: the great competitor was dead, and they had to get moving fast. Arango's articles, backed by the Havana oligarchy, glow with tragic joy. His uninhibited phraseology is eloquent: "The solid advantages we can draw from the very jaws of misfortune . . . this is the golden moment to expand agriculture . . . one must look at the situation with a political eye . . ."

The Cuban sugarocracy had a definite interest in the ruin of Haiti's sugar industry, and together with the English they helped it along to an extent which, while undoubtedly significant, we cannot measure precisely. They then dedicated themselves to seeing that Haiti would never revive—with Arango as a key man in the process. It was no accident that the most important diplomatic mission to Haiti at the time fell to this spokesman for the Cuban sugar producers. With the Haitian collapse the economic objective was attained: Cuba became the world's top producer of sugar, the new devourer of slaves. In the time of Someruelos French troops streamed through Havana on their way home, marching (according to their leaders) in "abject misery" after the vain attempt to reconquer their colony. The frustrated soldiers evoked pictures of sugar estates in flames, of devastated coffee plantations, while Cuban prices soared dizzily: 18 reales, 20, 24, 32, 36 an arroba! Cuban ports were glutted with slaves. The twenty-hour work day was initiated. Arango had said it well: "There is no doubt about it, the hour of our happiness has struck." [41]

The new cycle required a volume of investment such as Havana had never dreamed of. The promise of limitless profits shook the whole world with sugar fever. In Spain, Valencians and Andalusians strove to revive medieval production methods: at Oliva on the Mediterranean six ancient trapiches were patched up, sugarcane feverishly replanted.[42] The Italian Gaspare Vascari wrote a substantial sugar-production handbook, insisting that the world's leading sugar islands should be Santo Domingo and Sicily. He recalled the centuries-old *trappetos* of Ficarazzi, Trabia, Buonfornello, Pietra di Roma, Marina di San Fratello, Casalnuovo, and Trappetazzo and bewailed in tragic Neapolitan mood how they had been abandoned ignominiously "with humiliating indolence." The United States stepped up maple-sugar extraction, France experimented massively with beets, and Luis Proust in Spain and Domenico de Tommasi in Italy

with sugar from grapes, *"eguale al migliori di America."* [43] But only Cuba had what it took for a great and rapid leap forward in sugar.

From 1792 on, the island received large amounts of investment capital. The big merchants of New Spain, the magnates of Cádiz and Seville, the blossoming U.S. plutocrats, and the few Haitian sugarmen who had escaped ruin all joined in promoting Cuban sugar; local merchants and producers, with insatiable appetites for profit, kept reinvesting. José Sedano, describing events in Havana after 1792, spoke of the "furor" for starting new sugarmills. In fourteen years, from 1792 to 1806, the number of mills rose from 237 to 416 in the diocese of Havana alone. Furthermore, the new mills had a much greater production capacity and the old ones expanded theirs. The following average capacity figures sum up the change during the half-century:

Year	Arrobas per mill
1761	3,772
1792	5,063
1804	11,819

The giants of the period, as shown in the harvest of 1804, were: the Marquis de Arcos' San José de los Dolores, 40,982 arrobas; Bonifacio Duarte's San Miguel, 32,361; José Ignacio Echegoyen's La Asunción, 29,000; Arango y Parreño's La Ninfa, 29,179; and the Reverend Bethlehemite Fathers' San Cristóbal de Baracoa, 26,146.[44] Each of these had more than three hundred slaves.

The sugar boom distorted the island's economy by forcing the abandonment of many other activities, posing new supply problems, and radically transforming the landscape. Cuba went into a long sugar orgy which might be called "the first dance of the millions." Thus the sugar society was born—the semi-plantation which continued with few essential changes into our times. Abandonment of all that had no direct or indirect connection with sugar or coffee was rationalized as "disregarding the necessary to promote the useful." [45] The self-sufficient trapiche passed into history and the new mills imported all their maintenance needs. One product alone suggests the measure of the transformation: in 1761 Cuba was still exporting jerked beef; in 1792 it was imported by the hundreds of thousands of arrobas.

As the sugar industry grew and its export-import structure solidified, the merchant (in his dual role as banker) mushroomed in importance. He sold jerked beef for slaves, planks and staves for boxes and hogsheads, nails and hoops, clothing outfits, grinding mill parts and boilers; and he also advanced the cash for other operations. Into his sphere came innumerable functions previously handled by the owner. Sugar and molasses now had to be hauled by cart instead of on an animal's back: any average mill in 1804 spent more than 3,000 pesos a year on transport alone. The street floors of Havana mansions no longer sufficed for storage and it was necessary to use the merchant's warehouse.

This created serious problems for middle-sized producers, who saw prices sky-rocketing. Without any capitalist tradition, Cuba lacked the necessary mechanisms for technical and mercantile operations. The learning process was expensive, production costs were extremely high, and the small producer usually fell into the hands of powerful businessmen. On the other hand, the Havana oligarchy, which had been in the business for half a century and had accumulated capital, retained its economic independence and increased its resources. In the nineteenth century the story would be different.

The weight of commerce and of ruthless usury bore hard on the small and middle-sized producers from the beginning. The legal interest rate on loans was 5 to 6 percent, and the few agreements of this type which have survived for our study are drawn up on that basis. But the sham contract, which changed only the name and form of usury, was a routine practice. In the fine print of notarial documents we find loans at 30 to 40 percent interest disguised under contracts to buy sugar futures or to sell estates by retroactive agreement. This explains why the sugarmills were constantly changing hands. If we except high members of the Havana oligarchy, we find few cases of mills remaining under the same ownership for more than ten years.

The copious files of the commercial court are the place to study the usury of the period. There are concrete instances of 4,000-peso loans escalating to 20,000 (capital plus interest) in two years. The ordeal of José Antonio Bosque is one of many incidents which, while not recorded in standard heroic versions of history, indicate the facts of life in the eighteenth and nineteenth centuries. Bonifacio González Larrinaga, one of Havana's three biggest moneylending merchants, lent Bosque 1,000 pesos on a fake sale

contract for 800 arrobas of future sugar production from the Nuestra Señora de la Candelaria (alias Barandilla) mill. When the term expired the market price of sugar happened to be higher than the contract specified. In view of this, González Larrinaga demanded delivery of the 800 arrobas plus the difference in cash between the paid and the market price. Thus the moneylender would collect the high interest on the loan—around 25 percent over six months—and double the price differential. (Sugarmen had a word—"the difference"—for this juridical monstrosity, which was a run-of-the-mill usurers' gimmick.) Bosque balked and went to the commercial court. Success would have set a legal precedent contrary to the merchants' interests, and they presented a united front against him. To "protect his interests," González Larrinaga demanded that the court appoint a supervisor of the mill. The supervisor, with the court's compliance, assumed an administrative mantle, slowed down the work, raised production costs, and applied to González Larrinaga himself for a loan, thus facilitating total economic penetration. The drop in sugar prices in the next two harvests, while the lawsuit dragged on, put the mill decisively in the red and once again González Larrinaga defrayed imaginary losses. By 1805 he was the owner of the Nuestra Señora de la Candelaria estate, acquired with an original loan of just 1,000 pesos. In one of the documents appears this sad comment by Bosque: "There is no other business so stable, so smooth, and so sweet that it can garner such thousands without any risk . . ." [46]

Usury was one of the most potent brakes on the island's economic development. The lack of banks inevitably brought producers to the moneylender's door. But "usury, like commerce, exploits a given mode of production. It does not create it, but is related to it outwardly. Usury tries to maintain it directly, so as to exploit it ever anew; it is conservative and makes this mode of production only more pitiable." [47] Thus the moneylender-usurer had a special interest in maintaining the contradictions that choked the production system. Preservation of the sugarmill's negative elements assured his control of it. Perpetuation of slavery bred the continuously rising production costs, which became the basis of his total hegemony.

After the boom created by the ruin of Haiti, merchant-moneylenders and usurers grew immeasurably in importance. Controlling the slave trade from the first years of the nineteenth century, they were the suppliers of labor to the mills. The oligarchy's entrance into the world sugar market led to such intensive exploitation of the Negro that he stopped reproducing himself by normal procreation. Slave traders consequently had to import enough hands to cover the industry's prodigious expansion, plus replacements for the 5 to 10 percent of the slaves annually devoured by the Moloch of mill and canefield.

Those businessmen who played such a stellar financial and investment role in sugar stand out sharply at the turn of the century. Perhaps the most "modern" was Philip Allwood, an old partner in the British firm of Baker & Dawson who lived in the English Antilles and set up a business in Cuba when it blossomed as a market for slaves. A typical English businessman, with a sense of the future and of empire, Allwood combined with his basic economic activity a series of interesting sidelines. Apart from the slave trade, his name turns up in connection with the introduction into Cuba of various mango, coffee-tree, and sugarcane varieties. He was a leading figure in experiments with Otaheite cane. In 1792 he urged sugarmen to use mills with horizontal rollers. Allwood's significance is shown by the fact that, between 1790 and 1795, he imported and financed more slave cargoes than all the other Havana importers put together. The competition he offered the Spanish merchants maintained reasonable price levels and moderated the excesses of usury—which explains the big merchants' repeated efforts to expel him from Cuba. He was defended by Arango both in 1791 and in 1795, in the name of the Havana oligarchy, but, on the pretext of complying with the Laws of the Indies, and taking advantage of the international situation, the big merchants finally achieved his expulsion.[48]

With regard to direct loans for sugar investment and financing, the outstanding figure of the period was undoubtedly Pedro Juan de Erice. His investments exceeded 3 million pesos in the last five years of the eighteenth century. We have exact data showing that in three years he did 2,432 million pesos' worth of business—1.74 million pesos in one-year contracts, and 691,000 in four- and five-year contracts.

González Larrinaga loaned 1.78 million pesos

between 1789 and 1803. Juan de Santa María of the Santa María y Cuesta firm transacted many big deals and had enough cash in hand to make immediate delivery of hundreds of thousands of pesos. On April 26, 1799, for example, he furnished Nicolás Calvo with 300,000 pesos in a single transaction. The Seville firm which he represented negotiated more than 2.5 million pesos in sugar investments. Bernabé Martínez de Pinillos appears in contemporary documents as a merchant-moneylender in the same class. The large fortune he amassed gave his descendants politico-economic power and decisive government influence. Overall, we may say that sugar investment in the last years of the eighteenth century exceeded 15 million pesos. This is the highest figure for any business of the period anywhere in the Americas.[49]

THE SUGARMILL AS INTELLECTUAL ADVENTURE

If the objective problems of sugar expansion are interesting, the intellectual world of its progenitors is no less so. The sugarmill was an adventure of the spirit as well as an economic activity. Formation of the great production complex demanded wide reading, laborious investigation, and exceptional creative enthusiasm. When the Havana sugarocracy achieved the prototypes of large-scale production at the end of the eighteenth century, a special name was coined to distinguish them from all that had come before: they were called "sugarmills of the new type." These factories were an economic breakthrough, but they were also the concrete realization of an idea, the product of many sleepless nights.

From the intellectual standpoint it is important to separate the Cuban phenomenon from that of the Sugar Islands. The English Antilles were mere receivers of the Industrial Revolution, while the expansion of sugar in colonial Cuba did not originate in, but took place in spite of, the metropolis. It was not imported by the authorities, but it did come from abroad, thanks to efforts originating in Cuba itself. In a creative development that was unique, the Creole oligarchy took the reins and imposed their productive rhythm upon Spain. The material expression of this can be seen in the fact that the great technical motors of capitalism—the steam engine, the industrial use of gas and electricity, the railroad, telegraph, and telephone—were generally introduced into Cuba *earlier* than in Spain. Mechanical development in Cuba substantially loosened the bonds with the metropolis and widened the rift between Creoles and Spaniards.

The Cuban sugarocrat of the late eighteenth and early nineteenth centuries expressed himself in bourgeois terminology. A producer of merchandise for the world market, he had points in common with the European bourgeois. He lived in a period when sugar production was still a primitive task, to be performed by brute physical strength and by the quantity rather than the quality and technological state of labor. Since the industrial machinery for sugar production did not yet exist, slavery was a solution to the labor problem and the slave-master could permit himself the contradictory prerogative of talking and acting like a bourgeois.

The sugarocracy's bourgeois attitude made it strive incessantly to revolutionize its instruments of production. Its members fully realized that they could only maintain their predominance by abandoning primitive methods and obsolete mercantile relations. Economic transformation implied technical modification. Besides land, slaves, and money, they had to find thinkers, erudite men with some knowledge of the dark and remote world of figures and formulas. Who in Havana knew how to calculate the precise size of a mill drive shaft? The correct amount of lime to put in the cane juice? How much sugar the cane contained? The burgeoning sugarocracy exhausted all of the island's intellectual resources. They gave highly paid jobs to every technician to be found on the island and imported numerous experts from the other Antilles. The Haitian catastrophe made available many French sugarmasters, men accustomed to keeping sugarmill accounts, physicians versed in the illnesses of slaves. Much has been written about the impulse the French gave to coffee growing in eastern Cuba, but their contribution to Havana sugar was far more potent.[50]

This constant search for new techniques forced the Cuban sugarocrat out into the world. Now it was not only his merchandise that went abroad: he himself traversed the United States, Europe, and the Antilles in search of better machines, more productive varieties of cane, new chemical products, special measuring instruments. Thus he and his product broke the old isolation and cleared the way for the

global relations and interdependence that typifies the bourgeoisie.

As in every move connected with sugar, Arango turns up as a pioneer in this globe-trotting. In relation to his time his *Discurso sobre fomento de La agricultura en La Habana*, brief as it is, is the most finished example of sugarocrat thought produced in Cuba. He wrote it in a few evenings but its pages attain bourgeois altitudes rarely reached in our own day. It is a dry, candid lesson in economics, free from any ethical considerations or any basic aspirations, interested only in money and the low-cost production of sugar. For the first time in the literature of the Americas a work appeared which analyzed in a technically impeccable way the characteristics of a manufacturing enterprise. In the manner of the most modern industrial organization manuals, Arango begins with the flow of production and ends with a detailed study of every aspect of the labor force, supply, costs, investment, financing, distribution, and markets.

For the influence it had on the new intellectual world of sugar, and for its broad technical and political repercussions, the *Discurso* is indispensable reading. Arango demonstrated that, since foreign sugar enterprises were superior to Cuban ones in seven ways, it was necessary to study their methods, and he proposed a voyage for this purpose. Since the exclusive object was to steal technical data from competitors, he recommended that the voyage be made clandestinely—deception was an accepted principle among the ethical pace-setters of the rising class. In a spontaneous manifestation of the sugarocrat spirit, Arango suggested that the pilgrim or pilgrims should travel "as smugglers or whatever seems best to remain incognito."

Thus the first voyage of technical study was undertaken in 1794 by Cuban sugarmen: specifically by Francisco de Arango y Parreño and Ignacio Pedro Montalvo y Ambulodi, the Count de Casa-Montalvo. The trip took them from Madrid to Portugal, England, Barbados, and Jamaica. In Lisbon they gathered data on Portugal's slave-trading experience over a period of almost three hundred years. England broadened their scholarship, for Liverpool still led the world in traffic in black Africans, although what most interested the Cuban travelers there was the Industrial Revolution and its technical pivot, the steam engine. In the steam engine Arango saw

31

the solution to the "bottleneck" of the Cuban sugarmill, and with money from his cousin the Count de Jaruco—the Count de Casa-Montalvo's son-in-law—he ordered one from the firm of Reinold. This was only nine years after Watt achieved his last great patent. The steam engine was not an invention for specific purposes but a general industrial agent. Sugar production was not among the uses foreseen for it, despite the experiments of John Stewart and Dugal Clark. In using it the Cuban sugarocracy was to be a step ahead of its creators.[51]

Arango inspected English refineries with equally remarkable discernment (he left a superb technico-economic description of the biggest one) and sensed the role that the refining process would play in Cuban sugar.[52] He proved himself a born industrialist in his analysis—in 1794!—of the junior economic position and the fetters on development which would reward the seller of a semi-refined product. It was clear to him that from then on—later would be too late—not a grain of unrefined sugar should leave Cuba.[53] He was right.

Barbados and Jamaica had a lesson for the travelers that Arango would learn thoroughly twenty-five years later: despite the advances in metropolitan England, its colonies were at least as backward as Cuba in sugar refining if not more so, since they were turning out nothing but unrefined muscovado.* Slavery inhibited industrial development, while the metropolis' technical progress merely held the colonies back as suppliers of an intermediate product. Only two aspects of what they saw in the English islands had concrete value for the travelers: the practice of making one furnace supply heat to all the boilers, and the use of bagasse** as fuel. The distillation of molasses, although primitively performed, had become an interesting sugar sideline, but this was not a new discovery but a confirmation of Arango's own ideas.

Top sugarmen of the period made many journeys like that made by Arango and the Count de Casa-Montalvo. The fact of having visited Haiti, Jamaica, or Barbados was like a certificate of

industrial know-how, a special doctorate in sugar lore. It was something to which Nicolás Calvo, Martínez Campos, Antonio Morejón, and José Ignacio Echegoyen pointed with pride. While these men moved abroad on such study-trips, foreign technicians moved into Cuba, some brought for their qualifications, some arriving on their own in search of adventure. A few came from Haiti as a result of the tragic situation there. As was to be expected, they were of all sorts, from experts to charlatans. Many of them settled and made a solid contribution to building the industry. Julian Lardière, a good technician brought in by Nicolás Calvo, was the brains behind the construction of La Nueva Holanda and La Ninfa, two mills rated among the most productive of their time. He fared so well that by 1815 he was the owner of a mill. Dumont was a modest and efficient technician who left interesting practical works on sugar, coffee, and tobacco. Bernard Chateausalins, brought in as a doctor for the slaves, made his mark scholastically and left a manual of scientific distinction. La Faye, despite his fantastic idea of a pendular mill, was the most enlightened sugar technician of the period, the first to calculate yields on the basis of weight instead of caballerías of cane cut. His still-unpublished work on roads is admirable. In mill and city, these men created a cultural atmosphere far superior to that of the old sugarmasters, who were often illiterate.

The intellectual activity stirred by sugar also manifested itself in the series of publications on that subject. Up until the end of the eighteenth century, the technical bibliography on sugar was minimal. In French, Dutrone de la Couture and Corbeaux were considered classics.[54] In English, one good handbook was known: *The Art of Making Sugar.*[55] In Spanish there were two studies, one of 1719 and the other of 1766, both published in Spain and totally unknown in Cuba.[56] With the growth of the sugar industry the lack of technical knowledge began to come home. In 1792 Arango proposed the translation of Dutrone and by 1796 Paul Boloix had begun that task. But translating technical books is far from easy. As a Frenchman by birth Boloix had no trouble with the language, but he knew no chemistry. The translation job then passed to the Count de Mopox y Jaruco because of his "outstanding erudition in chemistry." He in turn asked, as a first step, to be sent to the United States to buy machinery against which

---

* Muscovado is unrefined sugar from which some of the molasses has been removed. (Trans.)

** Bagasse is sugarcane after it has been crushed and the juice extracted. (Trans.)

Dutrone's statements could be checked and corrected. The assembled sugarocracy finally agreed to found a school of chemistry in Havana—another example of the strong intellectual push given by sugar, and of the clear vision of a class seeking in science a solid basis for its production. For them, chemistry was the art of making sugar.[57]

In the century's last six years three sugar books were published. First, the magnificent handbook by José Ricardo O'Farrill;[58] on its heels, José Martínez de Campos' work on the best method of making sugar;[59] and in 1797, Antonio Morejón y Gato's study of the red-earth region, which speaks of "making analyses of the soil" for the first time in the Americas.[60] These works belong to a transition stage: the bourgeois spirit is there, but it is still chained to the Spanish feudal past and the Cuban slave system. Implied in them, however, is a profound change in attitude, and they initiate a totally new scientific prose. The authors write in a different way because the things they are saying are different. Morejón, a lawyer of the semi-feudal school, quotes the saying "agriculture ennobles the serf" and makes constant references to mythology, while Martínez de Campos, of the same school, mentions Osiris, Ceres, and Triptolemus in writing about sugar and Negroes; but O'Farrill and Calvo used a clear, clean, concise vocabulary with the flavor of an account book. They were the intellectual spokesmen of a class moving toward the exact expression of its ideas.* Arango provided the literary formula: "I submit that it is our duty to declare formally that we will speak here only in the simple language of the ordinary farmer and that, dispensing with preambles and idle digressions, we will approach facts with no other company than good logic and precise reasoning." [61]

LARGE-SCALE MANUFACTURE
IN 1800

What was gained by the studies, investigations, and experiments? They solved the fundamental quantitative problems. They created a simple but large-scale form of cooperation based on slave labor—a foundation on which nothing more could be built. Thus the sugarmill of 1800 closed the cycle of technical progress until such time as labor conditions changed. Physical effort remained the basis of production, routine the only agricultural law. When all its possibilities were exhausted, the contradictions that would end by destroying the sugarmill began to appear. Not going forward is the surest way of going backward.

In the eighteenth century the typical sugarmill had a certain flavor of domestic-rural industry. Field work was performed with rudimentary techniques, using either a pointed stake (a *jan*) to perforate the ground for planting cane or, at best, the "Creole plough," similar to the ancient Chinese plough. Only one variety of cane, the "Creole," was planted.

* The economic boom, the introduction of modern techniques, and the introduction of some aspects of capitalism made a "modern" dictionary of technical terms an absolute necessity. On October 8, 1795, Fray José María Peñalver—an eminent member of the consortium of sugar families—proposed to the Sociedad Patriótica a project for a *Diccionario Provincial de Voces Cubanas* to fix "the true meaning of technical terms in our country relating to agriculture, field work, island commerce, industries, arts . . ." He offered as examples two sugar terms, *guijo* and *machete*.

The transformation was most neatly reflected in this not unworthy anonymous poem published in the *Criticón* (Havana) on November 22, 1804:

Here, Celio, we look at the smiling picture of Parnassus
And see a crime, or at least madness.
Between youth and age, other passions sway us:
The rich harvest, what the earth's fruits will fetch in cash—
No other topic is of interest
When we gather at parties or to gossip.
To some peace is important, to some war,

Here we praise our pigs and calves.
One misery senses the approach of rain,
One has cut the cost of his harvesting,
This one samples new grinding machinery,
And that one plans to up the price of his crop.
A professor describes the heavy burden of toil
Which the intrepid genius of captive man
Has condemned him to bear.
One invokes heaven as witness
That he never stole another's property—
It was not high living that got him into debt.
One wishes he could find for his hacienda
An overseer who would not be lazy and would understand him.
One complains shrilly that he has lost his main grinding cylinder.
Another dreamer of golden dreams is furious
Because the earth does not belch forth pesos.
"How's your harvest going?"
Mileto has asked
"Not too bad," says Porcio,

Cutting and loading were manual tasks and cane was hauled to the grinding mill in loads averaging 80 arrobas, in little two-wheeled carts with a single yoke of oxen.

The grinding mills were of wood, with three vertical rollers between which the cane was crushed. Motion was imparted to these by a vertical shaft rotated by oxen attached to sweeps. The design and technical characteristics hardly differed from those used in sixteenth-century Mediterranean sugar areas. The juice, or *guarapo,* was expressed from the cane into open copper kettles where it was cooked until optimum concentration by evaporation was achieved. The fuel was wood, and each kettle had its own furnace. The degree of concentration was calculated empirically and, once attained, the syrup was emptied into a "cooler"—a wooden trough in which the concentrate was beaten with wooden bats until it crystallized. Since the physico-chemical composition of these concentrates was such that they could only crystallize partially, what remained was a thick mass of sugar crystals and non-crystallizing molasses. The final stage was separating the two, or "purging the sugar," an equally crude operation. The partially crystallized mass was emptied into clay containers, conical in shape and open at both ends, which were called *hormas* by the Cubans and "pots" by the English. The filled containers were stacked with the pointed ends downward and plugged with wooden stoppers. The molasses, of greater density than the sugar, settled to the bottom by gravity. After two or more days, according to the particular conditions of the product and technique of the particular sugar-master, the stopper was removed and the molasses flowed out, while the sugar grains, sticking together and solidifying, remained within the cone. Then a mass of watery clay was applied to the uppermost end of the cone and remained in direct contact with the sugar for thirty or forty days. The water from the clay filtered through the solid mass of sugar, dissolving and draining off much of the molasses that had adhered to the crystals.

At the end of all this the cones were exposed to the sun, and the sugar, taking the form of a solid loaf shaped like the container, was removed. The base of the loaf—the upper end during the purging process—had been in contact with the clay and had a lighter color than the pointed end in which some molasses still remained: in fact, the cone was a spectrum ranging from the bleached base to the dark point. The loaf was cut in pieces according to the shades, using a machete or hand spade. The light and almost molasses-free pieces were considered "white sugar." The points, darkened by their high content of molasses and impurities, were the brown sugar, known as *cucurucho, cogucho, culo,* or simply *puntas* ("tips"). The rest of the cone, of intermediate color between white and *cucurucho,* was the *quebrado* or

"Forty thousand arrobas so far. And yours?"
"How's things? Got as many arrobas as I said you would?"
That, my friend, gives you a rough idea
Of reigning tastes, passions that really sting the appetite.
The brimming cornucopia of Amalthea
Is indelibly printed on their hearts,
For the rest, they don't give a damn.
Nothing remains over in their abundant larders
To help the poor:
Nor do they hear the cry of the grieving widow,
Nor clothe the naked nor feed the hungry.
And so, Celio, what does it matter to these Señores
If Villegas listens to the lament of a little bird in a bush?
What do they care for the rustic love songs of Garcilaso?
For the savagely ardent stanzas of the divine Tasso de Godofredo?
Homer sang in vain of noble Achilles,
In vain the heroic soldiers of their Trojan captain;
And divine Anacreon with his subtle verses
Filling goblets with ambrosial wine
And weaving vine-leaves in his hair

Sings in vain to his handsome Batilo.
Such music makes them yawn,
The most charming epigram is a bore.
No image is splendid enough
To rouse in their starched hearts
That delight of the senses
To which the tender soul is susceptible;
Only the prophetic song of the cicada
Announcing happy seasons and bigger crops
Warms these Midas hearts.
Look, Celio, at my sad life;
Do I not have reason to complain,
To lie awake seeking, in your absence, some consolation?
So I write of my burdens and ask you
To find a way to ease them
Without forgetting me;
Take time to write to me
Invoking some exorcism from Apollo
For so many sectaries of Epicurus
And so few disciples of Horace.

yellow sugar. After separation the sugar was dried and rolled out. Because of the lack of any technical control for these operations, apart from the human eye, classifications multiplied until there were fourteen different kinds of sugar.

The general condition of the roads was too poor to permit the passage of carts, so the sugar was moved from the mill to Havana in five-arroba fiber sacks loaded on animals.[62] In Havana it was packed in wooden boxes of an average sixteen-arroba capacity. This task was performed on the street floor of the master's Havana mansion, where the sugar remained in storage until shipment. Serving as a packing plant and as a warehouse for sugar, jerked beef, clothing, and tools, the mansion was thus a Havana extension of the mill.

The large-scale manufacture of 1800 maintained the same production line and used these same methods, but with some substantial changes. Otaheite cane, taller and more robust than Creole and yielding a sugar-rich juice, was introduced. This new variety had been known in Cuba since 1780 and had been planted around 1795 in many parts of Havana's Barlovento zone.[63] In 1797 the Real Consulado, at the instance of Arango and with the cooperation of slave-trader Philip Allwood, brought in a quantity of the new seed and thereafter it came into general use. Many sugarmasters still preferred the Creole, however, and the usual practice was to maintain both varieties.

The introduction of Otaheite cane was a simple matter since it involved no change in work methods. Sugarmen merely used the new seed for new sowings while retaining the same old destructive routine in the fields. In those days when the yield of a tract fell, no special measures of irrigation, fertilization, or change of crop were taken; it was simply abandoned. Coinciding as it did with the great expansion of the canefields toward Matanzas, the innovation created no problem of substitution in existing fields.

The cutting, loading, and transport of cane to the grinding mill continued as before, but the grinding mill itself was the object of many studies, for it was the real "bottleneck" to large-scale production. The attempts to break it took two directions: changing the mill's mechanical structure, and finding a stronger, quicker, and more effective motive power than that of oxen. Through the former it was hoped that a system of gears or a way of placing the rollers

would be found to grind more cane faster with a minimum of power. Horizontal rollers were tried and the transmission system changed. Up until the first decade of the nineteenth century all the innovations failed. In 1798 a Junta de Fomento report reached the sad conclusion "that nothing was better than the simple vertical mill consisting of three rollers, as used here since time immemorial." [64] For a long time the mechanical characteristics of the grinding mill remained as of old, but it was definitely improved when metal parts were substituted for the old wooden ones. From 1783 on, United States smelters were marketing cast-iron shells to cover wooden rollers, and bronze or iron axles, blocks, and bearings became standard.[65]

A small but important implement was the so-called *volvedora,* or dumb returner. In the primitive grinding mill the three rollers were arranged in one line. Negroes fed the cane between two rollers, the main one and the *cañera,* which crushed it. On the other side of the grinding mill other Negroes took the crushed cane and fed it back, now between the main roller and the *bagacera.* Thus each cane passed through at least twice. The *volvedoras,* introduced in 1794, were wooden pieces which collected the cane after the first crushing and mechanically fed it back between the rollers. This brought a small saving of labor.[66]

The first effort in stepping up motive power was the substitution of mules for oxen. But in Cuba oxen were abundant and cheap and mules scarce and expensive: what was gained in speed did not compensate for the higher cost, and the idea was abandoned. In the end-of-the-century fever for more and better production there were attempts to use air and water power. Many projects came before the newly founded Sociedad Patriótica and the imperatives of sugar made it necessary to study the island's prevailing winds.[67] A wind-driven mill was built by Pedro Diago, one of the greatest industrial inventors who ever lived in Cuba. It was exactly the same as the ox-driven one except for the new-fangled transmission system from the sails of the windmill, which were made of mahogany and *quebracho.* The project failed.[68]

Water power was a solution for the sugarocrat invaders of Güines lands, where the copious Río Mayabeque flowed. The new mills, technically more sophisticated and containing numerous metal pieces,

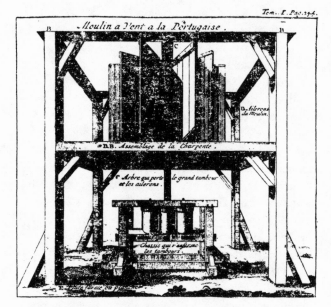

Moulin a Vent a la Portugaise.

D. *Ailerons du Moulin.*

BB. Assemblage de la Charpente.

c *Arbre qui porte le grand tambour et les ailerons.*

Chassis qui renferme les tambours.

A WIND TRAPICHE

Wind-driven mills were known in Persia from the eighth century on. In sugar manufacture they were introduced, according to Deerr, in Barbados around the middle of the seventeenth century. The only Cuban one we know of was that of Pedro Diago, described in the text.

were successful. The Amistad, Nueva Holanda, and La Ninfa mills were still grinding with them in 1840.[69] Around 1790 Havana had no water-driven mills—those which had been established of old along the Almendares had been abandoned—and the Havana-Matanzas sugar-expansion area had so few harnessable rivers that water mills were only a solution in isolated cases.

At about the same time, a foreign technician offered a miraculous solution: a mill to crush sugarcane without oxen or other animals, water or wind. Hopes soared high in the sugarocracy, for the proposer was a serious man, the French engineer La Faye, who had come from Haiti with the highest credentials. Miguel Peñalver quickly supplied him with timber, a house, furnishings, and slaves. The sugarocracy's hunger for more production made La Faye's workshop the most visited spot in Havana. Governor Luis de Las Casas, who at the time was developing his Güines sugar plantations, came every day, and so did his nephew and partner the Count de O'Reilly. Others cheering on the enterprise included the Marquises de Cárdenas de Monte-Hermoso and de Jústiz de Santa Ana, and the Counts de Buenavista and de Casa Bayona: in fact, all the high Havana

nobility whose fields were blazoned with sugarmills. On January 4, 1791, they finally saw the famous mill in operation. It was a machine with horizontal rollers moved by the swing of a large pendulum—although the pendulum was moved in the first place by Negroes, making it a man-powered machine. The experiment failed because the movement of the pendulum gave little speed to the rollers, but alert sugarocrats noted an innovation of enormous importance: La Faye introduced horizontal instead of vertical rollers. Here, in primitive form, was the blueprint for all future grinding mills up to our day. So the failure of the pendulum was forgiven and La Faye was urged to perfect his mill.[70]

Finally, in 1796, steam, the power source for big industry, reached Cuba. The machine, bought in London with the Count de Jaruco's money, was installed in a climate of tense expectation. It started functioning in the Seybabo sugarmill on January 11, 1797, and continued for several weeks. The experiment was not a success, but the sugarocrats were not disheartened; they understood that the problem was not the engine itself but the kind of grinding mill it was powering and the absurd transmission system. The problem was far from simple, but as someone

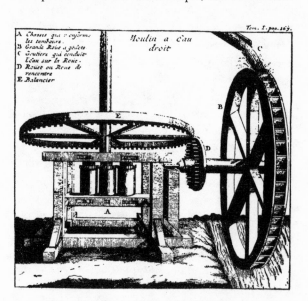

A *Chassis qui enferme les tambours.*
B *Grande Roue a godets.*
C *Goutiere qui conduit l'eau sur la Roue.*
D *Rouet ou Roue de rencontre.*
E *Balancier.*

Moulin a l'eau droit.

A VERTICAL WATER TRAPICHE

This was the design of the grinding mills installed in the Güines valley around the last decade of the eighteenth century. The use of water to move sugar trapiches goes back to 600 B.C. in the Euphrates Valley. The Arabs spread them through the Mediterranean area, whence they came to America.

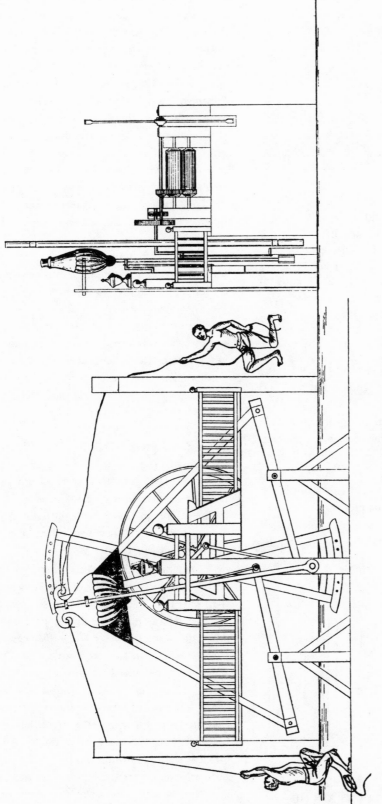

A PENDULAR TRAPICHE

This method was a great illusion and frustration of late eighteenth-century *hacendados*, although attempts to use the pendulum to move grinding mills lasted more than half a century. In 1837 José Francisco Othón built one for a Havana sugarmill near Jaruco, the design of which was published in the Havana *Recreo Literario* in 1837. The one illustrated here is a later model, patented by Hilario Rossi and Pedro Garola in Havana in 1839. The sketch was made from the original in the Archivo Nacional.

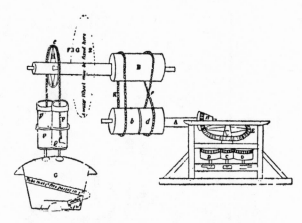

A STEAM ENGINE APPLIED TO TRAPICHE

Built according to Dugal Clark's design in 1769, this grinding mill was patented in the same year that John Stewart was trying to put his own model into operation. Both attempts, originating in Jamacia, failed. Primitive as it is, Clark's machine contained important technical elements which would be developed later.

wrote in 1798: "While trying to correct it and apply it more efficiently, nothing suggests that it is no good." [71]

In sum, the grinding mill used in large-scale manufacture remained the same as that of the small mill, although it was bigger and better made from more resistant materials. Its greater strength enabled it to handle more continuous and intense work loads, thus raising the amount of cane processed. But since the increase in production from this point on fell short of the sugarmen's expanded needs, the bottle-

neck remained and for a long time the only solution was quantitative—to install two grinding mills.

In the boiling room two substantial changes occurred, in the arrangement of the kettles and in the fuel used. As we noted, the standard eighteenth-century method of cooking the juice was the so-called "Spanish train," a series of kettles ranging from larger to smaller through which the syrups passed as they evaporated. The kettles diminished in size in ratio to the lessening volume of the concentrate, which moved continuously onward to the next smaller kettle. In the last one—the *teache,* or strike pan—it reached the "sugaring point." The only difference between the *teache* and the other kettles was its smaller size.

The "Spanish train" involved a separate furnace for each kettle, a system greatly accelerating concentration but requiring an enormous expenditure of fuel. For many years this was no problem in Cuba, for the splendid forests seemed able to provide endless firewood. In the Sugar Islands, however, rapid deforestation demanded a radical change of method. There they tried putting all the kettles in a line, heating them from one furnace. The fuel was fed to a furnace under the first kettle, and the others received the heat diffused from it along the line. This was a slower process than the "Spanish train," but it compensated by its much greater economy in the use of energy. It had another great advantage: it could function exclusively with bagasse as fuel.

These one-fire trains were introduced into Cuba around 1780, where they were called "French trains," partly because they were recommended by Dutrone de la Couture in his "sugar bible" of the period, partly because of the skill of the French in passing themselves off as creators of British inventions. But the system was not generally adopted until tremendous deforestation forced the *hacendados* to use bagasse as fuel. In fact, large-scale Cuban production was not characterized by any particular system of kettle arrangement: if firewood was abundant and cheap, the Spanish system was used; to the extent that firewood was scarce, the number of fires in the boiling room was reduced, creating the so-called "mixed train," burning both bagasse and wood. Furthermore, anyone who prided himself on being a sugarmaster set up his own kettle arrangement and named it after himself. Thus there arose the "Eche-goyen train," the "Arritola," the Montalvo system,

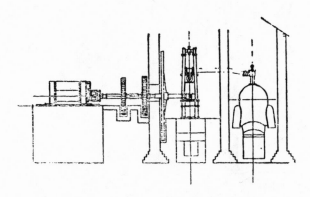

BOULTON AND WATT'S TRAPICHE

The steam engine and horizontal grinding mill designed by Boulton and Watt and tried out in Cuba.

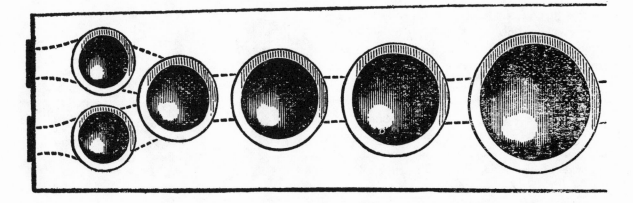

A JIMAGUA TRAIN

One of the many forms of the "Jamaica" or "French" train. Its only variant was that the final stage consisted of two kettles with a combined capacity equal to the one *teache,* for which they were substituted. Cuban sugarmasters called it the "Jimagua" or "à la Pacheca" train.

etc. When the shortage of firewood finally became critical in the Havana-Matanzas area, the sugarocrats returned to the "French train," but named it the "Jamaica train" because they were then copying from Jamaica. It was an unashamed step backward. Only our historians' total ignorance of sugar technology accounts for the assertion, maintained down to our time, that the Jamaica train was an "innovation." Facing the same primitive problem of timber shortage with the same primitive slave-labor system, Cuba resorted to an old Antillean solution.

In an action-reaction process, deforestation increased the sowing of Otaheite cane, whose woody stalk and great height made it an ideal fuel. But the use of bagasse created new problems, for it had to be collected in piles, spread over the factory yard for drying, and then stored in big sheds called *bagaceras,* or "bagasse houses." And *bagaceras* were the favorite hiding places of straying blacks and the easiest targets for firebug saboteurs.

In 1798 another innovation was introduced: the large-capacity pans known as "clarifiers," which received the juice directly from the grinding mill and in which lime was applied and scum removed. Their great advantage was in permitting the elimination of impurities by a simple decantation process. After adding lime to precipitate the colloids, the juice was heated short of boiling and left to stand; it then passed into the concentration train through an outlet at the bottom of the pan which was closed as soon as the first impurities floating on the juice appeared. This elementary mechanical operation was so com-

plicated under a slave-labor setup that use of the clarifier was soon abandoned. Thus the boiling room found the same sort of quantitative solution for large-scale production as did the grinding mill: more kettles. None of the changes in the shape and size of the kettles, in their arrangement on the furnace, or in fuel used changed in any essential way the system developed in eighteenth-century English mills.

Another technical innovation of the "new-type" sugarmill was using lime instead of lye to precipitate the colloids. Eighteenth-century sugarmills used a kind of lye which was an alkaline compound made by rural alchemistic techniques from the ashes of certain trees—preferably the *jobo, ceiba,* or *almácigo*—mixed with quicklime and a herb called "vixen's tail." In 1798 the application of lime was first introduced.[72] It was as elementary as all the other processes: quantities were calculated in "coconuts"— the shell of that fruit being used as a measure—and the degree of alkalinization was judged by the smell of the juice. A great advance at the beginning of the nineteenth century was in the use by some sugarmasters of a paper colored with *palo de tinte* (palo de Campeche tree extract), which tested acidity by its change of color, in the manner of litmus paper. But it was far from easy to detect these changes by the pale light of an oil lamp during the long night shift at the mill. And so the testing paper went out of use.

The use of the aerometer to measure density in the kettles was also recorded as a great step forward in 1799. The aerometer, or saccharimeter, was a device technically known as a Baumé's hydrometer, invented in 1768 and brought to Cuba by Arango. Progressive sugarmen rated it so highly as to be essential in controlling the density of the concentrates, but old masters with no school except experience regarded the little apparatus with skepticism and continued calculating by eye.

The purging process remained as before. For large-scale production the solution was again quantitative—more molds—but since the handling of thousands of clay molds involved much breakage, iron and tin-plated ones were substituted. The packing job previously done in the city was wholly transferred to the mill. Roads improved and carts could move into Havana.

This analysis explains why Cuba's large-scale slave-driven production of the nineteenth century can, without exaggeration, be called no more than a quantitative expansion of the old small mills: not because technical know-how was lacking—we have seen that it was not—but because a new technological process required the wage-worker. Small advances were always abandoned in the long run. The Cuban oligarchy's creative impetus at the end of the eighteenth and beginning of the nineteenth centuries got nowhere. Their bourgeois ideal of revolutionizing the means of production could not be realized because they were not pure bourgeois but masters of slaves. The unhappy contradiction in which they lived did not pass unnoticed by keen-minded sugar pioneers among them.

The great intellectual effort toward a better sugarmill failed because it could only start with the elimination of slavery. A discouraged statement comes down to us from the year 1798, when the creative passion was still at its peak: "The hands used by Cuban agriculture are certainly not ready to accept new inventions . . ." [73] Two years later Pedro Diago, after achieving technical improvements which required careful work, said: "It runs counter to the simplicity and practicality which our sugar trains

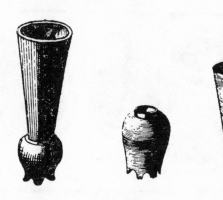

MOLDS FOR PURGING SUGAR
The cone on the right is a typical clay mold. "New-type" sugarmills experimented with clay receptacles (center), in which the molds were placed (as on left), instead of making a draining rack in the boiling room. These receptacles collected the first molasses; the second, which was mixed with the water from the clay application, was then obtained in the curing house. The experiment was abandoned.

require." [74] The words "simplicity and practicality" are euphemisms concealing the sad reality of slave labor: brute force and routine. Anyone wondering why the sugarocracy that politically and economically ruled Cuba from Las Casas to Vives (1790–1830) finally lost its privilege and wealth can find the precise answer in the history of sugar technology. The 80,000 arrobas of sugar produced in 1830 by large-scale manufacture were inferior in quality to what small, rural industry produced in 1761 under the semi-patriarchal slave system. The "little mills" that sold their sugar in the local market had put a certain medieval artisan's pride into their production. In those days sugar was no anonymous product, but came in duly labeled boxes guaranteeing the master hand of the small artisan. Its production used lyes carefully prepared from selected wood-ash and the excrement of hens, turkeys, or pigeons, and the syrups were bleached with the sap of *maguey,* white prickly-pear, *pitahaya* cactus, the guaiacum tree or the *hibiscus esculentus;* fresh or dried blood was also used, and the quantitatively small final product was white up to the cone of the mold. [75] But large-scale production, requiring much and ceaseless brute labor, destroyed the artisanal tradition and produced but one quality: the commercial.

The barbaric slave system held the industry back in another way: to achieve high-quality standards, the semi-elaborated sugar it produced had to be sent

SEPARATORS
These were used to pour green sugar into the molds.

for final processing to European refineries, whose workers worked for wages. The stagnation and technical retrogression of Cuba's large-scale manufacture reached the point where Pizarro y Gardín, writing a manual in 1847 on the process of liming the juice, could begin by asserting that this was "the only non-practical operation." [76] Even later, in 1864, sugarmill-owner Montalvo y Castillo admitted that all a sugarmaster needed to know in our mills could be learned in a week and set down in twenty pages.[77]

And we should add a word here on a point which will be fully developed later on: for those readers of the above who are thinking of the steam engine and big mechanized sugarmill of the 1840s: these were operated by wage-workers, not by slaves.

Technification having failed, and with a labor force consisting essentially of slaves, production could only be expanded by reorganizing the work. If hands and not machines were to be decisive, the big innovations had to be introduced into the work itself. A phrase of the period sums up the new attitude: "Sugar is made from blood." The cruel significance of the failure of the machine now becomes clear: the *hacendado* introduced into his mill the rigid disciplines of big industry. Along with the European bourgeoisie, he realized that seconds are bits of capital, and he began a special Creole speed-up system, or "Taylorism," which consumed Negroes as the trapiches consumed cane.

THE FIRST DANCE
OF THE MILLIONS

In the last decade of the eighteenth century, Havana was caught up in a wild millionaire orgy. The all-time-high sugar prices after Haiti's ruin distorted the island's economy and created problems beyond the power of existing resources to solve. To some extent the role in our history of the Haitian revolution resembles that of the English capture of Havana: it was the accelerator of a process already in the womb. It caused the sugar plantation to abort.

The sugar boom of 1792 quickly made obsolete all the colony's administrative and juridical forms. Changes which should have taken decades were made in a few years. From 1792 to 1802 life in Havana took on a new quality: the deep transformation created an exotic world of interrelations and

business deals hinging on sugar. It was a world of slave trading, of dried codfish and meat, of rum and molasses, of machines, of cloth for outfitting the toilers, of timber, land, and cattle, of transportation, of financial and trading transactions, of warehouses, road maintenance, merchant fleets and countless other subsidiary matters. And on top of all this were the non-economic repercussions: a gamut of secret, sordid deals born in the sugarmill and flowering in the University, the Cabildo, the royal medical college, the Audiencia,* the Cathedral.

The suspension of activities not directly or indirectly connected with sugar reached incredible heights in the 1792 boom. The nation became a burnt offering to the god sugar. José Sedano described it at the time as "the abandonment of the necessary to promote the useful," "useful" meaning the pursuit of the highest profits. Like all moments of economic intoxication, this one brought enormous inflation and a plunderous business rampage. There was an extraordinary demand for labor, opening jobs for everyone and circulating currency liberally among previously dispossessed classes. Money filtered down to technicians, workers, and apprentices, many of whom were free Negroes or mulattoes. White men naturally found work in sugarmills or marginal areas of the sugar business.

Peasants abandoned their fields to cut cane for 3 reales per 80-arroba (2,000-pound) cartload, a wage exceeding the profits they could obtain from their own produce. Many planted cane in their small plots, thus giving rise to an ephemeral form of *colono,* or independent cane farmer, contract. Others organized gangs to "cut and clear" forests, for which over 1,000 pesos a caballería was paid. White sugarmill employees' wages doubled, and overnight sugarmasters earned from 800 to 1,000 pesos per harvest. In sum, workers and peasants obtained more in months than they had obtained before in years.

In the backlash of this abnormal situation, production costs soared, especially for landowners owning few slaves. The price of land around Havana or in the great red-earth plain rose no less than 500 percent, and there was an inordinate, if smaller, rise in the cost of oxen and implements. Negroes selling in 1790 at an average of 280 pesos apiece now fetched

* The Audiencia was the court and the governing body under the Viceroy. (Trans.)

41

from 380 to 420 when sold in lots. Even priests reaped their harvest, hiking parochial fees for baptisms, burials, and masses at the sugarmills.[78]

The port of Havana hummed with increasing activity. With the Governor and Intendente now in the sugar-production business, the authorities could be bribed and freedom of commerce became an unalterable fact of life. When the war with France broke out in March 1793, Las Casas and Valiente assumed the responsibility of recognizing the right to trade with English and United States ships. Year by year, more and more ships entered Havana to load sugar and leave products from around the world.

The Basel peace treaty ended the war in June 1795 and opened the road to a new struggle against England. Legally the treaty put an automatic stop to the Cubans' right to trade with foreign ships, but in fact this trade continued to rise. The dance of the millions went on, if in an attenuated form. When the fabulous prices of 1792–1793 dipped slightly—although extraordinarily high averages were maintained—the producers, with incomparable cynicism, started talking of "a ruinous situation." To get an official green light for free trade, they addressed memos to the Court painting Havana in grim and terrible straits. It is interesting how even the most serious historians have fallen into the trap and written of the "depression of 1796" that resulted from the suppression of trade with neutrals.[79] Yet under the so-called "prohibition," of a total of 550 arrivals at the port, over 150 were U.S. ships entering officially, and prices were among the highest in world sugar history. So obvious was the mockery of royal ordinances that the Count de Santa Clara could issue a special permit in April 1797 for three months of free trade with neutrals, and it was automatically extended each time it expired. Sugar power was giving yet another demonstration of the liquidation of the old legal superstructure.

In the following years external maritime traffic (not including coastal traffic) continued to rise. The figures are:[80]

Year	Number of ships
1791	781
1798	800
1799	803
1800	771
1801	993

These figures are official and thus an understatement of the reality. The so-called authorization of trade with neutrals was the gimmick enabling the state-of-war regulations to be flouted. It provided a cover-up for trade with ships of any nationality that were registered in the United States. Thus the number of real or spurious U.S. ships arriving in the same years was:

1796	150
1797	383
1798	416
1799	558
1800	606
1801	824

In addition, there were the so-called *arribadas,* which do not figure in the Customhouse books— ships unauthorized to trade with Havana which entered the port to "take on water," "make urgent repairs," or "land a sick crewman." "Involuntary *arribadas*" were so scandalously frequent that one or two ships arrived every week on this basis, creating an enormous contraband traffic. They were finally prohibited. We also find numerous warships docking in the port. These were authorized to transport money and merchandise in exceptional circumstances, but in fact they did so all the time. In 1799 the Real Consulado in Vera Cruz, concerned about the constant movement of capital from New Spain to Havana, protested strongly against warships loading gold at Vera Cruz and dried meat at Tampico.[81] When Capitán General Marquis de Someruelos replaced the Count de Santa Clara, he had secret orders to maintain the ban on trading with neutrals at all costs. But the irresistible reality of sugar sky-rocketed this commerce 33 percent in the first year of his administration. With clear political vision, he noted that the Havana sugar oligarchy was the government, and that any ban on trading could only lead to the island's independence.

Like all economic booms stimulated by international conflicts, what we have called the "first dance of the millions" had a dizzy ascent, a glittering contrast of opulence and scarcity, and a vertical descent with a sequel of accumulation for some and ruin for others. At the top of the curve there was a desperate investing and reinvesting fever, the grandiose awakening of the Cuban bourgeois soul, still with unlimited faith in its own strength and an irrepressible propensity to expand. As always, money exercised its decisive corrupting influence and tore away the timid religious and feudal veils concealing the brutality of slavery. With the old morality shattered, and no bourgeois morality erected in its place, there were no limits on these new men.

Shady business deals started from the top, the Capitán General's office. Sugarocrats versed in the arts of bribery bought two clarifiers and much other equipment from Tomás Gimbal for Capitán General Las Casas' sugarmill. Soon afterward Las Casas was replaced, later to fall into disgrace. There being no further point in bribing him, Gimbal could not collect his bill and brought it to the front man, Joaquín Aristaraín, who had no intention of paying up but who knew how to arrange matters so that he would get the mill when Las Casas died.[82] The situation at the Treasury was no more hygienic: Pablo José Valiente, who already had his sugarmills humming, involved himself in shady flour deals.

The flour affair deserves separate treatment, for it developed with high Court connections. The Havana oligarchy had managed to move its chessmen into the Spanish Court and to interest members of the royal circle in their big deals. The monopoly on flour entering Cuba soon fell into the hands of the Count de Jaruco and his representative, Arango. In other words, the colony's most notable anti-monopolist was partner and administrator of a monopoly—only now the business was not that of Spanish merchants but his own.

As clear as it looks on the surface—a commercial concession to a private citizen—this flour business is one of the most confused of the period. We have, however, the documentation necessary to show who was involved. It was a long established practice, not a new business, but in Havana's period of splendor it assumed conspicuous importance. With the enormous growth of the slave population and the partial abandonment of the plots on which the slaves grew their own food, flour became Havana's most important food item after meat. The sugar-born abundance of currency assured its sale at almost any price. Thus the flour monopoly was especially interesting to the Crown. The Havana oligarchy, stronger than the Spanish merchants, took control of the business. The first shareholder in the concession made to the Count de Mopox y Jaruco was undoubtedly Godoy, Príncipe of La Paz; the intermediary was the Count de

Mopox; the key man in Havana was Arango; the U.S. representative was none other than Spain's ambassador to the United States, Carlos Martínez de Irujo; and moving in the background as liaison with various U.S. commercial concerns was José María Iznardi, a turbulent and mysterious character who was in the State Department's confidence and was U.S. consul in Cádiz. A business had to be substantial to involve such high personages: only plunder on a grand scale could interest a group in this economic category.[83]

During the "dance of the millions," flour was sold through a complex system of intermediaries. Various U.S. firms, especially Jos. Donath & Co., Robert Gilmore & Co., and Phillips Nicklin & Co., sold U.S. flour to Iznardi in Philadelphia or Baltimore. By arrangement with Martínez Irujo, Iznardi sent it to Arango. Arango sold it to Pedro Erice or Cuesta Manzanal, who in turn sold it in the local market or delivered it to other intermediaries to be sent into Las Villas province. The scale of prices, with normal oscillations, was as follows: the U.S. intermediaries bought at 1.50 a barrel and in the shady deal with Iznardi delivered it at 6; Iznardi billed it to Arango at 9; Arango cut in himself, the Príncipe of La Paz, and the Count de Mopox by selling it to the merchants at 16; and the merchants sold it to the bakeries at 24.

The Count de Mopox's royal concession was for a specified number of barrels, and these were transported speedily for fear of the blockade. Between July 28, 1797, and August 16, 1798, 47,389 barrels of flour arrived in Havana. The addition of these to what was already there glutted the city with flour. Since the Intendente Pablo José Valiente was also in on the business, the forts of Havana were turned into flour warehouses. Many a barrel developed worms and bakers refused to buy moldy merchandise at exorbitant prices. Valiente brought the army out into the streets and crushed the protests by force. In the end 3,680 barrels had to be dumped into the ocean as completely useless, but honest Valiente again saved the situation by charging them to the royal Treasury, for a total of 60,720 pesos.

The flour business had many facets. Various other contraband merchandise arrived in the barrels. Iznardi, whose faked invoices garnered him over half a million pesos, according to Irujo's charges, brought in large quantities of contraband in complicity with Arango. The Spanish ambassador to the United

States complained to the Marquis de las Hormazas about this "scandalous contraband, conducted with so much effrontery and so little discretion that it has become notorious among merchants of this city." He added—referring to Arango—that "top people in Havana were mixed up" in it. On one occasion Irujo surprised Iznardi with over 30,000 pesos' worth of merchandise earmarked for export in flour barrels, barrels which, on Valiente's instructions, passed through customs without invoices or documents. Slaves of the Valiente family were selling linens and fine laces in the streets and Spanish merchants had them arrested. The scandal could not be kept quiet by the Real Consulado.[84]

All this fancy speculation, still further enriching the Havana oligarchy, had its dire effects on the lower classes. The Capitán General had to recognize in mid-1799 that prices had risen outrageously and that the bread eaten in Havana was made with wormy flour. The report of the newly arrived Marquis de Someruelos is impressive.[85] But the toughest situation was in the sugarmills. The war had produced a scarcity of dried meat and fish. Undernourished Negroes, submitted to a twenty-hour work day, died by the thousands in the countryside. The physician Francisco Barrera y Domingo, an eyewitness to this devastation, left gruesome accounts of the Cuban sugar fields in 1797. In his analysis of slave diseases he noted as fundamental those caused by lack of food: if it were not for the sugar juice they chewed from cane, he wrote, "they would die of simple hunger." [86] For Cuba's toilers the "first dance of the millions" was a dance of anguish and despair.

2
THE CRISIS OF THE
SUPERSTRUCTURE
(1792–1819)

The story of a lump of sugar is a whole lesson in
political economy, in politics, and also in morality.
—*Auguste Cochin*

SUGAR INSTITUTIONS

By the end of the eighteenth century sugar expansion required the creation of official organs through which the new complex of activities could be channeled. There was a new situation which could not be resolved within the narrow confines of the old colonial organization. Cuban institutional forms corresponded with the concept of an incidental territory, a military bastion for the defense of the empire, an island producing tobacco. When the sugar boom posed the problems of large-scale manufacturing, and Cuban sugar invaded the world market, an organic crisis occurred which for lack of a juridical basis was resolved *de facto* by the governors of the island. Hence the transcendent importance of the transitional regimes of Luis de Las Casas and the Marquis de Someruelos.

The outstanding initial necessity was an institution which would encompass sugar production and its subsidiary economic world, one which would resolve such diverse problems as conflicts between merchants and producers, the financing of sugarmills, the maintenance of roads, the slave trade, and technical education. With the creative impetus of its new bourgeois consciousness, the Havana oligarchy wanted a radical solution, a completely new organism. But Spain, logically moved by defensive concerns, resorted to conservative measures.

Only two types of organization capable of partial adaptation to the new economic requirements existed within the American colonial superstructure: the Real Consulado and the Sociedad Patriótica, also known as Sociedad Económica. The Consulado, far from being a new institution, was an old Spanish organizational form which bore its fruits in the sixteenth century and almost disappeared in the seventeenth and first part of the eighteenth. Under Charles III it was given new life within a general policy designed to brake the inevitable fall of the empire. As for the Sociedad Patriótica, it was an intellectual institution which based agricultural and industrial progress on the enlightenment of the people. It stemmed from the French Encyclopedists and had been transplanted to Spain by Campomanes. These two organizations were the solutions Spain offered to Cuba's urgent needs.

Speaking bluntly and without euphemism for the Havana oligarchy, Arango propounded the uselessness of both. He made no bones about his disdain for the two metropolitan prescriptions. With his formidable economic mind, analyzing problems on the basis of the transformation process itself, he pointed out that Cuba's sugar boom had overtaken all of Spain's colonial formulas. Cuba had moved from a secondary and dependent position to become the world's first sugar producer. This radical change at the base had so upset the old juridico-institutional relations that it was as if the whole colonial framework had suddenly become obsolete. The leap forward was such that what Madrid proposed as a new formula was *passé* before reaching Havana. The manufacturing impetus raced ahead of formal plans. Those who lived the economic reality of the sugarmills understood this, but not those who studied it from documents in royal Court offices.

Arango, fighting and ridiculing the Spanish proposals, described the Madrid Sociedad Patriótica (which was offered as a model of what had to be founded in Havana) as useless. He added the lapidary comment: "If the model is no good, what hope for the copy?"[87] He was rougher on the Consulados, calling them "degenerate" institutions: as agricultural development agencies they were ineffective, and as commercial tribunals they merely inspired more litigation.[88] Such being the case, he suggested a Junta de Fomento on the administrative level and, on the juridical, the English formulas that had made possible the Industrial Revolution, or the Roman-based solution Montesquieu described in his *Spirit of Laws*.[89]

The Junta proposed by Arango was to be a completely new organ: an autonomous official body controlled by the Havana producers and capable of putting all national resources at the service of sugar—in fact, a budding Ministerio de Industrias with additional legal and banking functions. This symbolized the awakening of the new social class, deeply aware of its historic role, seeing the world as revolving around the production of merchandise. Fusing into one body all that Madrid hoped for from two, the project in fact dismissed the two as useless before they were born.

Royal authority could hardly accept this Junta, for it threatened to become an autonomous state within the colonial organization, despite the loyal patriotic blush its authors painted on its cheeks. Furthermore, such a body would take economic power from the merchants and put it in the producers' hands. All this is more complicated than appears on the surface. In a colony, commerce dominates over industry.[90] Sugar had created a new and lusty class, the producers—lords of the soil, Creoles, with potentially nationalist attitudes. The merchants, on the other hand, were Spaniards, since the metropolis controlled commerce. Thus the struggle between merchants and producers, common to all countries, had a definite political complection in Cuba—and hence the mutual support between merchants and the metropolitan government, with solid interests in common. For both of these the solution was the Real Consulado in its original form; while for the Creole manufacturer the solution was the Junta de Fomento.

Natura non facit saltus. Arango's solution was ahead of its time. The struggle between colonial-commercial and Creole-producer interests was resolved with an intermediate organization responding to the intermediate balance of power. The merchant had lost his old hegemony but the producer did not have the economic upper hand. Out of these two potencies—or perhaps these two impotencies—was born the strange hybrid of a Real Consulado with a Junta de Fomento appendage, plus a Sociedad Patriótica so exclusively devoted to sugar as hardly to resemble the Madrid model. Both bodies had specific functions, and assumed attributes, unlike those of any similar body in the hemisphere. They were organs of transition toward a capitalism, castrated by slave labor.

Let us glance at the birth of the two institutions. The Real Consulado began its labors on May 29, 1795, but not without an open battle between producers and merchants over its domination. The struggle was theoretically resolved in by-laws providing equal representation for the two groups. Arango, however, won control of the Consulado by smart political tactics. The rule for all overseas Consulados was that the Intendente should preside over them; Arango maneuvered the Capitán General into the *ex officio* presidency. This has been ingenuously interpreted in line with Arango's explanation that absolute neutrality, and respect for the highest general interests, would thus be guaranteed,[91] but the facts are otherwise. As a creator of sugarmills and an importer of slaves, the reigning Capitán General, Las Casas, was biased toward the Havana oligarchy, to which he was closely related (he was the uncle of the Count de O'Reilly, who was married to an O'Farrill). With his inclusion in the Real Consulado, the sugar circle, in a production and family sense, was closed.

Examining the first governing board, we find as its Prior or head Ignacio Montalvo Ambulodi, Count de Casa-Montalvo, owner of two sugarmills, five hundred black slaves, five thousand caballerías of land, and fourteen thousand head of cattle.[92] His deputy was his brother-in-law Antonio Beitía, Marquis de Real Socorro, whose escutcheon hung solidly over the San Telmo, San José, Santiago, and Nuestra Señora de la Concepción sugarmills, and who also had a slice of the San Juan Nepomuceno and Santísimo Sacramento mills and over another Nuestra Señora de la Concepción[93]—a whole constellation sacred to the production of sugar. The office of Cónsul Primero was held by the Marquis de Casa Peñalver, cousin of the Prior, whose son was married to a sister-in-law of the Teniente, or deputy chairman. The second councillor was the Cónsul Primero's son, Ignacio Peñalver Cárdenas. The indisputable Síndico was Francisco Arango y Parreño who, apart from being related to all the others, was the group's natural leader and political guide, thanks to his organizing ability and gift for seeing into the future.

This closed family group possessed no less than twenty-six sugarmills at the moment of the Real Consulado's founding, and would develop many more. The other key offices, Cónsul Segundo and Conciliario de Comerciantes, were held by Juan Tomás de Jáuregui and Pedro Juan de Erice respectively. Jáuregui owned two important Havana sugarmills, Nuestra Señora del Rosario and Nuestra Señora de la Soledad,[94] and his son Andrés consistently played front man for Arango.[95] We have already mentioned Erice as Cuba's biggest sugarmoneylender. For some twenty years the Real Consulado retained this family flavor, despite occasional interruptions by the aggressive merchant group.

A year and a half after its foundation, on Wednesday, December 21, 1796, the Consulado issued a report on its activities.[96] It had held eighty-four meetings and its essential work was made public in the form of twenty summarized points. At first reading, these suggest that the organization had many preoccupations besides sugar, and many a historian has been fooled into such a superficial analysis; but since the Real Consulado's archives have come to us intact, we can precisely evaluate each one and see that they are often euphemisms concealing a content of pure sugar. With one small exception, sugar was the *raison d'être* of all the matters dealt with in the eighty-four meetings; the fact that the wording does not suggest this merely shows the conventional linguistic hypocrisy of the rising class. This was still the period of the pious figleaf over economic nudity and few dared, like Arango, to express reality clearly. Here are the basic resolutions, with the Consulado formulation italicized to distinguish it from the real content which follows.

That there be a discount fund to aid hacendados: bank loans for sugar producers to free them from the usurious grip of the merchants. *That legal interest in this island be meanwhile raised by 10 percent:* a timid compromise in the struggle between producers and merchants. *That the sugarmills' privilege of not being auctioned off for debt be annulled:* liquidation of a feudal obstacle which inhibited the circulation of finance capital and fettered the development of sugar production. *That all disputes about refined products be resolved by the Consulado:* a juridical solution to the conflicts resulting from large-scale sugar export. *That the Junta should handle agricultural and commercial taxes following the practice with army equipment:* that sugar producers themselves should administer the tax on boxes of sugar. *That the sugar which the King's subjects export from this island be freed from duty:* another annulment of old laws hampering sugar development. *That means be studied of increasing the importation and lowering the price of Negroes:* more labor to become available at less cost. *Tighter and more equitable regulations on fugitive slaves:* agreement concerning upsets to production caused by the escape of slaves. *That the disadvantages of hacienda demolition and woodcutting practices be examined and corrected:* abundant land and firewood for the sugarmills. *That the tax on weight of livestock be lifted:* bullocks for the sugarmill and meat for the slaves. *That the number of farm workers' holidays be reduced:* slaves should work every day including saints' days, Sundays, and Holy Week, eliminating another religio-feudal obstacle to sugar production. *That the double tax collected from farmers be revised:* abolish the feudal tax on sales of land and sugarmills. *Installation of navigation lights:* for the benefit of U.S. ships arriving to load sugar. *Construction of roads:* lower the cost of transporting sugar. *Many resolutions on the slave trade:* the big problem of sugarmill labor. *Fugitive slave laws:* the same problem of labor costs. *Interior navigation canal project:* a means of getting sugar out of Güines, where the mills of the Consulado's Presidente, Síndico, Prior, Cónsul, and Conciliario de Consulado were situated. *Introduction of Otaheite cane:* a formula to raise agricultural productivity and at the same time have good fuel. *Construction of the Horcón-Guadalupe highway:* the road by which sugar reached Havana shipment wharves. *Finish the work on the wharves:* facilitate the loading of sugar. There was one resolution unconnected with sugar—on the cultivation of indigo.

A sample of the cynical sugar language was the use of the word "farmer." In one resolution it meant black slaves, in another sugarmill owners. In the case where it meant slaves, it was an attempt to use a

Spanish bishop's pastoral to Asturian farm workers as justification for some measure against blacks. When it meant sugarmill owners, it was aimed at applying to the wealthy Havana oligarchy a Spanish decree for the protection of landless peasants.

Like the Real Consulado, the Sociedad Patriótica of Havana gestated in the womb of sugar, and producers and merchants dominated it. In that sense it maintained the agricultural-industrial line of Campomanes. It sought to boost production through education and the practical application of pure science. At first there was some duplication of its and the Consulado's functions, but soon there was a natural division of labor. The Consulado dealt with basic problems, the many facets of the daily activity of sugar, the deep roots of the economic structure. The Sociedad Patriótica oriented itself toward theoretical studies, social repercussions, intellectual activities, and the effects of sugar on the outside world. But since these were all aspects of the same thing, the two institutions worked closely together. The Consulado was the place for men of action, the militant sugarocracy—producers, moneylenders, merchants, slavers; the Sociedad Patriótica was for intellectuals, for the ideologues who expressed in words what the Consulado expressed in figures.

Without going into the same detail as with the Consulado, let us recall the Sociedad Patriótica's first resolution at its first directors' meeting: to apply to sugarcane grinding mills the motive power of the pendulum. As noted earlier, this was La Faye's famous project, which Governor Las Casas and his nephew the Count de O'Reilly, among others, were interested in. The first resolution concerning books was to translate the works of Corbeaux and Dutrone de la Couture on cane growing and sugar manufacture.[97] The first resolution on education dealt with the establishment of a school of chemistry—and there was no doubt about the meaning of the word "chemistry." On page 17 of the first volume of the *Memorias de la Real Sociedad Patriótica* (Proceedings of the Royal Patriotic Society), published in 1791, it is defined as "the art of making sugar." And the Sociedad's first publication was José Ricardo O'Farrill's excellent work on Cuban cane-growing and sugar-elaboration methods.

The Sociedad Patriótica and Real Consulado were channeling institutions for the murky entrails of the sugar world. They acted as alchemists' retorts, in which producers and merchants integrated and contraposed their economic interests. They were the battlefields on which all conflicts rooted in the country's economy were fought. During the dominant stage of the Havana oligarchy, the Creole producers controlled the Consulado and their intellectuals ran the Sociedad Patriótica. As the combination of economic forces underwent a change in the nineteenth century, merchants replaced producers and slave-trade ideologists supplanted spokesmen for the sugarmill owners. The parallel developments in these institutions and in the national structure during the great transformation of Cuba from the Las Casas to the Tacón administrations (1790–1838) are easily followed. In the Consulado's first period the decisive figure was Arango, key man of the production sugarocracy. Arango spoke disdainfully of the Consulado once he lost his hegemony over it.[98]

Intellectual forms often survive by inertia the economic roots that gave them life, and the producers kept control in the Sociedad Patriótica after they lost the Consulado. They fought the last battle there in the 1830s. The fight raged around the Academia Cubana de Literatura, but this was a veil concealing stark economic reality. At that time José Antonio Saco was the Creole producing class's spokesman, while the merchants spoke through Juan O'Gavan, Cuban ideologist of slavery and the slave trade.[99] The conflict was resolved by Saco's expulsion from the island. In the arcane world of figures that was the Consulado, the shift of power proceeded discreetly; but the Sociedad Patriótica was an organ of ideology, communication, and message, and its internal struggles became something of a public scandal.

The fact that sugar was the *raison d'être* of both institutions will startle many students of standard histories, especially in the case of the Sociedad Patriótica, which has always been depicted as a cultural center outside of economic struggles[100]—as if a cultural organism in any period can avoid reflecting the doctrines of the ruling class. However, identifying the primary force, which showed itself in a thousand ways, does not make the Sociedad Patriótica and Consulado any the less important in our country's history. By pinpointing the sugar motivation, we do not minimize the great work these institutions performed in raising Cuban life to a higher economic stage. They were the sugarocracy's institutional vehicles, precise manifestations of the new juridical and social superstructure. Receiving, harmonizing, and channeling contradictory economic forces and conflicting ideas, they acted as crucibles in which the materials of the future were smelted. In this sense they played an indelible historical role. Having blossomed as the new creations of the militant sugarocracy, they lost their original meaning over the years and, like all human institutions, died a natural death of old age when the force that bore them expired. By the mid-nineteenth century both may be said to have vanished from public life. The Consulado was officially superseded after many changes in its organization. The Sociedad Patriótica expired when it became an "intellectual" organization in the bad sense of that word. From then on it was used to capitalize on its one-time prestige, as old and drained people are used. Such was its melancholy mission up until our time: in the republican period it began by defending the Platt Amendment and ended by supporting the policies of the government in power. The real Sociedad Patriótica—that of Arango, Peñalver, Saco, and Delmonte—had died in the previous century. What replaced it was a corpse: the myriad boughs of a great tree which still gave shade after one hundred years.

CHURCH AND SUGARMILL

Sugarmills were founded under the patronage of protecting saints, and as mills multiplied in the eighteenth century—Santa María, San Antonio, San Nicolás, San José, San Rafael, Santa Isabel—the Havana area became a celestial paradise with slaves. Some saints were extraordinarily popular, for reasons unknown to us, and their names were constantly repeated. In 1763 the Marquis de Villalta had a San Antonio mill in Managua, María de Meyreles had two San Antonios, and there were seven others owned by Antonio Laso de la Vega, Jacinto Barreto, María Teresa Pérez de la Mota, Luisa de Orbea, Antonio Alberto Acosta, Rafael de Cárdenas, and the Marquis de San Felipe y Santiago. There were ten called Nuestra Señora del Rosario, six called Virgen del Carmen, five called San Francisco, three called Virgen de Regla, and three called San Juan Nepomuceno.

When a saint proved less propitious than the mill owners hoped, the name could be changed. For example, in 1799 the buyers of the Victoria del Santísimo Sacramento mill decided to change its name, and five saints to whom they were partial—La Santísima Trinidad, San Pedro, Los Dolores, San Francisco, and La Purísima Concepción—were put into a hat. Two draws were made and, La Purísima emerging victorious in both, the mill was rechristened with that name. But since the old name had become familiar and had been used in all commercial transactions, the complete title was: La Purísima Concepción sugarmill, alias Victoria del Santísimo Sacramento.[101] This was not the only case in which it was deemed disrespectful for a new saint to replace an old and a new name was simply tacked on. Among sugarmill names we find San Antonio y Las Animas, Nuestra Señora del Rosario y San Antonio, Nuestra Señora de Loreto y San Nicolás, San Antonio y San Miguel. Like the mills, each canefield had its patron saint.

These complexities of nomenclature make sugar research extremely difficult. At times a mill appears under five different names in twenty years. Furthermore, since the names often failed to catch on, mills appear in maps and documents under the name of the owner; and when he owned more than one mill they would be known, for example, as "Diago Grande" and "Diago Chico"—"Big Diago" and "Little Diago."[102] In other cases the original name of the district or hacienda outlived all later ones, and *hacendados* had to speak of their mills as today we refer to criminals: San Ignacio, alias Jicotea, La Santísima Trinidad, alias Tinaja, Nuestra Señora de Regla, alias Retiro.

The end-of-the-century sugarocrat awakening immediately produced a series of clashes with the Church. Bourgeois revolutionary consciousness was confronting the last feudal superstructure. The Church-sugarmill battle occurred on a broad dogmatic-economic front, with questions concerning cemeteries, labor, and taxes among the gamut of problems, but with a jettisoning of saints from sugarmill names as its primary manifestation. The attitude was typical of a class with more faith in its organizational and technical capacities than in divine benevolence. Bishop Espada showed a clear vision of the future when he saw in this a first symptom of open irreligion.[103]

The first saintless mills belonged to the top men

of the sugar renaissance: Luis de Las Casas, Pablo José Valiente, Arango, and the Count de O'Reilly. Las Casas' mill, donated as a bribe to the Governor, was called La Amistad (Friendship), an exhibition of the sugarocracy's total shamelessness. Valiente's and Arango's mills, and the one belonging to O'Reilly, were given neoclassical names—La Ninfa (Nymph) and Amphitrite—as if to suggest that life in them was attuned to the French spirit.

From then on sugarmill names reflected the distress stage of the nineteenth century's fluctuating sugar curve: there were fourteen named Esperanza (Hope), one named Nueva Esperanza (New Hope), nine named Atrevido (Audacious), and five named Casualidad (Chance). Caught in the trap of producing merchandise with slaves, without the possibility of technology or capital, Cuban *hacendados* moved through a sea of noble titles and countless luxuries toward inevitable ruin. The residue of a faith which they could never quite lose was expressed in such combative names as Aspirante (Hopeful), Conquista (Conquest), Confianza (Confidence), El Buen Suceso (Good Results); but other names clearly betrayed the subconscious: there were three named Apuro (Wits' End), two named Angustia (Anguish), and four named Desengaño (Disenchantment). It is possible, though we have no documents to prove it, that Tinguaro (the name of the great Canary Islands rebel against Spain) was a timid Cuban message of liberation.[104]

What deep transformation of the Cuban superstructure can be seen through these simple changes of words? In the Spanish semi-feudal organization, the Church played a relevant role; hence sugar and Church were tightly linked. In 1602 the Governor had used that year's great sugar harvest as the main argument for bringing the Cathedral Church to Havana.[105] Until the first half of the eighteenth century, the Church stood out among the buildings in a sugarmill. Some of these sugar chapels were so important that they were maintained after the mills disappeared, and the people who grew up around them attend mass in them to this day—for example, at San Miguel del Padrón and San Miguel del Río Blanco. Such chapels functioned under special permit from the Episcopate, under which a *hacendado* undertook to maintain in his mill a priest to administer all religious offices. Since this privilege almost always gave rise to conflicts with the parish church's jurisdiction, permits were cautiously granted. Parish churches administered the religious offices in sugarmills which did not have chapels.

Until the mid-eighteenth century, when slaves were still few and had not yet submitted to a murderous work schedule and the mills were confined to a relatively small area, district parishes did an adequate job. But this semi-patriarchal setup was broken by the sugar boom; sugarmills spread far and wide and large-scale, three-hundred-slave production units were introduced. It was now clearly impossible to fulfill the Law of the Indies, the Good Government Decrees, even the Fugitive Slave Law of 1789, according to which Sunday and saints' day attendance at mass, baptism, religious indoctrination, confession, communion, confirmation, church marriage, and burial in consecrated ground were obligatory for slaves.[106] There was an odd intermediate stage during which the burgeoning sugarocrats tried to reconcile the rigid feudal superstructure with the intensive exploitation of the Negro. Especially after 1780, numerous permits for sugarmill chapels were granted and many impecunious priests emigrated to Havana from Spain and the United States. Francisco Barrera y Domingo, an eyewitness, tells how European priests settled in sugarmills and prospered in the Lord's service with masses, intercessions for the departed, marriages, baptisms, and Negro prayer-instruction classes.[107] They soon came into conflict with their superiors. The priests became sugarmill employees rather than members of the clergy, and this broke the hierarchical Church structure: while these men made their little piles in the sugarmill, and absorbed the religious offices in neighboring mills, cathedral coffers got a less than satisfactory share of the cash in circulation. Permits for new chapels were suspended and the old parochial system restored. But then the *hacendados* submitted that it was impossible to take two hundred slaves out of the mill each Sunday and march them four or five leagues to mass.[108]

In short order the insoluble contradictions between a merchandise-producing system and the Church's feudal superstructure became obvious. The modern sugarocrat, obsessed with raising production and lowering costs, needed to prune away all expenses which did not contribute to his merchandise-creating mission. The payroll item for "religion" was ridiculous from an economic standpoint and there was a not surprising tendency to suppress it. The first to open fire publicly was Nicolás Calvo, one of the most progressive sugarmen, who complained about the cost of maintaining a priest at a 400-peso salary plus emoluments in food, animals, etc., merely to say mass. The man also got separate and "exorbitant fees for burials, marriages, vigils, baptisms, and, if the truth must be told, even for confessions; in the aloofness of his office or his own pretensions, he always requires some gratuity, and much time is lost in having the slaves perform the penitential sacrament." To remove any doubt, Calvo presented in 1798 the receipts documenting his complaints.[109]

Obstructed on both sides, with no ecclesiastical interest in granting new permits and with the sugar producers steadily losing religious fervor, the Church began disappearing from the mill. The sugar-secularization process, which began at the end of the eighteenth century, culminated with the introduction of the steam engine in the 1820s.

In sum, we may mark three stages in the history of sugarmill chapels. First, their founding, with the bishop's permission and blessing. Second, the sugarmen's desire, during the end-of-the-century boom, to get free of the district parish and close the circle of their operations. At this point the Church began to resist further concessions and the sugarmen appealed to the Crown. Finally, the Real Orden of March 1800, conceding permission to erect chapels in the mills, came precisely when no more were being erected and the producers were daily showing less concern for religious matters.

Another cause of friction between the Church and the producers was the so-called indoctrination of slaves. The raison d'être of slavery was economic, but it needed religious justification. Here it is important to note that Spanish theologians had a long and distinguished anti-slavery tradition which could be summed up in the famous saying: "To save the soul it is not necessary to enslave the body." Nevertheless, the local Church dutifully built up a body of doctrine justifying slavery. It was based on the belief that the chief reason for bringing the black savage from Africa was to redeem him by work and teach him the road to Christian salvation. This lent the sugarmill the fragrance of a redemptive shrine and transformed the slave trade into a rosy-cheeked missionary society.

There is no doubt that in a remote stage of Cuban sugar life the Church's doctrinal principles were partially fulfilled. The tolerant atmosphere of the little production units before expansion made possible the minimal Christian instruction appropriate to a historical stage when religion was a spiritual category. When the mills had patron saints and the producers believed in God, there was time to spare and the hours dedicated to mass, catechism, or rosary were not stolen from production and did not affect costs. And in the long run this produced an atmosphere of greater tranquillity and better guarantees of the slaves' submissiveness.

In 1797 the priest Antonio Nicolás, the Duke de Estrada, published an *Explicación de la doctrina cristiana acomodada a la capacidad de los negros bozales* (Explanation of Christian Doctrine Suited to the Capacity of Simple Negroes).[110] Appearing in the middle of the sugar boom, the book already belonged to the past when it was printed. The author recognized this in addressing himself to sugarmill priests who, he suggested, saw as their chief object "to find a modest sinecure to keep the wolf from the door, and as a secondary one to indoctrinate the Negroes." But he also recognized a more solemn fact: that it is hard to teach religion to a man after a sixteen-hour work day, and still harder if it is at night and the man does not know the language spoken to him. The Duke de Estrada's ingenuous idea was that daylight was the best time for instruction since the blacks could watch the priest's mouth and learn to pronounce the prayers without having to understand them. Perhaps in this way an inner light would bring understanding of all that a Christian needed for salvation.

The Duke de Estrada was aware that religious instruction was in crisis. Sometimes this was the Negro's fault for not appreciating the good that was being done to him. For example, His Excellency the Count de Casa Bayona decided in an act of deep Christian fervor to humble himself before the slaves. One Holy Thursday he washed twelve Negroes' feet, sat them at his table, and served them food in imitation of Christ. But their theology was somewhat shallow and, instead of behaving like the Apostles, they took advantage of the prestige they thus acquired in their fellow-slaves' eyes to organize a mutiny and burn down the mill. The Christian performance ended with *rancheadores** hunting down the fugitives and sticking on twelve pikes the heads of the slaves before whom His Excellency had prostrated himself.[111]

In the face of such cases, the Duke de Estrada saw the need for a proper blend of discipline and Christian teaching. He recommended to the chaplains that they should never oppose the punishment of blacks, however unjust, and never argue with the overseer, who held all power in his hands. They should not appeal to the owner, for whom any other attitude was "morally impossible," and not get involved in slave quarrels but send them to the overseer. They should have no hacienda, farmland, cattle, fowls, not even a horse of their own. Above all, they should never put a Negro in the right but should say to them: "You yourselves are to blame because you don't all fulfill your tasks; you are many, overseer but one; today this one don't show up, tomorrow that one, next day one is naughty, next day another; overseer has to bear all this every day, every day, he don't want to get mad but he get mad. Ox him meek, but you kick him all time, he kick you. Overseer same, one day can stand it, next day has bellyful, can't stand nothing."

The Reverend Duke de Estrada also understood that the clearest examples for teaching blacks were offered by the mill itself. Sugar, he found, could explain the celestial paradise beyond. Life was a daily chore, an endless task like that of the blacks who went to the forest to cut wood. Firewood was measured in "tasks," of which the overseer kept careful count. Jesus Christ was like the overseer, noting everything down, forgetting nothing. One day the world will end and it will be like the day of the week when woodcutting ends. And just as the overseer punishes us if we don't cut the necessary amount of tasks, Jesus Christ will condemn us if we do not fulfill our spiritual duty. What must have been the slaves' conception, if they had any, of this Jesus-Christ-Overseer?

Even more graphic, however, was the portrayal of the Sugar-Soul. The clean, pure soul of the good man, the good slave, was like white sugar with its sparkling crystals untainted by impurities. No soul was all that pearly: all contained impurities, like

* *Rancheadores* were men whose job it was to pursue and capture fugitive slaves. (Trans.)

raspadura or the massecuite that came out of the *teache*. For purification it had to go to the purging house as souls went to Purgatory. Completely dirty souls were lost forever, condemned like burned sugar to be thrown out. But good ones went to be purged until no sign of dirt or sin remained, and then went to heaven like sugar to the dryers. Ah! Were there souls so clean as not to need purging it would be as if you could get white sugar without passing it through the purgery! Such sugar would make a beeline for Dryer-Heaven.

Other considerations apart, one must grant a certain beauty to this sugary explanation of heaven. Commenting years later on the Duke de Estrada's book, Domingo Delmonte wrote: "The author's aims, his correct performance, and the air of simple and ardent Christian charity he breathes do the utmost honor to that remote era when priests were posted in sugarmills—priests capable of producing such books, masters who hired and paid them, and theology professors who applauded and encouraged their perseverance in so saintly a mission." [112] Delmonte wrote these words at the height of slave barbarity, only thirty-odd years after the Duke de Estrada composed his book. But the transformation had been so cruel that those days already seemed "remote."

From the end of the eighteenth century, sugarmen stopped all religious practices in their mills except for those annual ceremonies which served as minimal moral figleaves. But they saw their mistake. If religion stole a few hours a week from production, it had been able to put a brake on black rebelliousness. One far from ingenuous sentence remained from the Duke de Estrada's ingenuous book: "God made me a slave, He wants me to serve my master, so I will work because God wants it . . . and God looks upon him with loving countenance because He sees into his heart." It was still advisable for someone to indoctrinate the blacks, and with the disappearance of the priests this high Christian task fell to the overseer. All the manuals of the period make this point. To cite only one, Montalvo y Castillo advises his overseers to read each Sunday one of the three mysteries and two pages of the catechism of Christian doctrine. Slaves should know how to cross themselves, the Lord's Prayer, the Ave Maria, the Credo, the Commandments, the Sacraments, the Articles of Faith, the Corporal Works of Mercy, the Misericordia, and the Mortal Sins, and how to make confession with the "Blessed and praised be . . ."; and mass should be obligatory on all saints' days.[113] In a word, the overseer should teach them all that they didn't know.

In the middle of the nineteenth century the sugarocrats again raised the problem of religion in the mills, explaining with total lack of modesty that it was a question of obedience. In the Real Consulado, the Síndico insisted that religion was fundamental, not merely to intercede for the spiritual welfare of souls, "but as a healthy influence in making slaves obedient and conscious of their duties." [114] This new tack was satisfactorily followed by ecclesiastics, by then firmly linked to the sugarmen. Some published their sermons to the Negroes, containing passages like this by the apostolic missionary Juan Perpiña y Pibernat: "My poor little ones! Be not afraid because as slaves you have so many burdens to bear! Your body may be enslaved, but your soul remains free to fly one day to the happy mansions of the elect." [115] Eduardo Machado was right when, with the liberal viewpoint of a man of 1868, he said of Catholicism: "Your ceremonies only serve to place a seal of approval upon our crimes." [116]

Another marginal rumpus with the Church arose at the end of the eighteenth century over meatless days in the mill. Once large-scale production did away with the slaves' self-maintenance plots, dried meat became almost their only food. After sixteen hours' work, it is a little hard to convince a hungry man that he must eat no meat on Friday. To deny this minimal sustenance was to provoke the outright mutiny of the empty stomach. *Hacendados* who were still religiously inclined resorted to dried fish, but fish was much more expensive and made meatless days a cost-raising luxury. Timidly, sugarmen took the problem to the Church. The Marquis de Cárdenas de Monte-Hermoso, for example, explained that he had to give meat on Fridays to sick and wounded slaves, who were swapping it with healthy ones so that his whole labor force was in a state of sin. For this reason he asked that meatless days be cut down to the Fridays in Lent, Holy Saturday, and Christmas Eve.[117] Always ready with pro-sugar solutions—divine or human—Arango added an economic argument: meatless days meant dried fish consumption, and dried fish was supplied by the English: if

we do away with Lenten fasting we take from the English the profit on fish consumed.[118] Finally, an assembly of theologians decided that only Fridays and Saturdays in Lent should be meatless, with no days of complete fasting. But since this was not a problem to be solved on the theologians' level, the resolution was not publicized.[119]

The other Church-sugarmill dispute was over cemeteries. Death was an ancient source of income which the Church was not prepared to lose. The problem had never arisen in the old days. A mill with fifteen or twenty slaves it did not exploit savagely had but one or two deaths a year, and the corpses were taken to the nearest cemetery. Since the mills were confined within a small area, the journey never took more than a few hours. But large-scale production, with its 10 percent annual loss of workers and its hoarding of every work-minute, could not afford the luxury of taking its corpses for burial in consecrated ground. When a Real Cédula of October 21, 1795, authorized the construction of cemeteries in Havana, the sugarmen applied it in their own special way, broadening it to cover cemetery construction at the mills. The Church's protests were answered with economic arguments. To carry a corpse in a straw basket on the back of a horse was undignified. If four men carried it in procession, the unhappy *hacendado* had not only lost the deceased worker but the day's work of four live ones. The battle of the cemeteries was another victory for the sugarocracy. The Marquis de Cárdenas de Monte-Hermoso contributed a touch to the controversy which was an indication of the barbaric attitude toward slaves: he noted that carrying a female corpse by a slave might provide an opportunity for sexual excesses.[120]

Longer and more polemical than any of the previous clashes was the one over holidays. The problem of a Church-producer agreement on the inhuman work regime was at first posed with the usual shyness: in 1789 the producers proposed "that the Negroes work on Sundays and saints' days for their own benefit." This was interpreted to mean raising their own food crops and pigs, an activity which also earned them money with which they might eventually free themselves. The producers' petition was shrewdly calculated. In fact, all mills stopped work one day a week, or every eighth, ninth, or tenth day. The off-day was called Sunday whether it fell on Sunday or not, although up to the end of the eighteenth century it generally did.[121] It was made necessary by the instruments of production themselves: worn wooden parts of the trapiche had to be adjusted and all the trains, troughs, pumps, skimmers, etc., on which the fermented juice left its mark needed thorough washing. Thus the Sunday stoppage was not religiously motivated but was determined by the conditions of production. On that day a reduced labor force was used.

As we have already seen, large-scale production brought the slave maintenance plots into increasing disuse. But the sugarmen saw that if the enforced off-day was used for the maintenance of minimal conucos, maize cultivation, or pig raising, the Negro would benefit by a small supplement to his wretched diet: in this way he would last longer, yield more, live more off the land, and cost less to maintain. This was the motive of the producers' plea that the slaves work Sunday for their own benefit. We must also note that during these production halts not only did a certain number have to work on repairing and cleaning, but a larger number of cutters, loaders, and haulers had to work on the so-called metida. By justifying the work of Negroes "for themselves," their work for the master was also justified. The Marquis de Cárdenas de Monte-Hermoso wanted only Christmas, New Year's Day, Annunciation, and Immaculate Conception as holidays—four days in the year.[122]

Large-scale production in the nineteenth century set precise work conditions in the mill. From then on any delay in production meant a large increase in costs. The hacendados realized that for a big mill it was more efficient to space out the production halts—one "Sunday" every ten days—and to limit them to fifteen hours. This clearly left no time for maintenance plots or pig raising. Furthermore, sugar-production labor was more profitable than minimal conucos, as marginal organizations now took care of the food supply problem. For the Negroes there were no longer any rest days. Bourgeois consciousness had evolved sufficiently to forget or ignore religious interdictions. Nineteenth-century documents show little concern about the matter. There is one memo from the Real Consulado to the "Most Illustrious Diocesan" seeking to reduce to ten a year the masses attended by slaves: Christmas, Easter, Pentecost, Epiphany, Ascension, Corpus Christi, Nativity of the

Blessed Virgin Mary, Purification, Annunciation, and Saint Peter and Saint Paul.[123] In July 1817 Pedro Diago again raised the question on a visit to the Diocesan Bishop. The Bishop agreed to the slaves working on Sundays and saints' days, but deemed it prudent to submit the issue to the Pope through the Ministry of the Indies.[124]

Among the thousands of sugarmill documents, none compares in tragic irony to these essays in sugared theology. The reader of the voluminous Real Consulado dossier on the abolition of holidays may gasp at a report beginning with a respectable quote from Saint Thomas: *"Quod non est licitum in lege, necessitas facit licitum"* (What is not just in law, necessity makes just), which reaches the hardly Thomist conclusion that "necessity knows no law." Since Saint Augustine says in the third chapter of *Decem Chordis* that work is just to avoid damage to the body, blacks should work on Sundays because their idleness exposes them to sin; between the two kinds of damage it is proper to choose the lesser— "let them work rather than sin." Sugarocrat cynicism reaches its zenith when—after citing Saint Matthew's ears-of-corn chapter (Leviticus, chapter 24, verse 9), the younger Pliny's 21st letter to Maximus, Seneca's 75th letter, and Sixtus the Philosopher—it is concluded that freedom is the most precious of all gifts: "Hence the slaves should work to win their freedom."

Each partial victory against the Church brought the sugarmen closer to their final target and toughest point of all, tithes. The Church had been gradually yielding its old feudal privileges and compromising on dogma, but giving up its income prerogatives from sugar was another matter. Since the start of the boom, the producers had raised continual protests against the high taxes on production, of which tithes were the largest. In Cuba they amounted to 5 percent of production, higher than anywhere in the Americas. Between 1790 and 1804 was waged what we may call the great war of the tithes.

To what extent were tithes actually paid? It is possible that up to the mid-eighteenth century they were one of the few taxes—perhaps the only one—paid with some regularity. The Church had penetrated sufficiently into the small pre-boom sugar-mill to be well-informed on production figures, and it was powerful enough to collect. Furthermore, a special organization existed to guarantee a specific collection. In a given area—usually comprising a parish or part of one—production was estimated over a number of years and the tithe-collection job was auctioned off. The successful bidder entered into commitments with the Treasury, putting up money and property as security. Thus the Treasury and the Diocese always made sure of their money, and the high bidder was obliged to make a thorough collection since it was his own loss if anyone did not pay up. As assurance that the job was done well, the collectors were always rich and influential members of the oligarchy, with resources to back their guarantees to the Treasury and power to make sure of payment.

The great sugar expansion sent this whole system into crisis. The proliferation of mills, their remoteness, the sugarocrats' growing lack of enthusiasm for religion and for collecting tithes made problems for Church and Treasury. There was a big increase in tithe collections but not in proportion to the growth of production. From the 1780s on, tithe collectors complained that the sugarmills were not turning in their production reports. Around 1790 only 30 of the 193 mills in the Havana diocese were complying with the regulations.[125]

The producers sent the King a number of petitions to lower the tithes. There was little result and in 1796 the Real Consulado, skillfully directed by Arango, asked that tithes not be collected from producers who were building new mills.[126] The King promptly asked the opinions of the Bishop of Havana, the Dean, and the Intendente. Meanwhile, the producers continued their policy of cheating on tithes, and in 1797 the first public battle occurred. Tithe collectors, who had paid exorbitantly for the office, demanded to see the sugarmills' account books to check statements on production. The accounts had until then been kept secret as a purely internal matter, and the request to make them public angered the sugarocracy. The Real Consulado called a special meeting on August 23, 1798, and all the producers attending declared themselves against this "new and immoral" practice. The most sparkling speech came from the Marquis de Casa Peñalver, who recalled that as tithe collector years previously he had asked the learned doctor Palomino, judge of the diocese, what to do in known cases of cheating. The learned doctor had replied: "Friend, welcome to your house the sugar they give you and keep your mouth shut."

The Marquis' advice to tithe collectors could not have been clearer. The hacendados closed ranks and refused to produce their account books. This was the first sugarocrat rebellion against the Church.[127]

Sugarmen had the edge in the tithe battle up until 1798. The man with the greatest influence in the Cuban Church, almost on a level with the Bishop, was Luis Peñalver Angulo, Bishop of New Orleans and brother of the Marquis de Casa Peñalver. His family formed one of the most powerful sugar consortiums in Cuban history. With such strong support, sugar-Church relations became increasingly tense, but always to the producers' advantage. The situation changed in 1798 when Espada y Landa—invested as Bishop by Luis Peñalver Angulo himself—took over the diocese. Espada y Landa fought hard against the sugarocracy in his first ten years in office. His reports to the Crown painted the sugarmen in the darkest colors, referring to their unconscionable greed for money, their vices, irreligiosity, and brutal exploitation of blacks.[128] From 1798 to 1804 diocese and Real Consulado were locked in inexorable struggle. The sugarmen pulled all their strings in Madrid and sought new solutions to the problem. Calvo suggested a transitional formula: part of the ecclesiastical tithes should be spent on building roads for the general benefit.[129] The Marquis de Cárdenas de Monte-Hermoso and Arango got the difficult assignment of convincing the intransigent Bishop.

A Real Consulado request for an interview with the Bishop went "mysteriously astray" and he never received it. The hacendados wrote to him again on March 16, 1802; the Bishop replied a month later that, as soon as some "little matters" were out of the way, he would receive a delegation with pleasure. The "little matters" took eight months: on November 12, 1802, the first interview took place, and was postponed till next day just as it was getting down to business. There was no next meeting because the Bishop, to the unconcealed fury of the Consulado, was "sick" for over a year. By the end of 1803 he had "recovered." But in 1804 Espada y Landa learned that the producers had won the day. By direct bribery in Madrid they had obtained a Real Cédula on April 4, exempting new mills from tithes and freezing the old ones' payments at a fixed amount based on 1804 production figures. The sugarmen had triumphed in the decisive battle,[130] and the new economy liquidated the most solid and visible of the old feudal superstructures; in the early nineteenth century only a few small skirmishes are recorded. No longer able to collect big sugar tithes, the Church tried to make up the loss with tithes on molasses, *aguardiente,* and all minor and maintenance products of the sugarmill. There was a new fight between Arango and Espada y Landa. In the end the sugarmen, euphoric in their power, took to sitting in on meetings of the Junta de Diezmos, the tithe body, to which they had never belonged. The Bishop personally ordered them thrown out, but they got royal permission to attend on January 24, 1805. After a report by the Bishop to the Crown the permission was revoked on August 2, 1807.[131]

At the zenith of sugar power, Church and sugarocrats made peace. They had many interests in common, especially when the bourgeoisie lost its revolutionary impetus and needed the cement of solid ecclesiastical tradition. The post-1820 harmonious stage was introduced by the Most Excellent Señor Dean of Havana Cathedral, who published the most grotesque pamphlet in justification of slavery ever to appear in the colony.[132] After this the Church, the sugarocrats, and the slave traders maintained amicable relations, disrupted only occasionally by some priest set on fulfilling Christian doctrine. Such was the case of the Bishop of Santiago, Antonio María Clarét y Clarat, who was expelled from Cuba in 1858 and is today venerated by the Church as a saint.

All these Church-producer squabbles are a miniature colonial version of what Groethuysen studied in France as the birth of bourgeois consciousness. The laws essential to the development of the bourgeoisie impelled the Cuban producer to shake free of religious tradition, even though he was no bourgeois in the full sense of the word. The simple fact of being a producer of merchandise for the capitalist market, and of having to be ruled by the laws of that market, made him a man with a bourgeois consciousness. The Cuban phenomenon, of course, had different characteristics from those in Europe. In the first place, the Cuban sugarman was no creator but an assimilator of what was useful in previously existing principles of autonomous life. His development resulted from his new economic conditions and from the imitation of his European confreres. And he did not have a strong religious superstructure to break with. The Havana Church had been character-

ized by a less than rigid attitude appropriate to a cosmopolitan population always open to the world. The lower clergy had lax habits, and the higher were linked to the sugar families. The Church had very substantial sugar interests. Santa Clara monastery alone received a slice of the profits of over twenty mills. It was an ancient custom to impose chaplaincies or quit-rents on the sugarmills for the benefit of a monastery, a saintly image, or a religious figure. We know that the statue of Saint Ignatius was a "partner" in the San Juan Nepomuceno mill in 1772. The monastery of Santo Cristo del Buen Viaje (Christ of the Good Journey) got part of the profits from the Cárdenas Peñalvers' mills. The Colegio Seminario collected 25,000 pesos in 1779 from only two sugarmills. We can understand why a priest—José Agustín Caballero—turned up as one of sugar's leading spokesmen during the boom.[133]

The Church-producer conflict is the most important external manifestation of the birth and rise of the sugar class. After the boom the existence of the sugarocracy was a solid fact: it had proved its right to exist by its activity in building a new world; it had shown that life could be organized in a new way. Now sugar was power, and the theologians had to take their hands off temporal matters. The new sugar producer had emerged in Cuban life proud of being the new world's true representative. To affirm this to himself, to show that he had built the sugarmill with his own hands, he had to eliminate the Church. Yet he was not blind: he knew the difference between what suited him and what was necessary for the slave and the wage-worker. *Their* religion was not to be suppressed—for could anything be more useful to preserve the social order he himself had created? To quote Groethuysen: "Property is much more secure under the protection of religion than under that of an emancipated lay morality. The dispossessed classes must not be deprived of their faith, or they may attack the property of others. The greater their misery, the more necessary to see that religion retains its hold over their souls." [134]

The Catholic faith in its most rigid form did not penetrate the sugarmill; but when slaves assembled in mill yards, its saints were effectively produced to the muffled sound of drums. Historical fate brought together men of the most diverse cultures, languages, religious ideas, and musical articulations, all for one annihilating task, all with the same terror and yearning for freedom. The mill came to resemble a demoniac temple where a new faith was being fashioned, with white gods and black gods, with drums beating time to Catholic prayers. Much later the city would provide a definitive form for this syncretism, but now they were pouring out their suppressed pain, returning to themselves and being reborn. The sugarmill was not only a tomb; it was a forge.

THE IDEOLOGICAL TRANSFORMATION

The sugarocracy could not express their germinating bourgeois consciousness exactly. Their end-of-the-century evolution was in fact too abrupt to allow time for outlining a body of doctrine, and codification and dogmatization came much later. The birth of large-scale manufacture was but a moment of affirmation. The construction of their economic world was the sugarocracy's proof to the metropolis and to themselves that the future held unsuspected possibilities and that they belonged to that future—and the proof was in solid cash. The economic victory was at the same time a first-class political one. They had made the world of sugar, an indigenous island world, with their own hands; they had not imported it from Spain.

Sugar put a widening gulf between the Spanish metropolis and the men of Havana. The sugarocrats were attracted by an industrial center of gravity based in England and France, and aimed point-blank at conquest of a market in the north. This would mean an investment in the fundamental values of life. The sugar producer was discovering himself to be an active, economically motivated man who owed his rise to the merchandise-producing process. This rise cannot be interpreted in terms of the old concept of "ambition." [135] He did not feel himself to be moved by dark impulses, by blind avarice and occult desires; he acted on precise principles and norms which he considered honorable and mandatory, and for which he asked recognition. Proud of being a Cuban sugar producer, he stood up against the convulsive situation in Spain: all of that belonged to an order of values which no longer applied to him.[136]

For the Spaniard and the Spanish government, the basic doctrine in America was their own primacy in history and their noble past. America was Spanish: they had discovered, colonized, civilized, and exalted it. Spain was the Mother Country and all the branches across the ocean extended from its generous trunk. But the sugarman countered this idea with a new concept of the past. He did not reinterpret it, he simply denied it. It did not exist. True history began after the capture of Havana by the English.

Placing the birth of Cuban history in 1761–1763 was a political invention on the part of the sugarocracy which endured as long as that class had the power—until modern times. As we have seen, Arango wore himself out hammering this point in; he even ended by calling the earlier years "primitive times." [137] Since he himself was born around then, the "primitive times" were those preceding his birth. Everything important in Cuba happened later, with sugar and the sugarmen; with them, history began. Erasing the past was also a spiritual revolution against the pattern set by the old noble families. Within the feudal superstructure the sugarocrat seemed like a *nouveau riche,* an upstart. To be rich without being noble was rather indecent, for rank was what legitimized nobility. Still without full self-confidence at the end of the eighteenth century, many sugarocrats breathlessly applied themselves to buying titles. Havana began to swarm with counts and marquises. Suspiciously near the end of the century (1795), the Crown decreed a "Tariff for Obtaining Honors," which set up a quick method to acquire a title and for a mulatto to convert himself into a Caucasian. It was a wise law, channeling the suppressed desires of many sugarmen whose class consciousness was still misty.

Since none of this title-fever corresponded with the sugarocracy's real ideological content, mockery of the purchasers of nobility became an intellectual trend as class lines sharpened with the passage of time. Pride in one's activity in the new economic life was proclaimed as the only true value: with the liquidation of the past, being a Havana sugar *hacendado* was a thing to boast about.[138] The new values were tangible. The sugarocrat class congratulated itself on having "things" which no one had in Spain. Thus when Capitán General Miguel Tacón opposed building the Havana railroad on the ground that it would be a gesture of superiority over Spain, he was right from the standpoint of external images.[139] After the sugar boom Cuba outdid Spain in welcoming many modern inventions, especially those which helped raise the standard of living of the wealthy classes. Miguel Aldama painted a remarkable psychological portrait of the new class in a letter to a cousin in Paris, describing the nature and function of the automatic "water closet" installed in his palace before these sanitary devices were known in Europe.[140]

The personal affirmation vouchsafed by material possessions necessitated a constant show of wealth. Nineteenth-century Cuba's prodigal luxury had psychological derivations but was also a means of strengthening credit. As Marx said: "Luxury enters into capital's expenses of representation."[141] Along with this philosophy of and for the dominant class appeared its counterpart—exaltation of labor and of saving. The reports on vagrancy are part of an ideological manifestation sharpened by an acute labor shortage.

One by one the sugarocrat assimilated the new forms of bourgeois consciousness, but he was still not a full-fledged bourgeois. The tremendous contradiction of selling merchandise on the world market and at the same time having slaves was painfully reflected in his ideological world. He had one foot in the bourgeois future and the other in the remote slave past. In this vacillating position he aspired on the one hand to the highest bourgeois conquests, all the superstructure made possible by free production; and on the other he wanted to keep the protecting shield of the slave-master. Thus when he appropriated the revolutionary cry of liberty he castrated it with an inevitable suffix: freedom for the white man. Sugar with its slave labor made the genuine bourgeois concept of liberty impossible in the island.

Despite its fast initial ascent, the sugarocracy did not take long to feel the frustration of its destiny. Like Prometheus, it had stolen the fire, and like him it was chained: slavery was the vulture that devoured its entrails. As usual, Arango was the first to note this when he referred to the rebellion of French slaves in 1791: "The slaves have aspired to civil liberty in imitation of their masters."[142] No political liberty could be on the agenda while civil slavery continued for a fundamental part of the population. The tragedy of this class, with its soaring bourgeois consciousness and clipped wings, was first pinpointed in a plea to the Cádiz Cortes by the Mexican Guridi y Alcocer, to abolish slavery in America. Freedom for

slaves was death for colonial sugar and for the social class based on the sugarmills. The Cuban sugarocracy rose in protest against Guridi y Alcocer's petition and again Arango was the chief spokesman.

The *Representación de la Ciudad de La Habana a las Cortes Españolas* (Representation of the City of Havana in the Spanish Cortes) is the first great document of sugarocrat ideology; it is the most sincere, and hence perhaps the most significant, the most cynical, and the most pathetic.[143] It broke with all established rules, speaking as equal to equal with no hint of the vassal. It was authentic political blackmail. It expressed the feudal scale of values and the sugarocracy's contempt for the old institutional forms. It reproached the King, the Church, the ministers, and flatly denied anybody's right to moralize about slavery or liberty. It stripped the past of all its ethical raiment and exalted cold money values as the one and only dogma. In this sense it is also the most disgusting document in Cuban history.

The Crown was reminded that blacks were in Cuba "in obedience to laws which not only authorized us, but commanded and encouraged us to acquire them." The Church was reminded that the blacks were there for a religion "which as we were told, and as many respectable authors' books still tell us, was very concerned to free souls from eternal damnation." Further on it was submitted that the blacks were there in fulfillment of a lofty ideal, "since all were becoming much happier than they used to be." What lends even greater importance to the document is that it reflects for the first time the absolute crisis of sugarocrat political values, the renunciation of all political liberty on the altar of sugar, the sacrifice of the nation to the plantation. Sugarocrats laughed at the purported democracy of the Cortes since "the absolute majority of votes, and even that of a single congress—however illustrious and numerous its members may be—has hardly ever produced good laws." They had to defend the omnipotence of the King, for their survival depended on a type of unipersonal legislation which would reconcile past and future, postponing to the utmost the inevitable crack of doom. Consequently, the top sugarocrats raised Ferdinand VII to a pedestal of glory, erecting a statue of him with a eulogy by Félix Varela in the Plaza de Armas.

Thus their political ideals boiled down to a glorification of liberty provided that slavery remained. Arango summed it up in one long paragraph:

Think, Señor, about the political slavery of these regions before civil slavery, about the Spaniards before the Africans, about the due rights and privileges of citizens here before determining the size and number of doors that should be opened or closed to people of color; about ways to breathe life into our inert police force, and all branches of our dead and decayed public administration, before increasing their risks and their burdens; define the role and powers of the Spanish and the colonial government before undertaking to cure ills which are neither urgent nor paramount; fortify the old government's corrupted organs and adjust its defective spectacles before exposing the wounds and infections of remote sectors of our social body.

The great sugarocrat formula was clearly delineated: reformism with slavery. Along with this devitalized and distorted reformism appeared other attitudes typical of the Cuban bourgeoisie: annexationism and independence. Even in 1811 Arango was proclaiming that the United States must swallow "if not all of our America, at least the northern part"[144]—a threat of annexation in case of abolition, which remained the sugarocrat position in mid-century. As for the threat of independence, the Capitán General himself saw, and advised the Cortes of, the need to stifle discussion about slavery "in order not to lose this important island." The following years gave sharp focus to these ideas. In Francisco de Arango y Parreño the sugarocracy had as their ideologist one of the most gifted figures in the history of America.

If on the political level the sugarocracy had to ask for reformism with slavery, on the juridical they had to reconcile bourgeois rights with defense of slave-owning. They first procured legislation assuring full enjoyment of land-property rights, obliterating the old land-grant concept. They then removed all obstacles to the devastation of the forests. And finally they achieved the expulsion of the few tobacco growers remaining on state lands. Roman law, the legal basis of capitalism, made its entrance on the Cuban stage; sugarocrats soon began to cite it as taking precedence over old Spanish law. José Antonio Saco translated Heineccio and observed that Spanish law was mortally wounded.[145] Under the new legislation the sugarocracy won its greatest legal victory: total condemnation "of all government

intervention in the management and development of private capital."[146]

The European bourgeoisie saw the inviolability of property as its prime juridical conquest. It was "the most sacred of rights, the one on which human societies were based and which most assures their duration and prosperity." But they also saw as fundamental to their system "the freedom of workers and employers to enter into contracts." Capitalism, that is, required as an indispensable premise the existence of the worker free to sell his labor. We are not concerned here with the extent to which this bourgeois "freedom" was real, only with its juridical form. While the Cuban producer claimed half of the pure bourgeois code—for his bourgeois conscience made him a champion of inviolable property in the means of production—the slave reality made him try to extend this right to the working man. He applied a bourgeois juridical concept to a situation which corresponded to the most primitive form of labor.[147]

The same insoluble contradictions arose in the field of education. Producing sugar for the world market implied running in the capitalist race. Once involved in it, the Cuban producer found himself harassed by the law of production costs and by the intrinsic need for continual replacement of old machines and for a new division of labor. This meant breaking the old organizational setup in the sugarmill. Until then production had depended on the technical expertise of the sugarmaster, but the very word "sugarmaster" betrays its feudal origins. These masters had operated within the limits of traditional functions known as "mysteries," which only professionally experienced initiates could penetrate. Large-scale production required that the veil that concealed his own process of production from a man's eyes should be torn away.[148] It became urgently necessary to reveal the exact scientific principles which ruled the manufacture of sugar, to develop technicians whose know-how would not be arcane but concrete, learned from schools and books; technicians who could be hired, paid a wage, and fired to be replaced by better ones. The "sugarmaster" was the despair of mill owners. To help break with his mysteries and liberate the Havana producers from his feudal secrets, the Sociedad Patriótica published a production manual and proposed the translation of Dutrone de la Couture. An attitude of deliberate hostility developed toward the sugarmaster, and in some manuals published by the producers he was repeatedly insulted. To puncture his mysteries, physics, chemistry, and botany schools were founded by the sugarocracy.

We have seen how the school of chemistry project of 1798 defined this science as "the art of making sugar." The concept never varied and determined the founding of the Instituto de Investigaciones Químicas in 1828.[149] The sugarocrats' first official chemist, José Estévez, proved highly frustrating. He was in fact a studious and responsible fellow who refused to bring out of the hat the sugar-rabbits expected of him.[150] The failure of these educational projects was soon obvious. The idea could prosper in France, where beet sugar was produced by wage-workers from whom a growing technical expertise could be demanded. Working with slaves, however, it was impossible to go beyond the primitive "trains," which needed no specialized knowledge. Technical instruction projects were born and died and Cuban sugar continued to depend on the old, abused sugarmasters. The influence of slavery on the mill owners was so persistent that when Constantino Bourbakis, one of the best sugar chemists ever to appear in Cuba, arrived at the Narcisa mill in the first years of the twentieth century, he still knew some of the sugarmasters, around whom clung an aura of respect. Bourbakis personally told me this, describing their frock-coats and mushroom-shaped hats and their furtive air about the mysterious powders they carried in purses tied to their belts, without which "you couldn't make good sugar."

Just as the first physics, chemistry, and botany schools failed, the first instruction in sugarocrat ideology was frustrated by slavery. The chairs of Political Law and Political Economy had hardly been founded when they vanished. The appearance and disappearance of the latter is especially eloquent of sugarocrat contradictions. Cuban sugarmen needed a special bourgeois-slave political economy which was never written down. Their great leap forward had one practical economic genius in Arango, but Justo Vélez, Havana's first political economy professor in 1818, was an egregious mediocrity. These theoretical economists did not really serve the oligarchy's ends but wavered within the net of contradictory interests. They tried to adjust Adam Smith and Ricardo to the slave traders and the Bishop, and ended as nothing better than bad journalists defending worse causes.

The founding of a chair of political economy in Spanish America in 1818 shows the prodigious strength of the sugar boom and its power to destroy old forms;[151] and the impossibility of teaching real contemporary economics shows the excruciating frustration of a class which wanted and was not able to be bourgeois. Vélez called economics a "charming and entertaining science." His use of these adjectives in the time of Ricardo and Mill underlines his total incompetence, especially if we compare him with the giant figure of his contemporary Arango. He was so innocuous that the Bishop showed great deference for his ideas and urged him to persist in his endeavors. But the professor and the Bishop received a shock at the end of 1818 when Spain suppressed all its chairs of economics and restored the scholastic methods of 1771. Vélez sailed for the United States, leaving his duties in the hands of Agustín Govantes, and the chair finally died of sheer disuse. Since it served no useful purpose, the sugarocrat-dominated Real Consulado blue-penciled its allocation of 500 pesos in 1825. The first authentic political economy lesson the sugarmen received was that the work system in their mills ran counter to historical laws. But by then they already knew it.

The continuing growth of sugar in the early eighteenth century only deepened the economic contradiction, and there was a long period of instability at the base which made its mark on the whole sugarocrat superstructure. This is the phenomenon which has distracted our political historians and prevented them from understanding the ephemerality of ideological forms. If we go to the roots of the sugar-production complex, we understand why Ferdinand VII began as an intelligent savior and ended as a rapacious tyrant, and why Arango, the most efficient organizer of the slave trade, ended up writing anti-slavery theses. Beneath this powerful tide of change a new, solid structural sediment was necessarily precipitated. But what characterizes the early days is the insecure feeling that gripped a whole class, convincing it to seize the fruits of the present because it did not trust the future. The lack of confidence took on a spiritual form. In the end, prevented by their own contradictions from building a body of positive doctrine, they could only produce a negative one. The sugarocracy knew quite definitely what it did not want to be.[152]

3
EXPANSION AND TRANSFORMATION
(1800–1860)

The inhabitants of Havana, Trinidad, or Matanzas do not represent, nor are they, the people of the island of Cuba. The people of Cuba include all its inhabitants; they should form one family, and it is among the members of this one family that the assets and liabilities should be distributed, without distinction or privilege.

—*Ignacio Zarragoitía y Jáuregui*

SUGAR OPENS UP THE ISLAND

With sugar, Havana lost its traditional hegemony and Cuba acquired a new dimension. A great green stain of canefields reached out from various centers, covering the island and transforming the whole environment—for cane meant destruction of the old landscape and the implantation of new human characteristics. At the outset, sugar had been almost a Havana phenomenon: the one hundred-odd mills existing in 1762 were all on roads radiating out from the city, not dispersed but like concentrations of small beehives.[153] Eleven mills operated around the town of Guanabacoa; then a second line of expansion extended eastward along the old Guanabo–Río Blanco–Jibacoa–Canasí road. Here were the famous San Francisco de Tivo Tivo; Peñas Altas, which had the eighteenth century's biggest slave-rising; and two giants of the same name, Jesús, María y José, one belonging to Miguel de Cárdenas and the other to Gabriel Peñalver. A third line spread from Guanabacoa along the road to Santa María del Rosario, Managua, and San Antonio de las Vegas. Finally, starting from Managua and tracing a big arc around Havana, sugarmills extended through Santiago, Rincón, Cano, Guatao, and Cangrejeras. This was the Havana sugar belt. Beyond were woods, tobacco, and cattle on ground not yet invaded by sugar. Güines had no sugar and Alquízar was still the shipyards' richest forest reserve. (Antonio Calvo de la Puerta's mill at Aguacate was south of Bejucal and should not be confused with the present area with that name.)

We have seen that forest, savanna, cattle, and seaport were the basic factors for the sugarmill planners. Transport was the producers' major prob-lem at the time, and the big ports became sugar centers. Rather than penetrate into the interior, producers preferred to make a jump and turn the ports of El Mariel and Matanzas into sugar nuclei. Thus in 1760 we find nine mills around El Mariel along the Guanajay–Quiebra Hacha road. Further east appear the Matanzas mills and an uncertain number of trapiches making or obtaining molasses for conversion into *aguardiente*.

In 1792, in the Havana area alone, 237 mills were actively operating. Sugar's grand march westward was already on, and to the east of Havana bay 45 mills covered the big Guanabacoa–Río Blanco–Canasí fringe. Seventy-six were built in the old production center of Managua-Cano. Mills were strung out in an almost continuous line from Havana to Batabanó, and canefields belonging to the Valiente family's mill, one of the eight to the south, extended to the edge of the Ciénaga. The most important original area of expansion, however, was along the coast west of Havana: 29 mills went up between Guanajay and Bahía Honda.

This somewhat disordered and impetuous growth took new routes at the end of the eighteenth century as the Havana sugar belt exhausted its forests and the mills moved further and further away. At the same time the development of Havana, now one of the largest cities in the Americas, called for ever larger maintenance areas, and land near the city soared in value. A process of concentration began, marking the transition from the little mill to large-scale production. Nearly one hundred mills disappeared or moved between 1792 and 1820,[154] but this was hardly noticed because new mills went up faster than old ones disappeared. Statistics at the end of each period show an absolute growth in total units. Typical was the Managua-Cano area, which had 76 mills in 1792; by 1804 it had less than 40, and in 1827 it had 13. The area had exhausted all its possibilities using contemporary techniques, and average production per mill in 1804 was only 89 tons of sugar, the lowest in the western zone.

Another totally exploited area was the mountainous belt extending from Havana to Matanzas. On this inadequate terrain, using the small valleys and flatter lands toward the sea, sixty-two mills managed to produce 7,227 tons of sugar in 1804;[155] after that the number of mills declined, although for some time it remained an important sugar region. As old areas were used up, expansion occurred along the Havana coast to the west and by 1804 this was Cuba's chief production center, with a total of 8,517 tons in fifty-one mills reporting the extraordinary individual average of 170 tons.[156] Here was the birthplace of large-scale manufacture. The ruins of the early nineteenth-century giants remain to this day. Planting cane between the Baracoa and Santa Ana rivers, in what is now the urban district of Baracoa, the Reverend Bethlehemite Fathers' San Cristóbal mill ground an average of 345 tons a year. To the north of the Sierra de Anafe, on the upper reaches of the Río Guajaibón, Sebastian Pichardo's San Antonio mill almost hit the 350 mark. The pride of the Guanajay jurisdiction, with an annual 440-ton average, was Bonifacio Duarte's San Miguel mill, in what is now the municipal district of El Rosario, exporting its sugar through the port of Cabañas.

Simultaneously with the westward expansion came the violent invasion of Güines, a story we have already told in part. Two mills appeared there in 1780, 4 in 1784, 9 in 1792, 26 in 1804, 47 in 1827, 66 in 1846, and 89 in 1857. There the red-soil myth was born.[157] From this center, mills invaded the red-soil savanna westward to Artemisa and eastward to Colón. The advance of sugar created or developed such communities as San Nicolás, Nueva Paz, Bermeja, Alacranes, Sabanilla del Comendador, Unión de Reyes, and Pedro Betancourt. In Bemba—the present Jovellanos—it combined with the sugar surge from Matanzas to spread along the Guanábana-Limonar road; the forest-destroying march continued until it founded Nueva Bermeja (now Colón) in

1836 and from there spread northward and southward.

But the Matanzas boom belongs to the nineteenth century. In 1798 the town of Matanzas only had three thousand inhabitants and all its houses were of straw. Its wealth consisted of three sugar mills, two cattle farms, and no coffee plantations, but its port handled the production of twenty-two mills in a sugar belt bounded on the west by Corral Nuevo and on the south by Guanábana. The total labor force was 911 slaves and 110 whites. It is never wise to rely on the census data of the period, but let us assume that the figure is reasonably realistic. Sugarmill development had already begun, and in the next years thirty-two were finished and fourteen more begun. Like Havana, Matanzas fulfilled all the objective conditions for development. Sugar growth inflated the town, so that in the same years 232 houses were built;[158] from 1800 to 1820 the urban population grew at the rate of 11 percent a year. The depopulated countryside was filled with saints' names which soon acquired key significance in sugar. New political and administrative divisions were periodically necessary, as mills proliferated like palmtrees by a stream.

Matanzas sugar expanded in three characteristic directions: from the city beside the hills to the southeast along the old Guanábana-Limonar road; from Güines through the red-earth savannas; and, the most important, southward through the old Cimarrones region to Bemba, using Cárdenas as its export outlet. Another branch brought Recreo (today's Máximo Gómez), San José de los Ramos, and Banagüises into existence. And just as small-mill production grew into large-scale slave manufacture in Güines and Guanajay, the definitive change from manufacture into big industry occurred in Matanzas at mid-century. The expansion showed itself more in volume of production than in number of mills. Insignificant in sugar history up to the end of the eighteenth century, Matanzas was producing 25 percent of Cuba's sugar by 1827,[159] and ten years later new areas had been so developed that the administrative district of Cárdenas had to be created.[160] Colón—which would be Cuba's number one sugar area twenty years later—was founded in 1837. At the time of the 1857 crisis, Cárdenas, Matanzas, and Colón were producing 55.56 percent of the whole island's sugar. At that time the Matanzas mills covered a total of 16,915 caballerías, 8,117 of which were canefields. Comparing this figure with the 9,918 caballerías (133,100 hectares) of cane cut in Matanzas a century later—in 1959—we see that by the 1850s Matanzas had stopped expanding because of the exhaustion of its soil.[161] Future sugar development would have to find new roads.

In Trinidad, an area of a very special kind, sugar developed at the same time, but in a world apart from Havana and Matanzas. On more than one occasion travelers from Havana were astonished to see sugarmills operating in the century-old community with the latest "foreign" Antillean techniques. On their way to Jamaica to study the design of the "Jamaica train," Pedro Bauduy and Ramón Arozarena touched at Trinidad and found it already perfected there.[162] Isolated between mountains, its port facing south—an ideal situation for contraband—Trinidad became an eccentric wheel on the Spanish colonial machine. It supplied oxen and cured meat to Jamaica, and for centuries had engaged in smuggling on an impressive scale. Its regular contact with the English colony brought it the indirect impact of the Industrial Revolution, and soon its sugarmills enjoyed all the improvements possible within the limits of slave labor. But its scanty savannas, and the diversion of the sugar trade to the United States, kept it from expanding as dramatically as the island's western areas.

In terms of its caneland possibilities, however, Trinidad was a production area of top importance, and its mills penetrated the valleys below the heights of Palmarejo and Caracusey.[163] Along the Río Ay, and northward to the jurisdictional border of Sancti Spíritus, two of Cuba's production giants were built—the Manacas and Güinia de Soto mills. This growth was almost as fast as Havana's. In 1790, 2,300 boxes of clayed sugar were officially shipped from the port of Casilda, plus a possibly much larger amount of contraband. In 1795 there were 32 mills producing more than 700 tons of sugar and some 1,000 barrels (11,000 gallons) of rum.[164] By 1803 there were several mills with over a hundred slaves, and not much later José Borrell founded the Guáimaro and Palmarito mills, two colossi of the day. In 1827 the Guáimaro mill was the world's champion producer, with 943 tons of muscovado and clayed sugar; few non-mechanized mills in Cuba would ever beat this figure.[165]

Trinidad followed the Güines pattern in that there, too, poor peasants had been growing tobacco and were unceremoniously ousted from their lands. Cattle, which had once been exported, did not meet the needs of sugar and had to be brought in from Sancti Spíritus. The social pattern was the same: slavery and wealthy oligarchy. Cintras, Iznagas, Borrells, and Valles decked themselves with noble titles and flaunted fortunes comparable with their Havana confreres. Trinidad, in sum, was a proud provincial replica of the capital.

Sugar development in Trinidad reached its zenith in the 1840s, when its forty-three mills produced more than 8,000 tons of sugar. The rhythm collapsed after the 1857 crisis and the town began to decline, until it gradually disappeared from the island's sugar map. *Hacendados* who had not capitalized on the boom were ruined; solid commercial fortunes emigrated in search of more propitious areas for investment, and Trinidad sugar names turned up in Cienfuegos, Sancti Spíritus, and Havana. The town began to take on the forlorn air that characterizes it today. Palaces built in the prodigal days were abandoned. The swollen peasant population, which had learned in the mill to hate the land, converged on the city: it became known popularly as the city of the "hads" (from the city whites' talk of some ancestor who "had and no longer has"). With its rancid colonial flavor, derelict houses, narrow streets impregnated with history, and conglomeration of churches reaching their pretentious towers to the sky, Trinidad moldered like an old sugar corpse.

The sugar-life of Cienfuegos was unusual. Although it lay between the island's most impressive mahogany forest and savannas that were ideal for large-scale production, sugar played no part in its beginnings: the city was founded in 1819 as a defensive white colony on the south coast facing the black world of the Antilles. But its large protected harbor—made to order for contraband slave traffic—and its woods, rivers, and savannas made it an obvious sugar zone, and at the end of the 1820s a fever of mill construction began. Capital converged on the area from Trinidad and Havana and the old sugarocrat names turned up again: Iznaga, Frías, Trujillo, Moret, Argudín . . . Contemporary data show the dizziest boom in Cuban history: in twenty years, from 1827 to 1846, production rose from zero to more than a million arrobas. By 1859, 9 percent of the island's production was coming from the new area. Between 1840 and 1860 Cienfuegos slave traders were the biggest and most accomplished in Cuba. One of them, Tomás Terry—justly known as the Cuban Croesus—was among the most important businessmen in the Americas, with capital accumulation comparable to that of Moses Taylor, the big New York trader who was his partner and *compadre*. English by name but Venezuelan by birth, Terry reached Cuba just in time to ride the Cienfuegos sugar wave. He became the axis around which everything revolved—the export of sugar and molasses, the import of machinery, slaves, and consumer goods—at the same time performing the function of banker. Despite his lavish donations, he died leaving over 20 million pesos, one of the greatest fortunes of his day.[166]

The Cienfuegos story was repeated in Sagua, although its importance as a sugar zone came much earlier: Arango was already pointing to its potential at the beginning of the nineteenth century. When the Matanzas boom embraced all the lands along the coast, Sagua became a new sugar zone by logical gravitation. The objective conditions for a boom were as excellent there as in many other Cuban areas. The first mill, founded in the 1810s, was symbolically christened Alpha by its owner, but the new inhabitants knew no Greek and changed it to Alba (Dawn)—a more fitting symbol, anyway, of the sugar awakening. Across from the Alba on the Río Sagua's lower reaches arose Guatá;[167] these were the only two mills in 1827, but five more were in construction. In the 1830s the area was invaded by restless capital from Havana and Trinidad, and the name of Iznaga appeared on various mills, as did those of such wealthy Havana sugarocrats as O'Farrill, Villa-Urrutia, Alfonso. The Count de Casa Moré played a Tomás Terry-ish role in Sagua. The growing community's history over many years may be read in the production statistics: 1827—two mills, a few hundred tons of sugar; 1846—59 mills, over ten thousand tons of clayed and muscovado sugar; 1859—119 mills, production nearly 46,000 tons. The rest parallels that of all sugar areas: the same wealth in the sugarocrats' hands, the same barbarous slave system on the land.

Over 90 percent of the sugar produced in Cuba during the nineteenth century came from the western and central areas we have mentioned. The rest of the island had a non-sugar economy. But sugar, even if

not decisive, had implanted itself in every community. Among secondary sugar areas, the town of San Juan de los Remedios played a relatively important role. We know that the sixteen trapiches grinding there in 1807 produced so little that sugar had to be brought from elsewhere to cover local needs, although this was perhaps because the trapiches were dedicated to producing molasses for rum rather than sugar. Coffee was important, however, and in that same year the area had over a million trees. The sugar curve later rose and at mid-century forty mills had a total production approaching ten thousand tons.[168]

The nineteenth century was well advanced before sugar impinged on life in the country around the old town of Sancti Spíritus. During Havana's sugar-boom decade, 1792 to 1802, the slow feudal rhythm continued there. Some small trapiches, using three to five slaves, produced sugar for local needs in typical rural-domestic fashion. The production fever brought a few more, and in 1807 there was one with thirty blacks and two with over twenty each; ten more with five to ten slaves completed the minuscule production picture. By mid-century Sancti Spíritus had grown in relative importance, accounting for 2 percent of Cuban production.[169]

Finally, in our survey of the island's central zone, we come to the Santa Clara district. We know that Trinidad sugar was being brought in at the turn of the century to supply inhabitants of the central town. Records of a lawsuit over excise taxes tell us that in 1776 the area's biggest trapiche was sold for 3,000 pesos and was located in Quemado Grande (today's Quemado Hilario). The poverty of this trapiche—the documents list its inventory and describe it as the area's biggest—shows the sugar situation in Villaclara.[170] The same conditions prevailed in 1807, when the inhabitants still had to supply themselves with sugar from Trinidad. There was no coffee and the commonest crop was wheat. Sugar, however, made its influence felt indirectly, sparking big sales of oxen and cured meat to Havana and Trinidad.[171] Modest later growth brought production to 288 tons of sugar in 1827 and 2,300 in the 1840s, but after the 1857 crisis the area quickly vanished from sugar geography. (Rebello reported a 11,500-ton production of muscovado in the Villaclara area, but this was produced in the Cienfuegos area of expansion toward Ranchuelos.)

Puerto Príncipe, the Camagüey of today, is one of

Cuban history's unknown quantities. In its extensive savannas volume rose appreciably at the beginning of the eighteenth century, and undoubtedly it had a much greater economic importance than we have ever been told. What we do have is a collection of disconnected data like pieces of a big puzzle. In *Espejo de Paciencia* (Mirror of Patience), written in 1608, seven poets show the kind of intellectual groping which is only possible in an atmosphere of solid affluence. From the end of the seventeenth century to the end of the eighteenth, there arose religious structures of a kind only seen in communities with plenty of capital accumulation. The Merced monastery, completed in 1748, was one of Cuba's largest; near it rose the imposing Parroquial Mayor—bigger than Havana's cathedral—and the parish churches of La Soledad, Santa Ana, and Santo Cristo, the San Juan de Dios Asylum, the Women's Hospital, the Iglesia de Carmen, the San Lázaro Hospital, and the Jesuit College. Donations and subscriptions for these edifices were very respectable sums in cash by current standards: on one occasion alone an Agüero gave 23,000 pesos, and 52,000 pesos were collected in a year for the Jesuit College. On top of all this there was work for three notary offices and in the eighteenth century two more were opened. In 1774 the La Torre census listed Puerto Príncipe as Cuba's second city with thirty thousand inhabitants, making it one of the largest in the Americas.

What kind of economic activity flouted the Laws of the Indies to create this little Cuban emporium? Sugar unquestionably played a major role in two ways. First, Puerto Príncipe must have supplied large Caribbean communities with cattle, oxen, and jerked beef. Haiti and the Sugar Islands totally lacked cattle land, but their sugar production could not but involve a high consumption of oxen—the only or almost the only power source—and of jerked beef, which was the slaves' main diet. Puerto Príncipe, Bayamo, and Trinidad all benefited from this trade, but there is no doubt that Puerto Príncipe excelled over the other two in contraband techniques. We must remember that Martín de Aróstegui, key man of the Real Compañía de Comercio of Havana, made his fortune in Puerto Príncipe. Varona, Agüero, Jáuregui, and Duque Estrada—to mention only some of the eighteenth century's top economic figures— also came from there. And secondly, sugar itself was produced in Puerto Príncipe. In 1715 many land grants were extended to develop sugarmills, and in 1729 the Cabildo recognized the existence of "sixty-one mills and much sugar." We have concrete data confirming the *official* production figure of 758 tons of sugar in 1760—and we know how official figures differ from reality.[172]

All this was part of an opulent extra-legal world which faced a crisis with the Havana boom. When the obstacles to export were removed, there was no reason to buy as contraband in Puerto Príncipe what was freely sold in Havana. However, the great demand for sugar, together with inflated prices, kept the ball rolling for a few more years. In 1795 Puerto Príncipe had 55 mills with a total production exceeding 450 tons, while cattle, now re-routed to Havana, continued as a substantial source of income. Since their economy was not based directly on sugar, Puerto Príncipe men did not acquire the plantation mentality.[173]

There is one more vital fact: Puerto Príncipe was the island's only important area totally dominated by Creole capital, without the smallest intrusion by Spanish merchants. The cattle-raising economy created an exceptionally free mentality, closer to bourgeois consciousness than was possible for the slave-owning *hacendado*. This, together with the feeling of Creole ascendancy without the clogging influence of the Spanish merchant, made the men of Puerto Príncipe a shock-force against the Havana plantation concept. The rise of western sugar produced a sharp rivalry between Havana and Puerto Príncipe, which found noisy official expression from the end of the eighteenth century. Its first big manifestation was Ignacio Zarragoitía y Jáuregui's remarkable report to the Real Consulado, dated Puerto Príncipe, March 8, 1805. His is the first piece of Cuban writing with a real Cuban approach that goes beyond narrow local limits; he is the only one we know in this period who can be compared to Arango.[174]

Zarragoitía posed all the problems of the hour from a non-sugar perspective, although on some points he could not help agreeing with the sugar producers. For example, he attacked the merchant thus: "It is too well known that business is not the businessman, and that the only positive result of exclusive privileges is the glorification of those who receive them and the misery and slavery of everyone else." He faced the fact that Puerto Príncipe was getting its consumer goods from others in the same province, adding that the hardship fell on the consumer. Then the definitive sentence: "The merchants' interests are absolutely contrary to those of the state." For the first time in Cuba he cited the example of the ascendant United States, "liberated in 1783 and already holding second place in trade." He denied that Cuba had progressed, "except for the four privileged ones." He demanded modern methods of economic control and a census of population, agriculture, industry, trade, and national wealth. He roundly disparaged Spain: "Hopes of help from the Peninsula are like the Jews' hopes for a Messiah." Finally, he expressed the first precise concept of a Cuban, the first full-throated cry of nationalism: "The inhabitants of Havana, Trinidad, or Matanzas do not represent, nor are they, the people of the island of Cuba. The people of Cuba include all its inhabitants; they should form one family, and it is among the members of this one family that the assets and liabilities should be distributed, without distinction or privilege."

Zarragoitía spoke not for himself but in the name of a Cabildo, and hence for a social class. Such a dramatic cry from the superstructure could only correspond with an equally profound economic transformation. Havana sugarocrats, prisoners of their slave system, could not have spoken such words at that time. We see now why Gaspar Betancourt Cisneros ("El Lugareño"), a Puerto Príncipe man *par excellence,* was talking about independence when Havana producers trembled at the mere mention of a war that might set their slaves in revolt. The conflict between the western sugar economy and the non-sugar mentality of Puerto Príncipe continued throughout the century. It emerged in the Real Consulado's aggressive and archaic reply to the petition to make Nuevitas a free port;[175] in the Havana *hacendados'* attack on Agüero for freeing his slaves;[176] in the conviction of the Capitán General that Puerto Príncipe was Cuba's chief source of revolutionary infection;[177] and, during the Ten Years War (1868–1878) in the attitude of Camagüey-born General Ignacio Agramonte and his men in compelling the easterners to declare slavery abolished in the rebel areas of Cuba.

Sugar also lent special characteristics to life in eastern Cuba. Canefields appeared early in the valleys around Santiago de Cuba on the southern coast, penetrating as far as El Caney. At the beginning of the nineteenth century there were many small sugarmills around San Luis; in the Bayamo area there

were thirty, and around Holguín some twenty.[178] Yet the sugar of the whole eastern region was insignificant compared with the west. Around 1820 the five large jurisdictional areas of the Departamento Oriental produced no more than 5,000 tons of sugar. Total Cuban harvests skyrocketed after that year, while Oriente developed at a snail's pace in comparison, so that relatively speaking the area went into a slump. In 1859, eastern clayed sugar was hardly 0.58 percent of the island's total, and in clayed sugar and muscovado together it was less than 10 percent.

As Cuba's most backward and least productive, the eastern mills were the first to face ruin when big industry invaded the countryside and beet sugar was perfected. In the mid-nineteenth century more than half the Oriente sugarmills were still using animal power. The area's average mill had from three to five caballerías of cane and less than fifty slaves, and produced some 250 hogsheads of muscovado. By an odd coincidence, this was the setup of a small mill which was grinding in 1860 in the Yaribacoa Partido of Manzanillo jurisdiction, owned at the time by Francisco Javier de Céspedes and called La Demajagua. It was here the Cuban war for independence began.

ALONG THE SUGAR ROAD

Until the end of the eighteenth century no solid concept of island unity existed. Cuba consisted of social nuclei differing in form and leading a special kind of autonomous life. This began to change under sugar's unifying influence: wherever it was implanted, the mill created the same physical and social framework, repeated with drab monotony. It also set up a community of interest, reflected in the same way in the most remote areas: Guanajay, Trinidad, Sagua, Matanzas. Green canefields and smoking chimneys homogenized the landscape.

Roads formed an integral part of this leveling process. The advance of sugar created, recreated, and transformed the geography of communications in four phases corresponding to the four stages of our economy: footpath, cattle and mule trail, cart road, railroad. The footpath was opened up by Negroes fleeing before the sugar tide, and was used by the woodmen who made the big clearings for the mills. Cattle and mule trains, the transport for sugar and molasses until the end of the eighteenth century, followed. In the words of the day, the products were measured by "loads," meaning the weight that an animal could carry. The nineteenth century's large-scale manufacture required the transport of heavy boxes, and the concept of "loads" changed to that of "hauls" in the transition to carts—which was also the transition toward a new economy.

The lack of roads was the large-scale manufacturer's biggest headache, and the first giant mills were established around Guanajay and Río Blanco beside rivers on which the sugar was moved to the sea, completing the journey to Havana by coastal ships. The sugar invasion of Güines made good roads an urgent necessity. Millions of arrobas of sugar and molasses could not be moved along the old trail winding its way through dense vegetation, constantly sprouting new weeds, washed out in the rainy season—a trail as mobile as the men who walked it.

The problem was an elementary economic one. The average mill had 100 slaves and produced 10,000 arrobas (115 tons) of sugar and 3,000 barrels of molasses. To move this by trail, it was concluded in 1795, the sugar had to be put in sacks and transferred to boxes in Havana. This was the first cost-raising upset. The 10,000 arrobas of sugar had to be divided into 1,000 loads of 10 arrobas each, since this was as much as a beast could carry on the long journey to the port. The molasses had to be carried in small barrels, four of which made a load. Thus transport to Havana required 1,750 beast-journeys with 1,750 loads, and supplies, cured meat, and clothing outfits required an additional 200 loads on the return journey. Adding to all this the laborious hauling of kettles, rollers, and other cumbersome implements, no mill spent less than 2,500 pesos per season—a sizable sum for the period—on transportation.[179] But as production grew and the mills spread out, costs multiplied and the problem became worse: there was more and more sugar, molasses, meat, and implements to haul over longer and longer distances while beasts of burden became increasingly scarce.

Hence the sugarocracy's anguished demands for immediate road construction. Without roads, no sugar; their whole "brain trust" met to consider the problem. Two studies were published in 1795 alone, written by Juan Tomás de Jáuregui and Nicolás Calvo, and there were five more unpublished ones, by Alonso Benigno Muñoz, Julián de Campos, the Marquis de Arcos, Juan Antonio Morejón, and La Faye. The one by La Faye, the famous pendular grinding-mill man, was among the most scientifically sound works ever presented to the Real Consulado.[180] All the top sugar intellectuals were talking about roads; inevitably, Arango wrote a report on the subject.

Having long identified national needs with the requirements of sugar, the producers spoke of roads as a matter of "general interest"; later they spelled out that "the mills need good roads most and expect the most benefit from them" (Morejón). The Marquis de Casa Peñalver summed up the problem concisely: "Harvests increase and with them the transport of products to the big capital market. Thus the need increases to replace animal by wheeled transport, in view of the shortage of beasts of burden; and equally to fix the roads for the use of carts, which cannot move over such rough trails as can animals carrying small loads on their backs."

These words were accompanied by noteworthy action. In the last years of the eighteenth century, all roads used for hauling sugar to Havana were reconstructed. The road to Horcón was given a surface eight yards wide, and the Guadalupe road was thoroughly made over.[181] The total repair job undertaken on the Havana-Güines road involved an unprecedented earth-moving feat in the stretch over the Candela hills—a job performed by Güines sugarmill and coffee-plantation slaves during the dead season. The Quivicán forests had been ravaged, so the Bejucal-Batabanó road was shortened. Road building ran abreast of sugarmill construction through the first half of the nineteenth century.

The cart was a big advance on the beast of burden, but sugar, with its fever for production, giant stature, and intricate interrelations, needed something more radical than animal-drawn transport. Arango had read Adam Smith's remarkable observations on water transport, and the Briare, Centre, and Languedoc canals in France offered a remote but splendid example of how merchandise distribution could combine irrigation with linking countryside and city. In the bourgeois sugarocrat mind arose the vision of a Güines canal, blueprinted by the Count de Macuriges and encouraged by Arango. This bold concept was born in 1795 and discussed until 1834, but never became a reality.[182]

Among the copious literature on communications,

José A. Saco's *Memoria de Caminos* (Report on Roads) stands out.[183] As in all else, the big spur was applied by the Industrial Revolution and came from Europe. The railroad was at the same time the sugarocracy's triumph and frustration. Unable to mechanize inside his mill, the *hacendado* did so outside it. He could not bring the machine to sugar while he still used slaves, but he brought sugar to the machine. The railroad was the great solution to the communications problem—hence the appropriateness of the name "iron road." This was not a mere Gallicism—*chemin de fer*—but the consummation of activity and creative study over a long period. Its debut in Güines cut inflated transport costs by 70 percent in the first year.[184] It removed the brakes from sugar expansion, causing mills to grow beyond all estimates; its mere presence made large-scale slave manufacture a viable proposition. It was not organic growth but a leap ahead, an overnight change in the whole economic scene. The railroad, not the steam engine applied to the grinding mill, was the first element of the Industrial Revolution to transform Cuban conditions of production. It was the foundation of the distorted growth of slave manufacture which sharpened internal contradictions to the maximum, and it also made possible the first steps toward big industry. Wenceslao de Villa-Urrutia, organizer and construction administrator of Cuba's first railroad, was at the same time the builder of our first highly mechanized sugarmill. It was no coincidence.

The railroad had a partially constructive influence on the countryside. It was no conquistador penetrating virgin territory, but followed the old cart roads between canefields over land that was already tamed. It soon united the scattered complex of mills. In the western area it was a pure appendage of sugar, the first line extending directly to the heart of Havana production, San Julián de los Güines. The initial stretch was inaugurated on November 19, 1837, in Bejucal; it reached its destination just a year later, on November 19, 1838, and in a mere twenty years all the Cuban sugar areas were linked by rail lines.[185] One line crossed the red-earth belt from Guanajay to Macagua beyond Colón, and there were connecting lines to Havana, Batabanó, Matanzas, Jovellanos, Cárdenas, and Júcaro. The railroad followed the Cienfuegos expansion as far as Cruces, whence a branch went to La Esperanza and another to San Marcos. Sagua mills were connected by a line from Cifuentes to the sea and one from Carajatas to Quemado de Güines. Smaller lines included a six-mile one linking Caibarién and Remedios and a double-track one via Regla-Guanabacoa connecting with the big sugar warehouses. The old rebel capitalists of Puerto Príncipe extended a forty-five-mile line from their city to Nuevitas.[186] In Oriente, the Cobre–Punta de Sal and Santiago–Santo Cristo lines and the big Guantánamo railroad had a more general economic significance. Behind the railroad came the telegraph, spurred by industry but made still more necessary by deepening political tensions.

By 1860 Havana was connected with all the island's main cities; from 1854 on modern sugarmills had a Morse telegraph, a cord-and-counterweight affair fed by sulphuric and nitric acid and mercury electric batteries.[187] By standards of the day Cuba had achieved physical unity, and for its backward communities there was a growing process of integration. Now thinking in terms of their whole country, the sugarmen projected giant mills in the virgin zones of Camagüey and Oriente. Vives' map, symbolizing the geographical integration, shows all the mills existing in 1827; after that year Pichardo periodically published new, corrected maps, following the expansion step by step. In 1862 Carlos Rebello published his *Estados Azucareros* (Sugar Reports), the first non-governmental work with statistics for the entire island. Sugar had united Cuba.

If sugar integrated the countryside, it physically transformed the city: Havana's streets were the final stage of its long journey. They had never been distinguished for their good condition, although the Cabildo and Capitán General had for some years made serious efforts, paving some with lignum vitae wood, gravel, and cobblestones. The end-of-the-century boom had made them impassable. There was a general overhaul early in 1798, but by September they were again in wretched condition, with cobblestones loosened and torn out and sidewalk slabs cracked and askew. A Cabildo report pinpointed the cause: "The normal loads of carts using the streets, which we may estimate at an average of ten boxes of sugar weighing two hundred arrobas"—this without including the loads of meat, sugar-box lumber, kettles for the mill. It was indeed a radical change from the neat little one-mule market carts of the old days.[188]

Town planners and economists went into action to

coordinate the beautification of Havana's streets with low transport costs. Sugar transport generally had been organized as follows: The ox-carts arrived from the mills at the city-wall gate near La Punta. There the cargo was transferred to mule-drawn market carts—four for the contents of each ox-cart—by domestic slaves under the eye of the sugarocrat's town-house major domo, and brought to the house, whose street floor served for storage. Finally it was taken from the house to the wharf. It was a sensible and efficient system for the small mill but ludicrous and costly for large-scale manufacture. The big mill owner who produced 40,000 or more arrobas, fed 350 blacks, and hauled 15,000 barrels of molasses faced the fact that moving his products in the city cost him almost as much as bringing them from the mill to Havana. The town-house street floor could not hold them, and all these complications called for a multitude of domestic slaves who most of the time were idle and unproductive.

The immediate solution was to bring the ox-carts into the city even if it tore up the streets. The Cabildo did its best: it banned metal sheathing on the carts' big hardwood wheels and limited cargoes to eight sugar boxes, 50 arrobas of coffee, or three casks of rum. But since urban sugar transport was a lucrative business, the finest mules were imported from the north; magnificent carts with metal-sheathed wheels replaced the old sugarmill carts within the city, and went much further out—generally to the Puentes Grandes or Arroyo Apolo toll stations—to fetch the sugar. Thus transport was speeded up and costs lowered. The discussion of this problem lasted four decades, from 1798 to 1835. The final problem arose when cart-owning concerns increased their vehicles' size to a capacity twice that of the ox-carts. The Cabildo was then forced to order the replacement of mules by oxen.[189]

The real problem was not the vehicle but the streets, so the final solution was to pave them—and this also turned out to be good sugar business in another sense. Cuba's exports far exceeded its imports and many ships arrived full of ballast. The ideal ballast was cobblestones, which served to pave Havana streets and enrich various businessmen: thus the San Francisco and Villalta wharves and the city's main thoroughfares came to be paved with Boston granite. There were the usual shady deals, and the joint Cuban-Yankee firm of Burnham & Co. was founded specifically to bring northern paving materials and technicians to fix the streets.[190] By mid-century the expanded industry had solved all these problems, for the railroads ran directly to the wharves. Furthermore, big commercial warehouses replaced the town-house street floor for sugar storage and thus reduced the absurd number of house slaves.[191] Sugar had put forth such a complexity of economic offshoots that its original root was all but lost to view.

Just as sugar unified the countryside, it served as a homogenizing influence on our cities. Apart from their size and formal characteristics, the great sugar ports—Havana, Cienfuegos, Sagua, Cárdenas, Matanzas—were redolent of jerked beef and fish. Here the railroads to and from the sugarmills had their rendezvous with the ships from the north. Each had a paved street up to a pier extending out on hardwood piles. Nearby were the big sugar warehouses. Each great sugar port—strange as it seems today—had a theater donated by a slave trader. These were cities of merchants whose disciplined Spanish employees worked fifteen hours a day, ate two meals on the job, and had Sunday nights "free." Cities of moneylending middlemen and speculators, with cash in a strongbox and credit in the major cities of the world. Cities of owners of distant sugarmills, who kept up the sugarocrat town-house luxury at all costs while looking with baleful scorn at the merchant-moneylender. Cities with an enormous floating population of soldiers and sailors who strolled through endless red-light districts. Cities, in sum, of cozy "morality" and real immorality, with bureaucrats, hack politicians, a nascent working class, patient artisans, and a frustrated middle class—and the marginal lives of their blacks and mulattoes. They were the reflection of a world that made sugar production the yardstick of all ethical and political values.

THE DEATH OF THE FOREST

Up until the end of the eighteenth century, Cubans took pride in their forests. The whole island was a stand of precious wood—mahogany, cedar, ebony, dagame, quebracho—among which soared giant palms. Early chroniclers could not suppress their amazement at our trees in whose shade, they insisted, one could walk from one end of the island to the other. The Laws of the Indies guarded this wealth jealously, taking the socially responsible position that the forests were not the landowner's property since they also belonged to future generations. Before sugar, before tobacco, before cattle, it was precious wood that symbolized the Far Antilles. From Cuban wood was carved the gorgeous ceilings of the Escorial, its still-intact doors and windows, and the incredible mahogany table, the world's largest made from a single piece. Boards from giant Cuban trees made the doors of San Francisco El Grande in Madrid, and Cuban wood abounded in the Royal Palace. Documents tell us that a typical form of English and French piracy was to plunder the forests of the semi-populated island: how much Cuban wood went into English and French palaces we do not know.

The protection of the forests was legally defined in the so-called Cortes de El Rey (Royal Timber Prerogatives) to be found in Law 13, Title 17, Book 4 of the *Recopilación de Indias*. These Cortes were the basis for setting up the Havana shipyard, which in a few years built 128 ships of all types and sent mountains of timber to Spain. The ships, ranging from 120-cannon giants to 30- and 40-cannon frigates, helped defend the Spanish empire; many went to the bottom at Trafalgar, but the exceptional timber used made them twice as durable as European ships. They derived toughness from *sabicú* and *chicharrón* bottoms and lightness from cedar planking.

Large-scale manufacture rang the forest's death-knell. The best sugarmaster of the early nineteenth century left us this crisp sentence: "The sugarmill's need for firewood is alarming—and where are the forests that can meet it?" He was José Ignacio Echegoyen, Arango's technician at La Ninfa, later proprietor of the giant La Asunción mill. Firewood consumption depended on the kettle system. The unit by which it was calculated was the "task," a cubic volume of 3 x 2 x 1 yards. A caballería of forest was estimated to yield about 1,000 tasks. The "Spanish train" consumed one task of firewood for each 5 or 6 arrobas of clayed sugar. Use of the Jamaica train more than doubled the yield, to 13 arrobas per task. We can easily calculate that at the end of the eighteenth century about 500 caballerías of forest were being felled each year to be burned in making sugar, plus many more for building new mills.

With sugar's advance, tree-clearing became a well-paid activity for the small Havana peasantry of the late eighteenth and early nineteenth centuries. They received between 300 and 500 pesos for "cleaning" one caballería. As prices rose over the years, the work became the speciality of teams employed on a piece-work basis. Although slaves were often used for wood cutting, it became more and more a free worker's job as the institution of slavery became bloated. Masters found that their blacks constantly disappeared into the woods and it was hard to catch them.

We must make a clear distinction between ground that was cleared for planting cane and building mills, and forests cut down for firewood. In the first case the method was simple. A machete gang first tackled the reeds and vines, leaving clear spaces around the big trunks. This "chopping" of the undergrowth was followed by the "toppling" of ancient trees. After thirty or forty days came the "burning" of the chopped, now-dry vegetation. If it was a "slash and leave" job, the trunks not consumed by the fire stayed where they had fallen and sugarmill slaves stacked them for use as fuel. If it was a "slash and burn" job, the fires were repeated and the trunks cut small so they would burn completely. When some of the timber remained unburned, it was piled into small bonfires (*fogatas*), a process known as *foguerear*. The most precious woods—ebony, mahogany, quebracho—were generally of great size and took two or three fires to burn.[192]

No one can calculate the extent of sugar's forest depredation. We have suggested that it ran to 500 caballerías a year in the late eighteenth century; by 1809 it was twice as much, and in 1830 sugarmen Andrés de Zayas and José María Dau estimated it at 2,000 caballerías—half for fuel and half burned up to make room for new mills.[193] The figure rose to 4,000 in 1844, at which point the Junta charged with protecting the trees announced that the forest laws had given "happy and satisfactory results." [194]

The right to destroy the forests was one of the sugarmen's great legal victories. The Cortes del Rey were a feudal privilege that was in open contradiction to the interests of large-scale manufacture and were interpreted by the bourgeois-minded sugarocracy as an encroachment on the "universal and sacred right of property." There was a stormy confrontation that took the outward form of a battle between the Junta de Maderas (Timber Board)—a feudal institution controlled by the Navy—and the Real Consulado. While the Junta was defending a privilege that ran counter to productive economic development, many of its arguments were well taken. It was undeniable that if the forests were unreservedly surrendered to the sugarmen's voracity they would disappear. Faced with this cold reality, the Consulado could only argue that Cuban forests were "excessive" and their total liquidation was "impossible, as the natural order of things attests." Meanwhile Arango was saying that many Havana *hacendados* did not have any forests or that those they had "did not contain a stick of any value." The sugar producers were caught in flagrant contradictions, but here was the confession of the death of the forest at their hands. Their power was decisive and on February 4, 1800, they obtained a Real Cédula, calling for a Consulado study of the possibility of withdrawing Crown timber rights to a distance of 81 miles from Havana. This was, in fact, a green light for free sugar expansion throughout the island's western area.[195]

On August 30, 1805, the sugar bourgeoisie secured the right to dispose of trees on their land with no limitations other than those in certain ordinances, which were never written. The final victory was won in the Spanish parliament: Cuban sugar spokesmen Andrés de Jáuregui and Juan Bernardo O'Gavan obtained the total repeal of all Crown timber privileges in the island. In Havana the Junta de Maderas, led by engineer Diego de la Parra, tried to resist the new legislation and was put to rout. A Real Cédula of August 30, 1815, summarizing the entire forestry code, put the finishing touches to the freedom of the bourgeoisie. The sole qualification was a new junta to study the results of the new forestry laws; its history is both long and short: it held its first meeting in the month of its establishment, May 1816, and its second and last in 1844, twenty-eight years later.

These legal comings and goings developed amid polemics which sometimes became violent. The battle, which appeared to be between the Navy and the Consulado, was in fact between the old feudal superstructure and the new wave of large-scale manufacture. As usual, the *hacendados* left no argument unvoiced in defense of their rights, so that—again as usual—startlingly cynical documents appear in the record. To cite just one, very representative of the polemical tone: the Consulado, by Real Orden of

October 5, 1795, issued a report on the production of wax. It said that the main obstacle to Cuban beehive development was "the trouble facing beekeepers in the matter of using cedar for their hives"; in order to produce wax and honey, permission to fell trees was requested. Las Casas, the sugar producers' staunch ally, accepted this as valid, but the forestry director, Pedro de Acevedo, replied with firm indignation. It was another pretext, he said, "to annihilate the forests." [196]

The many arguments used in the drawn-out controversy were summed up in a sage observation by Ramón de la Sagra: "At no time has the rational use of forest resources been discussed, only the question of who has the right to fell and raze." [197] As we have seen in other cases, so with forests: the legislation came *a posteriori*. The sugar expansionists ignored the Junta de Maderas, continuing to fell and raze through the great 1792–1802 boom. Throughout the eighteenth century, burning forests were a daily spectacle in the Cuban countryside. The name "Quemados" (burned) appears more than any other in Vives' map of the island, designating a host of places where memories of a forest in flames persisted.[198] Thus the new legislation merely recognized old and irreversible facts. If after its promulgation there was more destruction than ever, this was not due to the newly acquired rights, but to the steady growth of production, progressively claiming more fuel and land. The system resulted by mid-century in the conversion of the Havana area and part of Matanzas into treeless plains. In Cienfuegos, founded in 1819 beside forests "which the world envies," firewood had become a serious problem. The Sagua and San Juan de los Remedios areas presented the same vista of a land without shade.

Not until the disappearance of the trees began affecting production, did the sugarocrats begin to worry. Then they changed the kettle system back to the one-fire train, planted more Otaheite cane, and used bagasse as fuel. The more forward-looking ones wrote memos reflecting in part the outlook of the great manufacturing pioneers. The Count de Mopox y Jaruco and José Ricardo O'Farrill talked of replacing the stands of precious wood.[199] Others, thinking not in terms of forests but of firewood, proposed solutions to the fuel problem. José Pizarro y Gardín, for example, suggested extensive planting of royal palms—13,533 to the caballería, yielding "186,636 *pencas* [gigantic palm leaves] and the same number of *yaguas* [leaf sheaths]" annually for fuel.[200] Dau saw the best solution in wild indigo, one and one-half caballerías of which could yield 44,085,760 pounds of brushwood a year; or, if not, *paraíso*-tree plantations would give almost the same results.[201] Only one man of the time, Sagra, proposed untouchable forest reserves to safeguard the island for future generations. Realizing that this ran counter to the bourgeois concept of property, he made a socialist criticism of what he called "the vices of the economic theory of misconceived liberty" and demanded subordination of that liberty to the public interest.[202]

The death of the forest was also, in part, the long-term death of the island's fabled fertility. This was an old Antillean process with which our sugarocrats were already acquainted. Slave labor involved the use of crude techniques with a low yield. To compensate for manufacturing deficiencies, the highest agricultural yield was sought, but this was in no way the result of rational soil utilization, only of the exceptional richness of recently cleared virgin land. First plantings of a dead forest commonly produced well over 120,000 arrobas of cane per caballería. Annual cane cutting and neglect of the hilling and strawing of shoots lowered the crop of a field which was neither irrigated nor fertilized. When a critical point was reached it was abandoned, another forest was cut, and the fabulous cane production statistics were again repeated.

The Cuban *hacendado* did not invent this barbaric system: it was born with Antillean sugar, a typical product of the plantation. Technicians called it "extensive cultivation," while Liebig and Sagra gave it the more precise name of "plunder culture." The English used the same system in the small islands and were soon left without trees; by 1749 they were calling their once-fertile lands "poor and worn out."[203] French producers, one up on them at the time, were working land that was "fresh and fertile," but a century later a traveler noted that "the inhabitants can't even find roots to feed themselves." It was an exaggerated version of what had happened in Europe, attributed by Marx to the insuperable limitations with which private property always confronts the most rational agriculture.[204] On top of all the agricultural and economic motivations for destroying forests came the wars of independence. In the campaign plans drawn up by generals Concha, Valmaseda, Caballero de Rodas, Ceballo, and Azcár-

raga, it was estimated that 55 million trees would be felled for the various military arteries and roads.

A fantastic footnote on the contradictions of Cuban sugar production is that in the same years that the island was burning its own timber wealth, it was the top buyer of United States lumber. From the end of the eighteenth century, pine and cypress boards for making sugar boxes were arriving at Havana ports. The lumber trade was one of the United States' best-paying businesses. Imports, without counting contraband, ran between 600,000 and 1,000,000 pesos a year in the first two decades of the nineteenth century. José de Arango called this trade "shameful." He complained about the fate of our forests, "given to the flames or remaining in useless abundance while we empty our pockets for the foreigner's benefit." [205]

The excuse for importing lumber was simple—wood was needed which did not impart smell or taste to the sugar, so cedar and mahogany would not do—but the truth of the matter lay elsewhere. The sugar industry had absorbed the island's free labor and work had been degraded by slavery. This had so raised the wages for cutting and transporting wood that it could more cheaply be brought in from the north. In 1813 Havana had a steam sawmill—the first in Latin America—with no wood to cut. José de Arango did his utmost to convince the *hacendados* that because of its toughness, lightness, odorlessness, and ease in cutting, *jobo* was the ideal wood for sugar boxes. He presented testimonials to this effect by the Marquis de Arcos and the Count de Gibacoa. Little came of it and boxes continued to be made of northern wood.

But not only sugar-box wood was bought from outside: from 1837 on we find contracts for the importation of firewood to run the railroad. The Drake concern promoted the first deal at 14 pesos a cord: George Knight shipped it from New Orleans and sold it at 17 pesos. The cheerful slogan of this business was that "Northern wood gives more flame." Heavy imports of coal began later, reaching 92,000 tons in 1860.[206]

Sugar exterminated the forests. Deaf and blind to history, focusing on the present, the sugarocracy destroyed in years what only centuries could replace —and at the same time destroyed much of the island's fertility by soil erosion and the drying-up of thousands of streams. An extra debit item on the ledger of an irrational system of exploitation based solely on calculations of immediate profit was the resulting Cuban contempt for trees. Yet the poet Pobeda sang in praise of trees, and among other voices heralding the future was that of Sagra, who wrote: "At this stage of maturity, when man is enriched by the conquests of science and illuminated in his endeavors by moral sentiments, he faces the great enterprise of exploiting his planet not merely for his own generation but for those to come. This cannot be done unless individual, ephemeral, and transitory interests are subordinated to the general and eternal interests of all humanity." [207]

Of Cuba's forests, its legendary mahogany, almost nothing remains today. In 1962 one could still see the *palanqueros* at work on the Río Sagua, whose waters flow gently between treeless banks. They drive a long iron-pointed pole into the riverbed until they feel they have struck timber; they dive, secure it, and drag it to the bank. A hard, slow, monotonous job, like the throes of death. Day by day they bring up from the river bottom bits of the trees that sugar cut down. They live off the corpses of the forest. All that remains to them of the ancient wealth is the echo of an old folksong:

Tomorrow I go to Sagua
To cut me some boughs
To make me a house
On the slopes of Jumagua. [208]

4
A TECHNICO-ECONOMIC
PARENTHESIS
(1800–1860)

"Technology discloses man's mode of dealing with Nature, the process of production by which he sustains his life, and thereby also lays bare the mode of formation of his social relations, and of the mental conceptions that flow from them."

—*Karl Marx,* Capital (vol. I, p. 372)

INTERNAL DATA FOR
THE SUGARMILL

In search of criteria

There is a point at which Cuba's economic history becomes cloudy, when we enter the world of yields and techniques, the very heart of the production complex, a world in which words are superfluous and only numbers are eloquent. Without knowing the internal data of the sugarmill as a productive unit, we cannot seriously interpret Cuban history.

But the task is not easy: first, because published data were almost always false, and second, because the *hacendados* lacked real technical controls to arrive at an exact result. This remained the case throughout most of the nineteenth century and did not change until the dawn of big industry. Until then the measurements used were imprecise: cane was calculated in "cartloads," firewood in "tasks," bagasse in "baskets," lime in "coconuts," and the fire was controlled by the kettle-minder's shouts to the furnaceman.

Serious sugar producers despaired. The same mill, with the same equipment and human material and exploiting the same lands, produced 15,000 arrobas in one year, 24,000 the next year, and 18,000 the next. The quality of the product could go from the highest to the lowest in successive seasons. The proportion of white to brown sugar changed from month to month. One grinding used one thousand tasks of firewood, the next was done with nothing but bagasse. Every sugarmaster regarded his technique as infallible, and newspapers frequently published recommendations which contradicted each other. Echegoyen was convinced that cheap, high-quality sugar could only be obtained by constant use of clarifiers; Diago dismissed them as inefficient and costly. With regard to costs and slaves, everybody told lies.

How then obtain the internal data? There is no doubt that, amid this apparent or real chaos, the sugar producers had a series of solid norms to guide them, norms which they considered intimate industrial secrets. In their reports and manuals nineteenth-century producers published only lies or evident truths which their rivals already knew; they kept the real figures, to which they secured the ship of their calculations, to themselves. They used them as a basis for the really solid norms which determined what was good business, and it is essential that the historian find them.

Sources

Our first problem is that the works used by Cuban historians are crammed with errors. Writings about the sugarmill have been mainly based on the Baron von Humboldt, Jacobo de la Pezuela, Vázquez Queipo, Arango y Parreño, and José Arboleya,[209] but there are objections to all of these. The Baron, for all his perspicacity and steadfast skepticism, was sometimes fooled by the sugarocracy. His analysis of costs is based on a work written by Arango but falsely ascribed to Echegoyen.[210] Pezuela's data are good or bad according to the earlier source from which he took them, but as a whole they are a mishmash of contradictory figures used without discrimination or analysis. Vázquez Queipo shows such remarkable ignorance—real or feigned—that no one paid any attention to his report. Arboleya's descriptive passages are no more than picturesque. And as for Arango, who knew more about sugar than anyone in the Americas, we know how airily he manufactured his figures.

So we must be selective. The most reliable sources are the confidential ones of the mills themselves—their account books, slave records, daily harvest and grinding reports. Over a thousand such documents are at our disposal; they present a staggering picture of sugarmill life and only one special difficulty—the use of now-extinct terms and measures, some of which were generally used, others of which were used only in one mill. The many technical manuals published during the century are useful with reservations. As one would expect, none of them tells industrial secrets, but they give a generalized idea of sugar techniques as known to any well-informed contemporary. Examination of these together with the chief technical works of the day—Dutrone, Corbeaux, Porter, Evans, Wray, Soames, etc.—can give us a reasonably accurate picture.

We have noted, classified, and arranged all the figures at our disposal for each aspect of the mill and will indicate the high and low extremes. Figures under the various headings are confirmed by at least forty or fifty sources, and in cases where sizable differences occur we have relied on the internal sources in which there is rarely any great disparity. The reader interested in more details and in the exact manner in which each conclusion was reached should consult the notes at the end of the book.

Types of sugarmill

The *trapiche* was the minimal production unit. Its name identifies the whole industrial process with the one machine of the period, the trapiche or grinding mill. It had the same characteristics as in the smallest nine- or ten-slave unit of the colony's first years. It produced muscovado and raspadura from a maximum of one caballería of cane and consisted of a small animal-powered grinding device and two or three kettles of cast-iron or copper, operated by a crew of five or ten. Some examples still exist in the form of raspadura-producing units using kettles from the old mills. The word muscovado was applied to the imperfectly drained massecuite. Nowadays the word

has two meanings: in the English market it refers to the "common process" brown sugar, and in the Dutch market it refers to 96° test or refiners' crystals.* Raspadura is a solidified massecuite known in Barbados as "flavored" sugar.

Muscovado and raspadura being the sugar of the poor, we may say that these trapiches sweetened the palate of the island's lower class: they were the people's sugar world and their production figures did not appear in the statistics. Although economically they belong to our sugar history's earliest period, they were not replaced by large-scale production until the end of the century. They multiplied with the growth of the rural population and the city lumpenproletariat, for sugar at 14 reales per arroba could not compete with cheap raspadura. Their decline began when big industry lowered prices to the point where the poorest Cubans could afford sugar.

The trapiche cannot be seen as the germ of the sugarmill, for its efficiency lay precisely in its minuscule size. It was a distinct enterprise supplying diverse sectors of the population with different products. It was run by men of the lower classes and had a marked flavor of rural-domestic industry. The sugarmill was born and developed independently.

Trapiches were sometimes covered by the census, causing utter confusion to historians unversed in economics. Rebello, an expert in sugar technology, omitted them from his reports of sugar production in 1859–1860; but the Comisión Estadísticas, concerned not about sugar but about tax collection, did include them. This explains why Pezuela, who copied official data, speaks of 2,050 sugarmills in the same years that Rebello lists 1,305.

The animal-powered sugarmill. This was rural manufacture of a certain technical complexity, a type we have studied early in this book.

The semi-mechanized sugarmill. This was almost the same as the larger examples of the above type, with the difference that the steam engine replaced animal power. Coinciding in time with forest destruction and the consequent firewood crisis, these mills

* 96°, or pol. 96, refers to the sucrose purity of the crystals as measured by the polarization of light on a polariscope and a saccharimeter, respectively. Sugar which measures 96° or over is considered refined sugar. (Trans.)

Table 1[211]

The Average Production Capacity of Cuban Sugarmills, 1800–1860
(*tons of sugar per grinding season*)

Year	Average production capacity	Type of mill
1761	49	Animal-powered
1792	58	Animal-powered
1804	127	Animal-powered
1860	113	Animal-powered
1860	411	Semi-mechanized
1860	1,176	Mechanized

brought the "Jamaica train" into general use in an attempt to rationalize fuel consumption. They raised production and sugar-per-man productivity but not per-cane sugar yield.

The mechanized sugarmill launched Cuba's industrial revolution, doubling industrial yields and notably improving quality. It brought about the crisis of slavery and the separation of the agricultural and manufacturing sectors. It was the germ of today's big sugar *central*.

We must note that while these three sugarmill types followed each other, the later type did not always replace the earlier in the 1800–1860 period under study. That is, the process was not one of animal-powered mills successively becoming semi-mechanized and then mechanized—although such was usually the case with the first two types. Generally speaking, the mechanized mill was a separate phenomenon, requiring such a radical transformation that it could not grow upon the narrow foundation of the old type. Apart from certain aspects of the initial stage, it was a new kind of mill. It is impossible to mechanize a method of production designed for manual labor, and thus there could be no such thing as industrialization of the large-scale slave-manufacture routine. It was simply liquidated. The big sugar industry was a separate phenomenon, springing from new concepts and using none of the elements of the old mill. All that went before— grinding mills, kettles, scummers, and buckets—had to be demolished and a new factory built.

A chaotic situation resulted from the coexistence of various types of factory all producing different qualities of sugar at different costs, and the *hacendados* proceeded to spin scientific lies about it. As we propose to show, they either took data from one type of factory, or took an arithmetical average of all of them, which is a statistical absurdity. An example of this technique was Juan Poey's request for certain tax exemptions in 1862.

Average capacity

In the 1800–1860 period the average productive capacity of Cuban sugarmills is shown in Table 1.

In modern times a mill's production capacity is calculated in the crushing capacity of the milling equipment each twenty-four hours, a calculation almost impossible to make with the data available on eighteenth and nineteenth century mills. For this reason the figures in Table 1 are mere arithmetical averages of the total known production in the given year and the number of mills functioning. But as mills generally worked at full pitch, these indices can be understood as production capacity per season of six months, the longest period then customary. Using modern terms, we can suggest that there was an enormous underutilization of installed capacity as a result of a labor shortage. The chronic scarcity of hands led Cuban producers to use "one negro" as the measure of capacity: that is, they based their figures not on equipment but on men. This economic enormity is logical if one realizes that labor was the major item in a slave sugarmill's fixed capital, an item which one bought and sold like a kettle or a log of wood.

Changes in production, 1800–1860

Factory capacity in 1804. The average size of a Cuban mill in 1804 is clearly reflected in the figures in Table 2.

Table 2

Table 2
Distribution of Cuban Sugarmills According to Production
(Animal-powered mills, grinding season of 1804, Havana area)
(tons of sugar per grinding season)

Production per mill	No. of mills	Percent of mills	Total production in 1804	Percent of production
1 to 50	26	14.94	876	3.98
51 to 100	44	25.29	3,246	14.73
101 to 150	44	25.29	5,415	24.58
151 to 200	35	20.11	6,055	27.48
201 to 250	16	9.20	3,574	16.22
251 to 300	4	2.30	1,081	4.91
301 to 350	3	1.72	940	4.27
351 to 400	1	0.57	372	1.69
401 to 450	—	—	—	—
451 to 500	1	0.57	471	2.14
	174	100.00	22,030	100.00

Production in 1860. Between 1804 and 1860 these changes occurred: (1) The animal-powered mill was changed with the application of the steam engine to the horizontal grinding mill, initiating the semi-mechanized sugarmill. (2) Beginning in the 1820s, all large animal-powered mills became semi-mechanized, but small mills of less than a 170-ton (15,000-arroba) capacity per season continued with their old ox trapiches. (3) Almost all the recently built mills in the western zone were semi-mechanized, but in the central area—Sagua and Cienfuegos—many new animal-powered mills were built. (4) Beginning in 1839, with installation of the first "Derosne train," there appeared the germ of the mechanized mill, which was further developed in the 1840s and 1850s. (5) With four different types of mills, 1860 production totals can be seen in Table 3.

Factory capacity in 1860. With three types of mill—excluding the non-representative water-powered mill—grinding in 1860, the size of the semi-mechanized and mechanized mills—which between them represent 91.43 percent of the harvest—can be seen in the following figures. The maximum for animal-powered, and the minimum for semi-mechanized, mills seems to have been two hundred tons.

Table 3
Sugar Production by Type of Mill, Grinding Season of 1860
(in tons of sugar)

Type	Number of mills	Percent of mills	Total production	Percent of production
Animal-powered	359	27.24	41,625	8.07
Water-powered	6	0.45	2,567	0.50
Semi-mechanized	889	67.45	395,273	76.64
Mechanized	64	4.86	76,276	14.79
	1,318	100.00	515,741	100.00

Table 4
Frequency Distribution of Cuban Sugarmills According to Production, Grinding Season of 1860
(in tons)

Production per mill	Animal-powered				Semi-mechanized				Mechanized			
	No. of mills	Percent of mills	Tons	Percent	No. of mills	Percent of mills	Tons	Percent	No. of mills	Percent of mills	Tons	Percent
Under 100	209	15.93	11,671	2.27	46	3.50	3,269	0.64	—	—	—	—
101 to 200	105	8.00	15,693	3.06	133	10.13	20,349	3.96	1	0.08	162	0.03
201 to 400	42	3.20	12,722	2.48	335	25.53	112,560	21.93	2	0.15	642	0.13
401 to 600	3	0.23	1,539	0.30	192	14.63	101,844	19.85	7	0.53	3,478	0.68
601 to 800	—	—	—	—	95	7.24	66,023	12.86	7	0.53	5,247	1.02
801 to 1,000	—	—	—	—	57	4.34	52,440	10.22	10	0.76	9,554	1.86
1,001 to 1,200	—	—	—	—	22	1.68	26,129	5.09	10	0.76	11,649	2.27
1,201 to 1,400	—	—	—	—	5	0.38	6,613	1.29	7	0.53	8,809	1.72
1,401 to 1,600	—	—	—	—	4	0.30	6,046	1.18	9	0.65	13,512	2.63
1,601 to 1,800	—	—	—	—	—	—	—	—	7	0.53	12,039	2.34
1,801 to 2,000	—	—	—	—	—	—	—	—	1	0.08	1,905	0.37
Over 2,001	—	—	—	—	—	—	—	—	3	0.23	9,299	1.81
Totals	359	27.36	41,625	8.11	889	67.73	395,273	77.02	64	4.86	76,296	14.86

Technological evolution, 1800–1869. Table 3 shows that semi-mechanized and animal-powered mills were responsible for 84.71 percent of 1860 production. Thus it is here that we find the key to the great sugar crisis culminating in the Ten Years War (1868–1878). Only technology can show us the economic root of that crisis. In our analysis we start from the classical division between agricultural and manufacturing sectors.

The agricultural sector: cane

Varieties of cane. Villa-Urrutia said in 1843 that "the sugarmasters owe their know-how to land and weather conditions more than to their own expertise." [212] He was expressing the reality of the rise of Cuban sugar, which resulted from natural elements and not from the producers' technical efforts. Agriculturally, the only specific ripple on the waters was the importation of other varieties of cane—not based on internal experience, but in the hopes of reproducing the real or supposed successes abroad. This yearning for new varieties began at the end of the eighteenth century when Havana producers, noting the rapid growth of Otaheite cane planted in Baracoa (Havana province), made a seed expedition to the Danish island of Santa Cruz de Tenerife in the Canary Islands.

By the 1860s Cuban mills were using five varieties of cane.[213] One was Creole cane, also called "native cane" and "La Española cane." It was the first variety to arrive in the Americas (brought from Spain by the Conquistadors) and possibly the original of Linnaeus' *Saccharum officinarum.* It grows only six or seven feet high and has yellow-white skin and fairly straight leaves. The nodes are very close together—the more so the more it is cut—and it sends out abundant shoots, but it has little resistance to low temperatures. According to Dutrone it matures slowly, taking from twelve to twenty months; in end-of-the-century Cuba it was always cut after twelve months. It was ideal for the old wooden mills since its fibers offered little resistance to the grinders, but for the same reason its bagasse had little value as fuel. From the first sugar factories until the 1780s it was the only variety known in Cuba, and its replacement by other varieties continued throughout the nineteenth century. Even in the 1860s, some animal-powered mills in the central area producing muscovado preferred this crude type of cane for its ability to stand up to numerous unplanned cuttings. In the big Matanzas area its cultivation for sugar had stopped by the mid-nineteenth century, but it was still retained as cattle feed.[214]

Another variety was Otaheite cane. Although it could be either white or yellow, nineteenth-century Cuban references are exclusively to the yellow, which grew much higher than the Creole variety—up to an average of thirteen feet in some canefields. It was thicker (five to six inches in circumference) with more widely separated nodes (six to seven inches), and it matured faster. It allowed the early nineteenth-century producer to have two canes of different maturing periods, and in many Cuban mills it solved the chain-reaction problem of fuel. Although known in Cuba since around 1780, it was not at first used because wooden trapiches extracted little juice from its thick and woody stalk. When grinder pressure was stepped up, roller shafts often broke. Around 1790 iron sheaths became standard, and they kept evolving in the nineteenth century until they were all-metal. The trapiche transformation generalized the planting of cane whose bagasse could best be used, as it increasingly was, to fuel the trains.

We have seen that yellow Otaheite cane did not displace the Creole variety even in the Havana-Matanzas area until the 1820s. Then, the larger and more mechanized the mill, the more it predominated. The purple-striped or "Borbón" variety was known in Cuba in 1820 and its large-scale planting began in mid-century.

We do not know when crystalline cane was introduced, but Dumont and Echegoyen mention it, which shows that Havana mills were growing it around 1825. After 1830 it spread through the red-earth belt into the Matanzas area. By 1860 white Otaheite and crystalline had absolute preference in the west. The latter yielded less than the former in tons per area but was much easier to grow, especially in soil that was becoming exhausted; it was also more resistant to drought. It was, however, rapidly destroyed by mosaic, one of the worst of the cane diseases (its name derived from the German *Mosaik-krankheiten*—mosaic disease), and hardly a sample has been preserved. (In Java, where mosaic was first observed in 1890, it was known as *Gele Strepenziekte,* meaning the yellow-stripe disease.)

Ribbon cane, also known as striped or Batavia cane, was introduced into the French Antillean colonies by the naturalist Cossigny in 1782 and reached Cuba between the last years of the eight-

eenth century and the beginning of the nineteenth. Saco refers to it in Oriente province in 1812 or 1813. In 1820 it was planted in Güines, brought there by the Count de O'Reilly for his Alejandría mill. It is reddish in color, with numerous vertical lines, to which it owes its name; it grows over three feet in height and has an average stalk diameter of about four inches. It replaced Otaheite cane in exhausted lands but, despite its fervent initial welcome, mill owners soured on it because they said it turned tough and low-yielding after the fourth or fifth cutting. In the confusion of nomenclature at the time we find Dau calling the ribbon or striped variety "Batavia cane" in 1837,[215] while in 1862 Reynoso used the name "Batavia cane" exclusively for purple cane.

Purple cane was introduced around 1820, and is first mentioned in an unpublished agricultural handbook of 1828 preserved in the Sociedad Económica archives. Originating in Java, it reached Cuba via the French colonies. It has a very tender stalk and puts out abundant shoots. Despite its richness in sucrose, it was not widely grown for sugar and Reynoso recommended it as suitable for animal feed.

Through most of the past century the sugarmen concentrated on the manufacturing aspects of production and much less on the agricultural. All the world's sugar producers did likewise. Almost the only agricultural preoccupation was the search for a marvelous variety of cane: experimenting with new varieties was an obsession of men hoping for a sugar miracle. Especially in the last half of the century, France and England, and then the United States, carried on continuous research and Cuba copied the results with the necessary years of delay. The great imperialist expansion into the Pacific opened up a fabulous sugar panorama. Colonists on Réunion and Mauritius in the Indian Ocean were impressed by the extraordinary cane grown by the Melanesians in New Caledonia and the New Hebrides. In 1863 Vieillard, and then Delaplanche, described forty varieties; in 1884 De Greslan and Sagor noted sixty. At that time the United States was making an exhaustive investigation in Hawaii.[216]

Sugar being one of the world's richest industries, discoveries in the field became a theme for sensationalist journalism. The first big sensation was the total degeneration in 1855 of Otaheite cane brought to Louisiana, which obliged the United States to import 440 million pounds of sugarcane. Part of this was brought from China and was of the species then improperly known as Sorghum. This so-called Sorghum was clear evidence of the highly industrialized colonial powers' concern about sugar. It was brought to Paris by Count Montigny, France's consul in Shanghai, and to the United States by Jay Browne in 1854. In less than a decade some twenty monographs on the new cane were published, among them the voluminous works of Sicard, Stansbury, and F. L. Stewart.[217]

Cuba was a marginal part of these sugarcane events; during the nineteenth century no official or group action was taken to seek new varieties. Only in 1798, in the case of Otaheite cane, do we find any coordinated activity of an institutional kind. Yet in many areas Cuban cane was meanwhile diminishing in size, robustness, and sugar yield, and there began to be talk about its degeneration. It was then that Sebastián de Lasa wrote letters to the Real Consulado requesting the introduction of new seed, and Count Saguins de Vasieur mounted a grandiose expedition to Tahiti "with the aim of renewing our sugarmills' cane seeds." The long list of share-subscribers in the enterprise was headed by top sugarocrats.[218]

Reynoso charged that the alleged degeneration of Cuban çane was the result of irrational farming. In no country in the world, he insisted, did cane develop better than Cuba. This was a kind of return to the starting point. The slave monstrosity had removed all possibility of technical development, and the mid-century sugarocracy, its creative impulses thwarted, sought miraculous formulas for salvation. Well acquainted with *hacendado* psychology, as well as being an agricultural expert, Reynoso summed up in a shrewd paragraph this anguished experimentation with new varieties. It had, he wrote, "the curious aim of finding such a supernatural variety as to produce in limitless abundance, despite the neglect of the soil it grows in. A delightfully simple and well-adapted variety which will grow equally well in the most exhausted soil and with the worst kind of farming, producing giant stalks crammed with the richest sugar juices." [219]

Planting in cleared forests. As forests were felled, new plantings were made. In our "Death of the Forest" section we indicated the three stages of the destruction process—chopping, felling, burning. The fellings had their *raison d'être* in the island's exceptional conditions, its apparently inexhaustible forests.

The first subsequent cane yield was so extraordinary that, at least for the moment, it compensated with interest for the sacrifice of the strip of forest; furthermore, the mill's fuel problem was solved for a long time by the firewood obtained. Reynoso noted the following as typical of sugarman thinking at the time: "Time must not be lost cultivating exhausted, old, already exploited land, and it is better to fell trees than continue using such land. . . . To reverse a mill's falling production, and indeed to increase it, planting in cleared forests is indispensable." [220] This barbaric custom lasted as long as a single forest remained.

Canefields and guardarrayas. The size of the canefields was ruled by the contour of the land; certain standards were, however, normally observed where lands permitted regular division.[221] The mill of the end of the eighteenth century, which only needed a small area and had no serious slave-rebellion problems, carved out large rectangles 333 yards long—a measure generally known as a "square" in seventeenth, eighteenth, and early nineteenth century technical parlance. The *guardarrayas,* or spaces between the fields for roadways or fireguards, were 7 yards wide, except for those bounding the estate itself, which were twice that width.

As the sugarmills, their production, and the slave system grew, the canefields were reduced in size. Up until 1860 the usual measures were:

$$
\begin{array}{llll}
18 & \times\ 4.5 & cordeles\ = & \tfrac{1}{4}\ \text{caballería} \\
18 & \times\ 6.5 & cordeles\ = & \tfrac{1}{3}\ \text{caballería} \\
13.5 & \times\ 6 & cordeles\ = & \tfrac{1}{4}\ \text{caballería} \\
9 & \times\ 4.5 & cordeles\ = & \tfrac{1}{8}\ \text{caballería}
\end{array}
$$

The first of these sizes predominated through a good part of the nineteenth century. The $\tfrac{1}{8}$ caballería was only planted in the 1830s and 1840s when canefields were daily being burned in slave uprisings. At that time it was also mandatory to leave a completely clear 15-yard strip on the canefields' boundaries with other estates.[222] Throughout the nineteenth century the old custom was maintained of raising plantains along the edges of the *guardarrayas,* which solved three of the producers' problems. The leaves were used to wrap the stoppers plugging the sugar molds, they served to put out fires, and the fruit was fed to the slaves.

Seedlings and planting. As far as planting was concerned, the scene in 1860 exactly reflected agricul-

PLANTING CANE

tural practices of the previous century. Some of these were the result of age-old experience in cane planting and thus scientifically quite valid. Others were the offspring of routine and ignorance. The immigration of French sugar technicians at the end of the eighteenth century brought something new, but the end result was simply an amalgam of two routines. Without detailing the techniques, let us note what changed and what remained the same through the 1800–1860 period.

From the seventeenth century on we have references to four classifications of seed cane corresponding to the crops harvested: *caña de planta* (cut for the first time), *soca de planta* or *socaplanta* (cut for the second time), *soca* (cane from *socaplanta* fields), *resoca* (cane from *soca* fields). These definitions appear in O'Farrill's handbook of 1792 and also in Reynoso's great work of 1862; both explain why *caña de planta* is the ideal seed cane, although Reynoso does it scientifically while O'Farrill merely writes of an old-established custom: *hacendados* used it for seedlings because other canes were "old, and the offspring of old mothers don't live long."

Experience also taught the best seasons for

planting, and throughout the period the same customs which have come down to us prevailed. There were "cold plantings" beginning in September and ending in December, and "spring plantings" from mid-April to mid-June. Due to a chronic labor shortage, many mills only practiced the former because it occurred in the dead season; in springtime arduous harvest and grinding tasks occupied all the slaves. Furthermore, cane planted between April and June could hardly ever be cut in the next harvest and tended to give low yields if not irrigated.

In the nineteenth century the shortage of hands and the imperious need to continue expanding production initiated a new and vicious practice. Defective steam engines and clumsily unreliable trapiches caused frequent interruptions in the grinding process, and whenever these occurred the whole idle labor force would be taken out to plant, replant, and weed. Thus every second of a slave's work time was made use of, but the field jobs were not always performed at the right moment. As Reynoso accurately observed: "They plant when they can rather than when they should."

Four of the most primitive implements known to

88

agriculture were used for all these tasks: the *jan,* the hoe or spade, the Creole plough, and the machete. In the early nineteenth century the *jan*—the Cuban version of the digging stick with which prehistoric tribes made holes for planting—was a hardwood stake about one and one-half feet long, with a pointed end and suitable thickness at the top to be grasped by the hands. The one innovation the industrial era provided to the Cuban *hacendados* who planted their fields this way was an iron *jan* of the same size weighing some fourteen pounds, a more solid instrument for breaking the ground. The *jan* was especially used after the end of the eighteenth century. The slaves first marked out the ground with cinder lines or ropes of *majagua* bark and then set to work with their *jans,* a task described thus by Reynoso: "To *jan,* the worker either spreads his legs, leans forward, and pushes the implement in toward the rear, or moves forward and, standing half sideways and leaning over slightly, drives it in. This latter position is more convenient and most used. The workers advance the right foot, leaving the left at the point where the hole is to be made; then they move the left foot forward and open another hole next to the right foot."

The hole was made at the maximum possible angle. Sometimes the slave put leverage on it and almost lifted out the soil. He drove the *jan* down several times and moved it in all directions to deepen and widen the hole. He stuck in the seed cane and, so as to leave none of it exposed, cut it with his machete at ground level, then used the machete to cover it with earth and trod it down with his foot.

This absurd planting system was used in numerous Cuban mills, including the mechanized production giants of the second half of the nineteenth century.[223] Many *hacendados* defended it, since excellent yields resulted. As Reynoso pointed out, however, this high production merely showed Cuban soil to be so fertile that even with methods running counter to all scientific agricultural principles it gave optimum results.

Planting with the hoe repeated the same routine as *jan* planting. It was the eighteenth century's standard method, but in the nineteenth was only used in cleared forests or very stoney lands which the feeble Creole plough could not furrow. Hoe men generally opened holes in the ground at irregular intervals, but sometimes lines were traced out beforehand, as in the *jan* operation. The holes had to be deep enough to receive whole pieces of cane minus their tender, low sugar-content tops. The work team consisted of choppers, hole makers, planters, and coverers. The first, beginning at the estate boundary, cut off the tops and chopped the cane in pieces if it was too long. The second opened up holes no more than six to eight inches deep. The planters put two, three, and sometimes four (!!) parallel canes in the holes at two fingers' (1.5 inches) distance from each other. The distance between holes—*narigón*—was one or two spans (between 8 and 18 inches). Through the years, from O'Farrill to Reynoso and Montalvo, the only recorded variant in hoe planting was in the number of canes per hole. In 1792 four were recommended; in the 1860s two, or very occasionally three, were customary. Those who used this method and planted four canes were dubbed "cane buriers" by Reynoso.

Plough planting was the great taboo of the period. An eighteenth-century phrase was still being repeated in the second half of the nineteenth: "Experience has confirmed the short duration of these plantings." [224] But the labor shortage made the use of the plough necessary and many producers convinced themselves that the taboo had no basis. The plough, of course, was the Creole one which scratched rather than penetrated the soil. The planting operation was repeated in the plough furrow, and the plough could then cover the cane used as seed. The only difference was that the furrow replaced the hole.

The various superimposed methods, the old Spanish farming habits taught to the blacks, the lessons learned from the English and French Antilles, and, over all this, the deadweight of the slave routine, created the absurd principles described by Reynoso as "a monstrous system." [225] It was not an extensive system and it was even less an intensive one. Sugarcane is one of the so-called "selected" crops which need the most careful attention, fertilization, and crop rotation. The intensive method is the natural one, but Cuba preferred the extensive, which is above all a way to cut production costs. Thus slavery was the father of bad farming. Sagra frankly called the system stupid, insisting that no reorganization was possible while the work was done by slaves.

Progressive *hacendados* saw an economic abyss opening before them and tried to adopt rational methods involving mechanization of the mills. The records of the Real Junta de Fomento contain articles about new agricultural implements, especially one

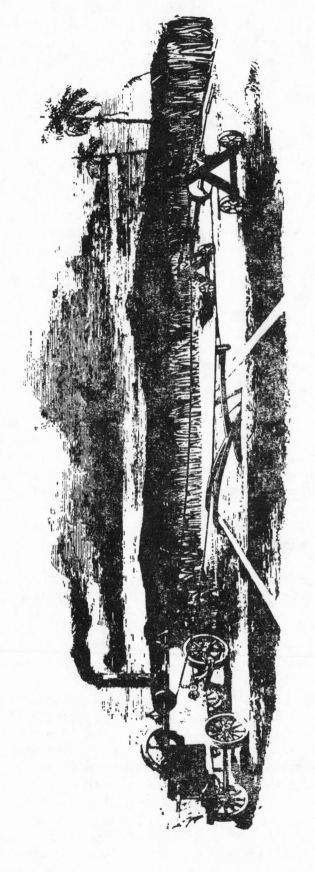

FOWLER PLOUGH

A drawing of the steam plough tested in the Aldama family's Concepción mill. The political and social importance of mechanizing agriculture was not lost on the *hacendados*, who knew how changes in production methods must transform the superstructure. In the exchange of toasts celebrating this occasion, José Silverio Jorrín pronounced these words: "I drink to the eternal memory of this agricultural milestone, the first such machine in Cuba. I drink to rapid propagation of the theoretical principles of scientific agriculture and their practical application as foundation stones of an economically, politically, and socially solid future."

about the use of steam engines in the fields.[226] In the group of Cuban sugarmills described by Cantero, we find ploughs, harrows, rollers, weeders, and rakes made by the various English and United States factories of the period. The Count de Fernandina bought Croskill rollers, Howard harrows and ploughs, a Coleman cultivator-extirpator-scarificator, and a Garret distributor. On Friday, April 24, 1863, the first attempt in the Americas at cane cultivation with a steam plough was made in Miguel Aldama's Concepción mill, and soon afterward José Melgares tested another steam plough made by Howard.[227] In both cases wage-workers had to be hired to run the machines.

Such isolated experiments in scientific farming were frustrated by the grim reality of slavery and the island's astounding fertility. Reynoso crowned his writings with his great *Ensayo sobre el cultivo de la caña de azúcar* (Essay on the cultivation of sugarcane) of 1862. It was a sudden flash of light illuminating the sugarmen's ignorance and the depths to which slavery had reduced agriculture. Reynoso's only worthy predecessor, Sagra, had been pointing to the abyss since the 1820s and crying out for scientific methods. The *Ensayo* was of the greatest economic importance; a second edition appeared in Madrid in 1865 and, translated into Dutch, it soon became the sugar bible of Java.[228] Reynoso advocated deep-trench cultivation by working the soil and planting in furrows—as against the obsolete *jan*–hoe–Creole plough systems. It was the world's first study of the whole sugarcane problem, decisively surpassing the foreign works by Porter and Wray. In our day big English agricultural-implement factories still produce machinery "for the Reynoso system of cane cultivation."

Apart from its global technical importance, inside Cuba Reynoso's book was a political manifesto. Cuba's reformists and frustrated and castrated bourgeoisie saw his doctrine as a partial solution to their problems—although in fact it was an epitaph for their class. But since it seemed at first to be good for everyone, it was greeted with enthusiasm: slave traders and solidly capitalized *hacendados* appear in the subscription list, and the ruined Count de Pozos Dulces, a representative of those producers who had gotten out of their depth, wrote the introduction. The book set standards for scientific cane farming, but they did not conform with the island's objective conditions and hence triumphed in Java and the United States but were forgotten in Cuba. Reynoso spent his last years in wretched poverty and could fittingly apply the farmer's analogy that he had been ploughing in the ocean. Slave labor continued to cultivate Cuban sugar. When slavery was abolished, his influence continued to be felt in the island but the absurd methods went on. Forty years after this luminous book, when Reynoso's system had gone around the world, Fernando Montes de Oca published a *Tratado de agricultura* (Treatise on agriculture) for our republican agronomy schools. It began with precisely the ideas Reynoso fought: "Cane is planted in two ways, with the *jan* or hoe-hole."[229] That was in 1903.

Cane yields. Cuban mills of 1800–1860 did not weigh their cane—the big sugarmill scale was introduced and came into general use immediately after that period. Yields were calculated on the basis of caballerías of cane processed and sugar obtained. These were the terms accepted by Humboldt, who showed such enormous differentials as 1,500, 3,000 and 6,000 arrobas of sugar per caballería. Figures of this kind can only serve as working tools for later calculations, not as definitive data. Since we have analyzed them in detail under the heading "Industrial Yields," we will limit ourselves here to agricultural yields and stress these points: First, that for 1800–1860 we have found no source giving the weight of cane harvested in a given area. Second, the first calculation of this type for which we have references is the French technician Dumont's estimate in 1830 that the cane in one caballería of land must have weighed about 74,648 arrobas (a figure he arrived at, however, by a scientifically worthless mathematical process).[230] Third, the Spanish technician Casaseca obtained the following figures for the 1850 grinding season in the mills of the Banagüises area:[231] *

Table 5

Sugarmill	Arrobas/caballería
San Narciso	110,933
Urumea	105,286

* See notes for conversions to tons per hectare for Tables 5, 6, and 7.

Santa Elena	103,567
Alava	97,500
Ponina	81,250
Belfast	34,664

Casaseca's figures cannot be called exact either, since they were obtained by indirect calculation. In each case he obtained the sugar production figures and the number of caballerías of cane processed. To these numbers he applied a *possible* index of industrial yield to obtain the agricultural yield by an elementary mathematical operation. Had the industrial-yield index he used as a base been scientific, his method would be unobjectionable; but it was no more than an approximation based on the experience of, and given him by, a Banagüises *hacendado* named Diago. Except for the Belfast mill, however, the error was undoubtedly not very great, and Casaseca's figures provide us with a guide to cane yields in new lands where only Otaheite cane was planted.

Fourth, a newly installed scale in the Macagua sugarmill in 1876 provides our first concrete figures for that mill's highest-yielding canefield: 142,000 arrobas/caballería. Fifth, the first complete series we have is in the 1877–1878 harvest records of the Las Cañas mill, for which we have the following figures shown in Table 6.[232] These yields were described by its sugarmaster "as merely average and without irrigation."

The sixth point is that despite the lack of data from scales, uncertainty about the size of canefields, and variations in industrial yields, we can easily fix the limits within which the producers of 1800–1860 moved. These limits seem to have been:[233]

Table 7

	Arrobas/caballería
Plantings in cleared forests	120,000 to 140,000
Good lands	90,000 to 120,000
Average lands	70,000 to 90,000
Ordinary lands	55,000 to 70,000

When production fell below 55,000 arrobas per caballería, the tendency was to abandon the land and cut down another forest, to move the mill, or to stop grinding. These figures, which seem extraordinary today, were therefore normal.

For the 1880s, with scales installed, we know the exact cane yields of many mills; they are very similar to our own calculations, and there is no reason why those of the immediately preceding period should have been lower. In the century's last two decades there was a new expansion of canefields around Camagüey based on a goal of 100,000 arrobas-per-caballería yields. The average yield a century before the period under study was only 47,963, and in recent years minimal yields of 41,255 have been recorded.[234] What with the disappearance into the sea of thousands of tons of our best soil through erosion,

Table 6
Yield of Las Cañas Mill Canefields, 1877–1878 Harvest

Yield in arrobas/caballería	Number of canefields	Percent of total
40,000 to 50,000	8	5.0
50,001 to 60,000	8	5.0
60,001 to 70,000	38	23.8
70,001 to 80,000	39	24.5
80,001 to 90,000	14	8.8
90,001 to 100,000	10	6.3
100,001 to 110,000	15	9.4
110,001 to 120,000	16	10.0
120,001 to 130,000	10	6.3
130,001 to 140,000	1	0.6
	159	99.7

VERHANDELING

VAN

DON ALVARO REYNOSO,

OVER DE

CULTUUR VAN SUIKERRIET,

MET EENE VOORREDE VAN

GRAAF DE POZOS-DULCES.

~~~~~~~~~~

NAAR DEN TWEEDEN DRUK

(DIE, EVEN ALS DE EERSTE, OP KOSTEN VAN HET GOUVERNEMENT
VAN SPANJE HET LICHT HEEFT GEZIEN)

UIT HET SPAANSCH VERTAALD

DOOR

SERVAAS DE BRUIN,

EN

voor het *wetenschappelijke* en *praktische* nagezien

DOOR DE HEEREN

Dr. J. E. DE VRIJ en J. MILLARD.

—◆◆◆—

ROTTERDAM,
H. NIJGH. — 1865.

Title page of the first translation of Reynoso's work into Dutch.

WEIGHING CANE

A Fairbanks scale of the type first installed in Cuba at the Las Cañas sugarmill around 1870. Scales multiplied from that time on.

with land impoverishment through the "monstrous farming" and "stupid planting" noted by Reynoso and Sagra, and with the whole agricultural structure being built "on the absurd foundations of force, ignorance, and improvisation," sugarmen were plundering the earth like thieves. Today the Cuban Revolution picks up the bill and the peasants, masters of their land, have to set themselves as a high goal figures which were formerly below the normal average.

Cutting, loading and hauling. These were aspects of canefield work which hardly varied. Cutting was done with machetes supplied for many years by the English and Spanish and, from the second decade of the nineteenth century, by the United States. At that stage it became a rite to use the Collins machete.

Cutters and loaders left for the canefields in carts at dawn. It was a fixed rule starting in the eighteenth century that "some cut and some load." Their number varied, of course, according to the distance from mill to field and the need for cane. The labor force's strongest members were chosen to drive the carts, not because it was hard work but because this job alternated daily with boiling-room jobs. That is, a man spent eight or nine hours driving a cart and eight or nine in the fierce heat and exhausting rhythm of the "Jamaica train." [235] The next strongest men did the cutting, though this was not a fixed rule.

In Arango's La Ninfa mill, for example, cane was cut and loaded exclusively by women—who cut an average of 300 arrobas (3.5 tons) a day. In the Trinidad Río Abajo mill, the daily average per cutter was 400 arrobas. All technicians and sugarmill documents agree on these figures. In canefields yielding 80,000 arrobas of yellow Otaheite cane, a good cutter averaged 600. [236]

The method was the same as today. The cane was cut as low as possible—Reynoso said "the ideal would be below the ground"—with one sharp blow. Leaves were removed, the top (which went to feed the animals) lopped off, and the cane cut into lengths of one to two yards. Loading was for weaker workers, and thus some *hacendados* assigned it to women. Creole children and *macuencos* (injured slaves) went out to collect the "stray cane." The ox-herds were children four to seven years old. [237]

There was little variation in the carts in this period. Up until 1800, the prevailing type had two wheels, one yoke of oxen, a four-foot-wide floor and $7\frac{1}{4}$-feet-high poles. It was loaded in two layers and carried an average of 80 arrobas (2000 pounds). Four-wheel carts were tried out at various times—the Gener family bought twenty in the United States in 1859—but failed dismally. Oliván returned from his futile technical trip to Europe with ox-harnesses which he hoped would substitute for the old yokes

CUTTING, LOADING, AND HAULING

and improve haulage.[238] The harnesses do not appear to have been used. Dau proposed that cane be hauled on the backs of oxen instead of in carts, but no one paid any attention.[239] One *hacendado* group had the inspiration of importing camels: the San Ignacio mill in Matanzas had thirty-six of these beasts around 1845.[240] Of all these ideas only one caught on: broadening the carts, which began to be built two yards wide around 1850.

To establish the exact weight of a cartload of cane is necessarily difficult, but study of countless documents leads me to believe that these figures are not far off the mark:

1 cartload = 80 arrobas or 2,000 pounds (in all animal-powered mills between 1800 and 1860, and in semi-mechanized ones up to 1850)

1 cartload = 100 arrobas or 2,500 pounds (in nearly all semi-mechanized mills after 1850)

1 cartload = 120 arrobas or 3,000 pounds (in the production giants of 1860: Progreso, Ponina, Flor de Cuba, Alava)

To sum up, the old routines were maintained. In the 1860s the usual innovative voices were raised. First Reynoso explained the simple mechanism of the scale and told the *hacendados* that they should weigh their cane. He also had the vague hope that a cane-cutting machine would come along to solve the labor problem, "for there is nothing that time and man do not permit us to hope for." Sagra followed with a more definite proposal to try out the recently invented cutting machine.[241] Both were ahead of their time, and the only modern device that rapidly came into use was the cane railroad, which began to throw out its network from the mill yard to the remotest fields. It was the seed of the latifundio on iron rails.

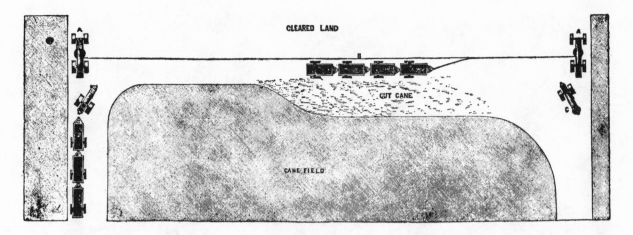

THE MECHANIZATION OF HAULAGE

A cane haulage system patented by Greig in 1866. In Cuba the Concepción mill tried it out, using Fowler machines bought for hauling ploughs.

The agricultural sector: firewood and brushwood

Fuel was one of the producers' biggest worries in the 1800–1860 period. Lack of firewood often resulted in the demolition and removal of a mill. "Mill after mill has to be abandoned for lack of wood," wrote Echegoyen in 1827, "and all we do is clean up and clear off."[242] Until the 1820s the solution to the firewood shortage was to install a system using one furnace, which could be kept going with nothing but bagasse supplying heat to all the boilers. Introduced in Havana mills in 1780, this system spread as the pressure of the firewood shortage sharpened.

As we have seen, the island's forests were so extraordinary that the sugarmen called them excessive. Felling forests every so often to plant cane, the *hacendados* had a permanent reserve of firewood until the day of crisis dawned. On top of this, they resisted

Greig's wagonette, similar to Fowler's, conceived for the transport of cane.

using bagasse because it had to be dried in the sun and stored in big sheds—to which it was easy to set fire. And just when the mills did begin to adopt bagasse-burning trains, the steam engine arrived, and this new source of heat required thick firewood.

Three fuels were in general use—firewood, bagasse, and brush. There were two kinds of firewood: "thick" or "machine," and "thin" or "furnace." The term "brush" covered such light combustible vegetation as small branches, grasses, dry millet, cane leaves, etc. All were measured by volume, not by weight. Villa-Urrutia was already noting this in 1843 as one of the many factors making it hard to calculate yields.[243] The measure of thick or machine firewood was: 1 task = 6 cubic yards. The task was a cubic measure 3 yards long, 1 wide, and 2 high. Reynoso offers a slightly different measure, 3 yards long x 5 spans wide x 2 yards high, or a volume of 9 cubic yards. The first measure, however, is the one frequently appearing in sugarmill documents. Other measurements were:[244]

1 *cajón*	= 2 cubic yards
1 task	= 3 *cajones*
2 tasks	= 3 cartloads
1 cartload	= ⅔ task = 2 *cajones*
1 *carga*	= 40 logs (*rajas*)

The *carga*, or animal load, was also called a *caballo*, and was the amount of firewood a normal beast could supposedly carry. The *raja* was supposed to be 3 spans long and at least three inches thick:

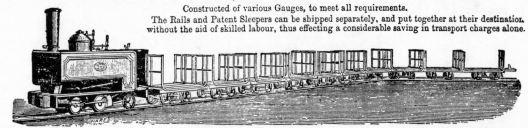
PORTABLE RAILWAY

The definitive mechanical solution. This was the type used in the Hormiguero sugarmill around 1885.

1 *caballo*	= 1 *carga*	
1 *cordel*	= 8 *caballos*	
1 cartload	= 15 *caballos*	

As for the amount of firewood obtainable from a caballería of forest, calculations differed enormously but were made from figures based on forest-felling experience. We have figures from the end of the eighteenth century which seem to have some solidity. According to them a caballería of "good forest" should yield 2,750 tasks of firewood. Reynoso's calculations in 1862 hovered between 2,430 and 2,592—that is, an average of 7.5 to 8 tasks per *cordel*. Some manuals lower this average to only 1,000 tasks per caballería.[245]

Bagasse was generally measured by *canastas* (baskets), since it was brought to the furnaces in baskets. Contemporary calculations were that a cartload of cane furnished sixteen baskets of bagasse. Brush was also measured by basketfuls, or else *brazadas* (armfuls). According to Dau an armful weighed 10 pounds.[246]

Needless to say, accuracy about the sugarmills' fuel consumption is difficult with measures of this type. It also depends on a series of highly variable factors: the number of fires, the kettle system used, the steam engine, the sugarmaster's work habits, etc. Yet many sources offer certain constants. For example, one fire in the boiling-room required the following amount of fuel for one hour:

Using bagasse:	50 baskets
Using firewood:	2 *cajones*
Using brush:	5 cartloads

On this basis, the estimate for "Spanish trains" was between 5 and 7 arrobas of sugar for each task of firewood.[247] With wood-burning Jamaica trains, consumption was 1 task of firewood for each 13 arrobas of sugar. Early nineteenth century large-scale manufacture, working with mixed trains, consumed rather more than a caballería of forest for a 30,000-arroba harvest. Semi-mechanized mills maintained this figure because although they reduced the number of fires when they introduced the Jamaica train and the burning of bagasse, the reduction was compensated by the installation of the steam engine. At this rate of burning the sugarmills annihilated Cuba's forests, and the figures are astounding. In 1828 alone the Guáimaro mill burned two caballerías of the best Trinidad forests; La Ninfa started its 1827 grinding season by cutting 2.5 caballerías to obtain 6,201 tasks.[248] Untechnified mills kept no account of the wood they cut; instead of measuring it in tasks, they stacked it in disordered heaps around the mill. Since the firewood came from fellings, the wooded slopes were called *tumbaderos* (felling-places). According to

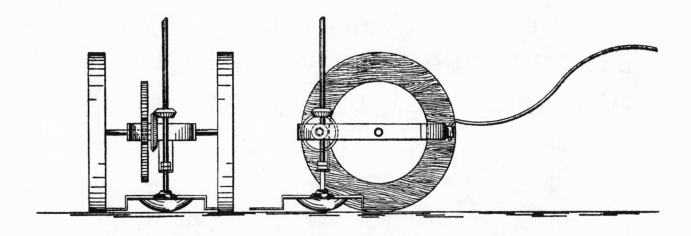

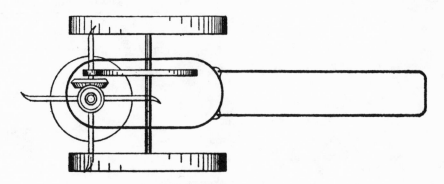

THE MECHANIZATION OF CANE CUTTING
William H. Rastrick's attempt at mechanization, patented in Havana in 1866.

an 1823 report, they were used by slaves as meeting places to practice their clandestine sexual acts: hence even now in Cuban vernacular the words *tumbadero* and *palo* (log) have a sexual connotation—*tumbadero* refers to a house of prostitution and *palo* to sexual intercourse.

With characteristic lack of foresight, the producers always felled but never replanted. By a curious psychological transmogrification they substituted the idea of "firewood" for that of "forest." In the few cases where they talked of reforestation they continued thinking of firewood: Dau, for example, recommended only the types of trees suitable for fuel, such as the *paraíso* and wild indigo.

Slave sugar production—the plantation economy —gave rise to the same problems wherever it was installed. Cuba's fuel problem had already arisen in the English and French Antilles, and had been partially solved there. An English sugar handbook of 1752 says that the kettles should be boiled with one

furnace,[249] and in the mills closest to Havana, situated on deforested lands, the system of burning bagasse and using only one furnace already prevailed in the 1780s. But the problem kept growing and repeating the same cycles. When a mill started grinding there would be plenty of firewood from fellings carried out to erect the buildings and plant the cane. Original land calculations would include 8 to 10—and sometimes more—caballerías of forest for fuel. Since these were consumed in as many or less years, the day of crisis had to come. Cuba's forests were estimated at more than 400,000 caballerías, so there were always more to destroy. But in Jamaica, where there was much less forest, it had all been cut down by the early nineteenth century.

In 1827 the Junta de Fomento sent Arozarena and Bauduy on a trip to Jamaica to study "how to make white sugar with no fuel but bagasse." The first lesson they learned was that Jamaica was not producing white sugar; the second, that its one-furnace trains were inferior to those used in Cuba. What had happened was simply that those Cuban producers who had run out of firewood had already copied and improved the sugarmill's final recourse for survival. In the Trinidad canefields they had seen that Angela Borrell and Pedro Malibrán heated their kettles with nothing but bagasse. The proof was there that all that Humboldt and Echegoyen had said about the technical superiority of the Antilles was completely false. They were as backward as Cuba.

The lesson they did not learn—or at least did not transmit—was *why* Jamaica was so backward: because it had run the same cycle the Cuban producers were running now. The curve was the same, only Cuba was at the zenith and Jamaica at the nadir. Jamaica only used bagasse for fuel because it had already exhausted all its forests after pursuing the same monstrous system that Cuba continued to pursue. Jamaica only produced muscovado because under the slave system in deforested lands there was more

profit in offering only raw materials and semi-refined products. In the 1870s Cuba's western zone would present the same dismal picture.

The agricultural sector: oxen, pastures, and maintenance plots

An old-time sugarmaster observed: "A mill's oxen are second in importance to its blacks, and deserve particular attention both for their value and for their scarcity." Montalvo y Castillo was more explicit: Slaves, he thought, should be given a taste or two of the whip to liven them in their work and twenty-five lashes as castigation, but "no ox must be beaten, on pain of severe punishment." [250]

The ox was the mill's motive power: it moved grinding mills and carts, hauled cane and sugar, ploughed the land, and when it died its flesh fed blacks and its skin, used as straps, fastened the boards of the sugar boxes. Some of the small mills that

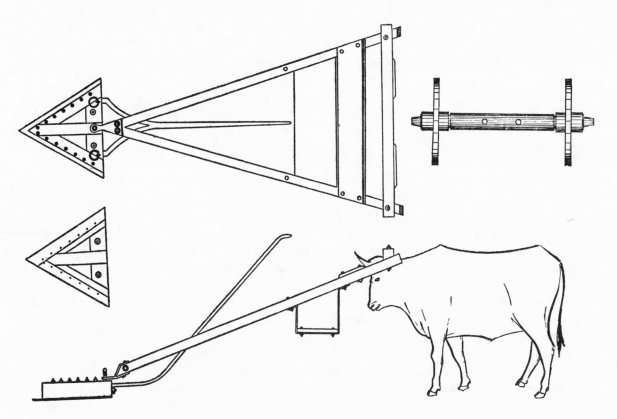

THE MECHANIZATION OF CANE CUTTING

A cane-cutting knife moved by animal power—a rudimentary attempt to mechanize—patented in Havana by Enrique Araujo in 1883. In the same year Luce in the United States was patenting the first cutting machine, which was tested with relative success in Louisiana. Other patents of the period were those of Dollens and Zschech, which failed in the canefields but laid the foundation for modern cutting machines.

prided themselves on their top-quality white sugar used its dried blood in the clarifying operation. The number of oxen depended, of course, on the sugar-mill's capacity and type of crushing equipment. In the early nineteenth-century production boom, the average would be 120 yoke where there was a water-powered grinding mill (as in La Ninfa, La Nueva Holanda, La Amistad) and many more where the grinding mill was ox-powered. The typical horizontal mill of that period needed a minimum of 26 to 30 yoke. The number rose when plough-planting of cane came in. For a 25,000–30,000 arroba production, 40 to 50 carts, with an equal number of ox teams, sufficed. Annual depreciation was figured at 10 percent.

Large ox herds needed a large amount of pasture-land, especially after the semi-mechanized and mechanized mill raised the requirement to three hundred, four hundred, or more yoke. In the late eighteenth century, guinea grass was introduced with the new cane varieties and proved a fine solution to the cattle-feeding problem. In the same period the last molasses run-offs were tried out as cattle feed. The massive use of oxen and their continuous exportation to the foreign Antilles created a buoyant cattle business alongside that of sugar. Without going into details, we may say that the same routines obtained here as in sugar production: the extensive system of cattle-raising, as practiced since the birth of the colony, was maintained. The high prices prevailing after the 1830s made cattle-raising so lucrative that *hacendados* made serious efforts to technify it. Many studies on the subject appear from this period on, and the cry for new systems came from the same throats that clamored in sugar: Sagra, the Count de Pozos Dulces, Reynoso, etc.[251]

Between 1840 and 1860 specimens of the Durham, Devon, and Hereford breeds arrived. Few survived long, since they were turned out indiscriminately into Cuban pastures and the tick transmitted to them all the diseases to which local cattle were immune. In the same period Brazil or Para grass (*Panicum barbinode*), and the rice grass (*Leersia hexandra*) of Puerto Rico, called Scottish grass, were introduced. Attempts to select and improve breeds were concentrated almost entirely around Puerto Príncipe. On western sugarlands cattle were in slave hands and the ox herds were scrawny and beaten. Pastures were hopelessly neglected and it was the general custom,

at the end of the harvest season, to put the oxen in some neighbor's field and pay a standard fee for the privilege. Reynoso complained that many producers were turning the *guardarrayas* into sugarmill pastures. During the harvest cane tops were the main cattle feed.

Care of the cattle fell on a *boyero,* a word with a different meaning in Cuba from what it had in Spain. The *boyero* was responsible for all the cattle and carts, a sort of administrator of this whole department of the mill. He was generally white and always worked for wages. The actual ox-herd was known as a *narigonero* (nose-ringer) or *boyerito,* a diminutive originating from the fact that slave children almost invariably performed this job.

There were no fixed rules about maintenance plots in the nineteenth century. We have shown that a basic characteristic of the mill of 1760 was its self-sufficiency in food. While the early nineteenth century's large-scale producers did away with this, they retained certain elements of it. In the early days the slaves' *conucos*—the little plots given them to raise crops, fowl, and pigs—were part of the scenery. Furthermore, mill owners would then buy the products of these plots from their slaves, thus tacitly recognizing the property rights.[252] With the great growth of sugar and the increasingly cruel treatment of slaves, there was a decided tendency to eliminate all Negro property and the *conuco* system. In the long run the new system proved totally negative, since it suppressed the one fragile link binding the slave to the mill. Constant uprisings, shortages of food, and other factors led to the resumption of the old practice. By the 1830–1850 decades the more intelligent *hacendados* had restored *conucos*. Canefields in the Cárdenas area were in fact being set on fire so persistently around 1840 that something had to be done, and the extent to which the maintenance of discipline figured in this decision is shown by the Real Consulado's advice to the *hacendados*. A commission named to study the problem reached these conclusions: The best way to avoid canefield fires was to feed the slaves better, and the bagasse-shed fires could be stopped by turning the immediately surrounding areas into corrals where the slaves could raise pigs. The conclusions were impeccable sugar-logic, based on the same fatal slave premise.[253] What was fed to the slaves was once again bought from the blacks themselves. The super-barbarity began to decline and the masters began to think seriously about their slaves' survival. The complicated problem was how to squeeze the most out of, and at the same time preserve, property which daily rose in value.

The manufacturing sector

The grinding mill. This was the most radically transformed of all sugarmill equipment between 1800 and 1860. The "bottleneck" of early nineteenth-century large-scale manufacture was a heavy machine of wood and iron which squeezed out the cane passing through its vertical rollers. The rollers, 25–30 inches in diameter, were set in a row and moved by oxen.[254] With a vertical mill, the best technical know-how of the period could only grind about a 15,000-arroba (170-ton) harvest, so large-scale production solved the problem by installing two and sometimes three of them. In thus breaking the bottleneck a new circulation and work problem was created, since between fifty and eighty yoke of oxen had to be used merely for grinding power.

The Industrial Revolution quickly provided the necessary elements to improve this sector of the mill. First, iron shells protected the wooden rollers; then metal parts replaced their wooden equivalents; and finally there were all-iron horizontal mills, which were a real technical revolution. It should be explained that the "horizontal mill" is a machine which survives to our day and consists of three rollers whose axles form the vertexes of an isosceles triangle. They are not to be confused with the horizontal-roller mills whose axles were mounted in a straight line, and which had the same characteristics as vertical mills. These were of very ancient Antillean origin: descriptions of them appear in Père Labat's *Voyages*.

The first "modern"-type horizontal grinding mill we know of was designed in 1754 by John Smeaton for a Jamaican sugarman named Gray.[255] John Collinge began producing it in bulk in 1794, but the model was almost certainly tried out between 1754 and 1790 in some French colonial factories, for it was already known by sugar technicians who fled to Cuba after the Haitian revolution. We have seen that in 1792—two years before Collinge—La Faye presented such a model for the consideration of the Real Sociedad Económica, this being the first horizontal

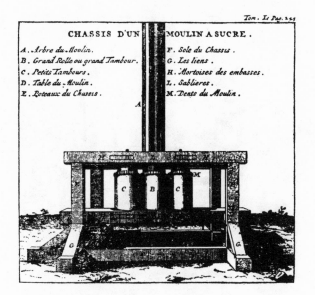

A PRIMITIVE TRAPICHE

A typical trapiche used in the Antillean sugarmills up to the end of the eighteenth century. In Cuba's crude sugar terminology, the central cylinder (B) was known as the main roller, the one on the left (C) as the cane roller, and the one on the right (C) as the bagasse roller. The platform on which the trapiche rested was called a *bancazo*, and the four supporting beams (E) were "virgins."

mill recorded in Cuban history. Ten years later, in 1802, another horizontal mill was designed by another French technician, Esteban Boris, who gave the blueprints to the Real Consulado.[256]

Horizontal mills were soon manufactured entirely of iron and sold in bulk by the chief implement concerns of England and the United States. The new machine showed great superiority over the old. It was more durable and the transmission mechanism was much better, lightening the work of the oxen. The horizontal roller placement allowed better distribution of the cane, avoiding a concentration of the wear at one point and exerting pressure on only one of the shafts. In vertical mills the pressure on the cane was regulated by the distance between rollers; these could be brought closer together or further apart, but once the distance was fixed the pressure was constant. The horizontal mill, on the other hand, had a simple spring-and-weight mechanism which yielded when irregular cane was fed in. This mechanism was the oldest ancestor of the modern hydraulic pressure-regulator. Finally, the horizontal position made it possible to slide the cane down a board in front of the mill, thus avoiding accidents to

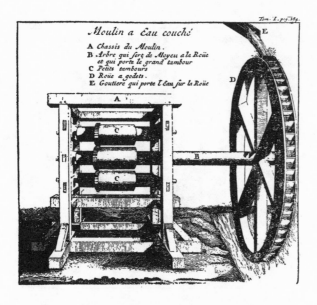

Tom. I. pag. 364.

Moulin a Eau couché

A *Chassis du Moulin.*
B *Arbre qui sert de Moyeu a la Roüe
et qui porte le grand tambour*
C *Petits tambours*
D *Roüe a godets*
E *Goutiere qui porte l'Eau sur la Roüe*

AN OLD HORIZONTAL-ROLLER
GRINDING MILL

This is the "horizontal" grinding mill referred to in eighteenth-century documents but very little used. It was technically similar to the vertical one except for the position of the rollers. It is not to be confused with the "modern" horizontal grinding mill, whose rollers rest at the vertexes of an isosceles triangle.

black "feeders," whose hands were often caught between the rollers. The first moving belts, or "cane conductors," made their appearance around 1840.

All these advances put Cuban grinding techniques, after 1820, on a level with the best of the day. Both mechanized and semi-mechanized sugarmills generally installed grinding mills that far outstripped those of the beginning of the century. Many of the sugarmills depicted in Rebello's reports as working with oxen had good horizontal animal-powered mills, and at least in the western area the three-roller horizontal mill involved not a complication but a simplification of the work: it was stronger, not weaker, than the old wooden machine and hence could stand up better to slave treatment. Furthermore, it did not change the rest of the work in the sugarmill in any way. Cane was still brought to the grinding mill and fed between the rollers to obtain bagasse and juice. As with the iron *jan,* the new apparatus preserved the production system intact.

Like many other sugarmill features, iron horizontal mills did not totally replace the old kind: much three-roller vertical grinding continued into the 1860s, even though the new machines predominated.

From early in the century the English firm of Fawcett, Preston & Co. sold grinding mills schematically similar to the most modern ones of our day. In 1830 Fawcett, Preston brought out a perfected model, the first units of which were bought for Cuban sugarmills by Joaquín Gómez and José Aizpurúa.

There is sad historical confusion in studies of this process. From a technical standpoint until 1840 there was no difference between the quality of the product and the sugarcane/sugar yield of a steam-powered mill and an animal-powered one—granted, of course, that we are referring to iron, horizontal-roller grinders of the type made by Fawcett, Preston, Derosne-Cail, etc. Indeed, up to 1840 no grinding machines were manufactured exclusively to be driven by steam; all were adapted for any kind of motive power.

This involves a total revision of the view maintained until our day concerning the steam engine's influence on the Cuban sugar industry and thus on the island's economy. In its initial stage, steam produced no upset in the rhythm of production.[257] We have seen that sugar's first steam engine began functioning in the Count de Mopox y Jaruco's Seybabo mill on January 11, 1797; it was a failure, but over the next twenty years more than fifteen other types were tried out until one worked—in Juan Madrazo's sugarmill in Matanzas. Madrazo had bought it from Fawcett, Preston for £1,050 in December 1816, and it went into action in 1817. Like three others bought from the same firm in 1817 and applied to horizontal mills, it worked by a condensation system.*

The success of Fawcett's engines brought in its wake the utilization of that firm's fine horizontal mills. Deerr says that Fawcett sold sixty-three horizontal mills and only eleven vertical ones, eight of which came to Cuba. Our *hacendados* soon realized

* Technical documentation on these machines, and all data on their sale and transport, appear in the superbly organized archives of Fawcett, Preston, who generously photocopied all the references to Cuba. It is impossible to pinpoint the first successful application of the steam engine to a grinding mill in Cuba since four Cuban sugar plantations—Madrazo's, Pérez de Urria's, Peñalver's, and Diago's—began their 1817–1818 harvest grindings with a Fawcett machine. As will be seen below, the only one that failed was that of Diago, who has always been cited as the first to introduce a steam engine in Cuba. It should be noted that a steam engine had been driving a sawmill in Havana since 1810, so that 1817 is the year of steam's first application in a sugarmill, but not in Havana industry.

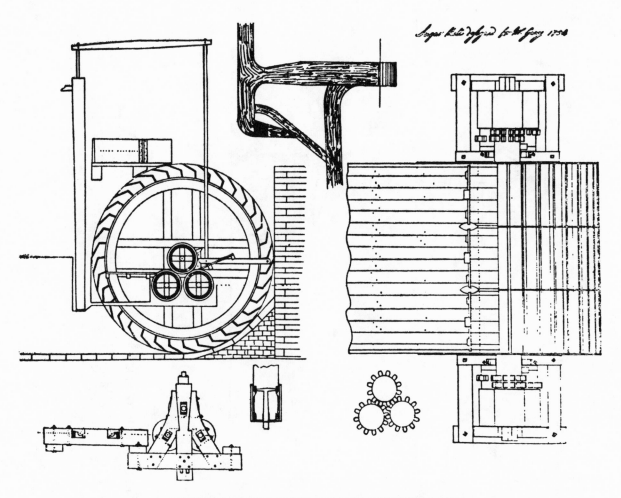

Sugar Rolls Designed for Mr Gray 1754

A MODERN HORIZONTAL-ROLLER GRINDING MILL

According to Deerr, this is the first known horizontal grinding mill of modern design. It was built by John Smeaton for the Jamaican planter Gray in 1754. The sketch is taken from Deerr, who in turn took it from the Royal Society's Smeaton Collection.

the great advantages of the horizontal type. In 1817 Diago unsuccessfully applied a magnificent 12-horse-power steam engine to a vertical mill. He consulted the English technician Joseph Hibberson, who diagnosed the engine as sound and the grinding mill as needing to be changed. A horizontal mill was ordered from Fawcett (the first of its type to reach Cuba), with rollers 26″ in diameter and 48″ long, and the Cambre sugarmill ground cane with this for more than fifteen years. Fawcett then became the king of mill mechanizers, selling sixteen of the horizontal type and fifty 8–12-h.p. steam engines. Thus the process of industrial germination in our sugarmills, begun in the Seybabo plantation in 1796, came to fruition.[258] Yet in 1833 Alejandro Oliván was still claiming that "the ox-powered horizontal mill is best for Cuba and more fitted to a rural

industry."[259] And Villa-Urrutia, who had eliminated oxen from his La Mella mill and gotten worse results, ended by agreeing in 1838 that "a good ox mill is better than a bad steam one."[260]

The main reason for the rise of the steam grinding machines lies in the economization of oxen and labor and the comparative ease of production. They eliminated fifty to eighty yoke of oxen and the corresponding personnel to care for them, and the saving was particularly great after six yoke instead of four became necessary for the large iron mills. The big plantations' final solution was one steam-driven machine and a smaller ox-driven one in case the machinery broke down.

On the labor level, the steam-driven horizontal mill created two contradictory trends. On the one hand, it required the presence of a machinist and

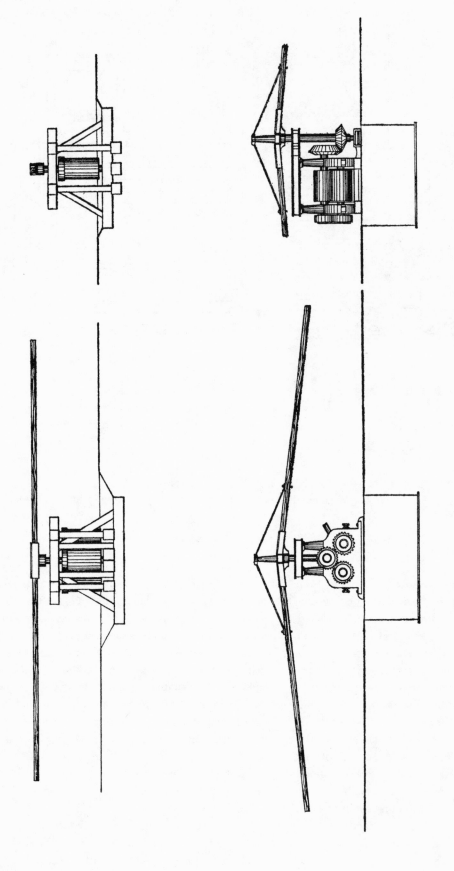

FAWCETT GRINDING MILLS

These are examples of both the horizontal and vertical type sold to Cuba by Fawcett, instantly adaptable to either oxen or steam. The favorite in the island was 22" in diameter and 32" long. Pedro Diago brought the first Fawcett horizontal grinding mill to Cuba by order dated March 20, 1821, paying £600. It was 26" in diameter and 48" long, and was installed in El Cambre mill.

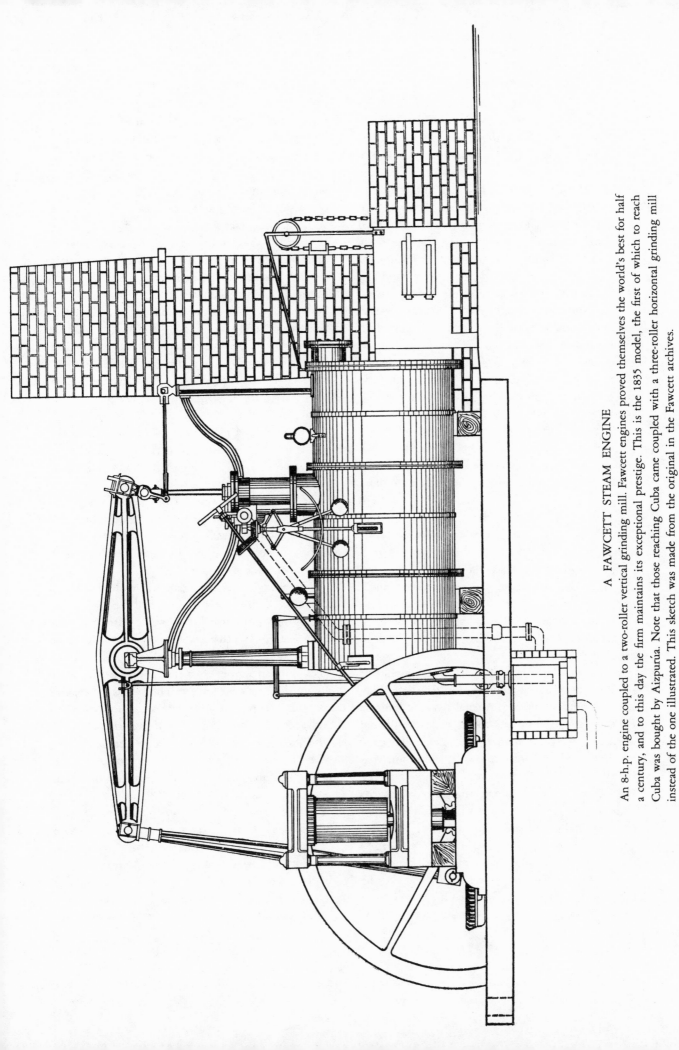

A FAWCETT STEAM ENGINE

An 8-h.p. engine coupled to a two-roller vertical grinding mill. Fawcett engines proved themselves the world's best for half a century, and to this day the firm maintains its exceptional prestige. This is the 1835 model, the first of which to reach Cuba was bought by Aizpurúa. Note that those reaching Cuba came coupled with a three-roller horizontal grinding mill instead of the one illustrated. This sketch was made from the original in the Fawcett archives.

assistant, initiating an autonomous cell of wage-workers within the slave establishment. On the other, it called for far more slaves, for one large steam mill broke the bottleneck and brought a fast rise in the production curve. In a 30,000 to 40,000-arroba plant the new system must have cut the number of oxen by several dozen and displaced into other activities not less than thirty slaves. It also speeded the production rhythm by allowing for fixed or moving cane carriers to feed the mill—previously impossible because of the constant circulation of oxen. Black cane feeders and bagassemen could slip in and out without passing under the driving sweeps.

Iron steam-powered mills raised production capacity but hardly affected the sugarcane/sugar yield. Contemporary investigations both in Cuba and the foreign Antilles show that good grinding machines extracted 60 to 65 percent of the juice in the cane whether oxen, steam, or water provided the power.[261] Not until the end of the century, when the first tandems of several grinders appeared, did this percentage increase; and only in the twentieth century was the process completed with revolving knives, shredders, and crushers. The grinding mill on Poey's Las Cañas plantation, powered by a high-compression steam engine bought in West Point, New York, was the best there was in 1860. Consisting of three horizontal rollers with a small peripheral groove, it passed the cane through once, ejected the bagasse whole, and used neither imbibition nor maceration.[262] This seems to confirm Casaseca's estimate of the grinding mill as the point in the flow line where there was most loss in extracting sucrose.

Although the new mills left the productive structure intact, slaver-producers resisted the inevitable modernization process. Around 1850 the Junta de Fomento was still worrying about pendular mills and miraculous perpetual-motion machines.[263] To compete with the speed of steam power, José Montalvo y Castillo, a collateral descendant of the Count de Casa-Montalvo, fitted up San Miguel de las Caobas with an ox grinding mill which had an iron cogwheel and transmission, and no sweeps. As usual, the attempt to stop the clock of history failed.[264] Other industrial-minded producers toured Europe in search of better and more powerful machines. At the time the French firm of Derosne-Cail turned out a six-roller horizontal grinding machine unrelated to the classical Smeaton design. This mill gave excellent results and the first was installed in Villa-Urrutia's La Mella plantation at Limonar.[265]

In sum, the sugarmill of 1860 with a big iron grinding mill and a steam engine could appreciably increase its production and to a very small extent its yield; but in terms of the production line the organism remained intact. The slave had no contract with the machine, which was operated by one or more wage-workers; nor did he have any new or different jobs to perform. He did have to multiply the old jobs drastically, pacing his muscle power to the steam pistons. Despite the steam engine and the iron grinding mill, sugar manufacture continued to be a manual and routine task. Increasing production in a particular unit meant more arrobas per Negro. But since methods did not change, this could only be achieved by more pressure on the slave, by longer and heavier tasks, draining the last second of his useful life.

Steam-powered mills started a process which led in the end to the abolition of slavery. But in their first stage they only magnified it in an exploitation process that was progressively more bestial. In that sense the machines were a curse to the slave. The wisest question of the period came from a priest in the novel *Cecilia Valdés*: "Why are there more slave risings in steam-powered mills than in those which grind their cane with oxen?"

The boiling room. The place where the juice was defecated, clarified, and concentrated, known as the boiling room or sugar house, was a basic part of a sugar factory. The changes in it up to the 1840s were more nominal than real. A typical eighteenth-century sugarmill had a series of smelted copper kettles, each mounted on its own furnace. The kettles, where the concentration process took place, were of varying size and generally grouped in sets of five; the first one, which received the raw juice, was the largest, and the others became smaller as the syrup evaporated. In the last, called the *teache* or strike pan, the optimum point of concentration was reached.

When a group of kettles was placed on the same fire-ditch it was called *tren* (train) or *reverbero* (reverberator). In the English islands the term "copper wall" was used, as well as "Jamaica train." In Louisiana this group of kettles was generally referred to as a "set of kettles," or merely as the "set." The first trains in Cuba were the so-called

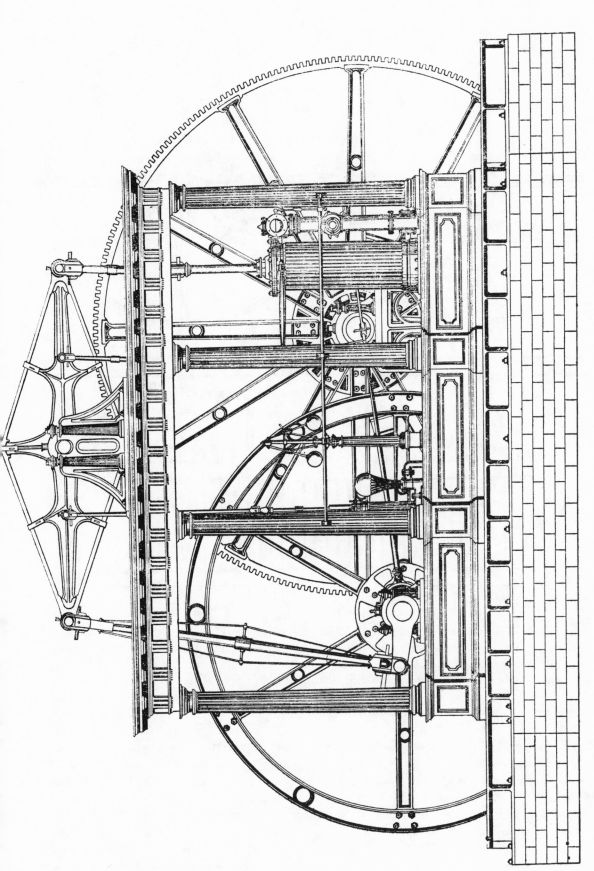

THE STEAM ENGINE IN A LARGE MECHANIZED SUGARMILL

With the appearance of vacuum trains and the great increase in the productive capacity of completely mechanized mills, ever larger grinding mills had to be used. The above is typical of a big mill of 1860, bought in that year by Julián and Aniceto del Valle for the Yankee Girl, or La Crisis, mill, and manufactured by the Washington Iron Works of Newburgh, New York. The rollers were 36" in diameter and 78" long.

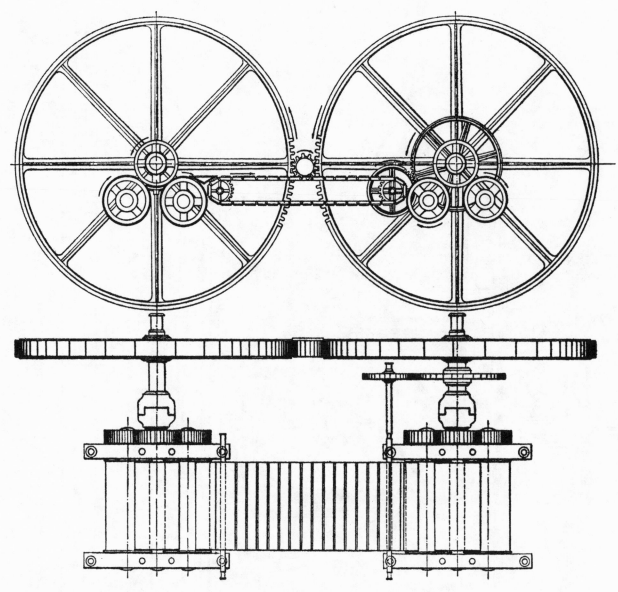

VILLA-URRUTIA'S TANDEM

A most interesting but almost unused device which was Villa-Urrutia's exceptional solution to the problem of loss of sucrose. It is a tandem of two horizontal grinders powered by the same steam engine and joined by a link belt which carries the bagasse to the other grinder. Maceration and imbibition occur as the cane passes over the belt. The only known imbibition precedent is James Robinson's patent of 1840; as a tandem it is the first of its kind. In fact, tandems were not built until 1870, when Cail began making the first two-grinder model; in 1892 three-grinder ones began to be made. This is the most serious Cuban contribution to global sugar technology.

French ones, comprising five successive kettles. French trains were universally known as *Equipage du Père Labat*, and the kettles as *grande, propre, flambeau, sirop,* and *battérie.*[266] We do not know exactly when this system was introduced into Cuba, but there were already French-train sugarmills in Havana in the 1780s.

Early nineteenth-century large-scale manufacture copied and extended the French train, adding two or three clarifiers: these were pans of smelted copper 70 to 80 inches in diameter to which the juice came directly from the grinding mill; there it was heated short of boiling after lime was added. The syrup was then allowed to stand, and was finally released into the first kettle of the train through an outlet some three inches from the bottom, thus separating off the

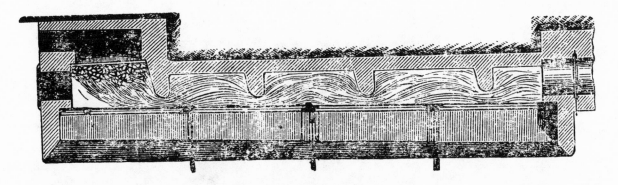

A TRAIN OF SQUARE KETTLES

One of the Jamaica train's many variants. Its only advantage over previous systems was in presenting a bigger caloric surface, thus speeding evaporation. With small changes, this system was sold in Cuba around 1860 as the Arritola train.

solid elements by decantation, and the colloids—in the form of scum—by precipitation. In their original form, clarifiers filled the role of today's juice evaporators and at the same time were defecators and decanters.[267] They were first used in Jamaica in 1778 by a *hacendado* named Sainthill,[268] and Arango brought them to Cuba after his famous voyage of investigation. In terms of the period's crude technique they were a notable advance, but they were soon abandoned since they necessitated a degree of care not to be expected of a slave.[269] During the nineteenth century the *hacendados,* starting from the idea of trains or sets of kettles, tried out countless different arrangements—the "French," "Jamaica," "mixed," "scissor," "Ramos," and "Arritola" trains, etc. All the combinations were the result of the same routine and the stark impossibility of technifying with slave labor. Normally a production of 10,000 arrobas per harvest could be obtained with one train of five kettles and one or two auxiliary boilers. Large-scale production was achieved by increasing the number of kettles, and some plantations ended up with ten Jamaica trains.

Furthermore, apart from in the few highly mechanized mills, secondary operations in the concentration process did not change in any way in the first sixty years of the century. The removal of scum, which had at first been attempted with clarifiers, continued to be performed with scummers. The transfer of syrup from one kettle to another was normally done with a long-handled paddle called a *bomba, bombo,* or *bombón,* giving the name *bombear* to the operation. Some producers invented a sweep-type *bombo* with a metal handle, two or more yards long

and worked like a lever. Another idea was placing the coppers at different levels so that the syrup passed along the line by gravity, but this was abandoned since it created a problem with respect to the fire.

It should be stressed that early nineteenth-century Cuban mills had no standard way of arranging kettles. The system of several kettles on one furnace prevailed because of the fuel shortage, and the Jamaica train, with its four kettles and two defecators, was the most common arrangement. Technically unversed historians have presented the Jamaica train as a step forward in sugar production. In fact it was no more than a return to the English system used in Barbados in the first years of the eighteenth century, transmitted to the French in 1725, and copied in some Havana mills in 1780.[270] This is why Arozarena and Bauduy's voyage was a complete fiasco: the few advances made by the English had already been copied in Cuba, and further technification was as impossible for them as for us while the slave system continued.

From the 1820s on, Sagra was insisting that the island needed a totally new juice-evaporation and concentration system,[271] and as an example he cited European beet sugar factories. This is one of the oddest facets of the global sugar struggle: Two

A HAND PNEUMATIC PUMP

A BIG JAMAICA TRAIN OF THE MID-NINETEENTH CENTURY

The interior of a typical semi-mechanized mill's boiling room at mid-century. This is a big mill with four to six Jamaica trains, two of which are in foreground and two more in rear to the left. The device on the right is a cooler. A *bombón* rests on the edge of the first train, and a set of two clarifiers can be seen behind each. The sketch was carefully copied by Modesto García from a watercolor of 1845 by the English painter Sawkins, who lived in Cuba for several years.

sugars appeared in nineteenth-century European markets, different not only in their sources—beets and cane—but in the type of labor used to make them—wage in the first, slave in the second. Each had its advantages and disadvantages. Cane sugar was produced on extraordinarily fertile, often virgin lands; several harvests were gleaned from one planting; the cane was above ground and merely had to be pressed to extract its pure juice. Beets needed annual planting; being a root, they had to be carefully washed; and they could not be pressed like cane, but had to undergo a complicated slicing and maceration process. This gave cane a clear head start over beets despite the slave labor system. On the other hand, slave labor itself stagnated Antillean sugar production while European factories steadily progressed. From the first years of the nineteenth century, every technical advance in sugar production originated in European factories, and America's slave factories could but partially imitate such new processes as were viable with slave labor.[272]

It was for the European sugar beet factories that the first system of vacuum concentration, invented by Howard in 1812, was destined. Like all its successors, the Howard apparatus was based on the low-temperature evaporation of the liquid while it was subjected to below-normal pressures—that is, on the simple physical principle that a liquid's degree of evaporation is in constant relation to the atmospheric pressure exerted upon it. Sagra's publications made Howard's apparatus known in Cuba. It was a large closed boiler with a double bottom through which steam circulated. Syrup evaporated in it at 72°C. after a pneumatic machine created the vacuum. Roth's later apparatus perfected this by adding a coil which contacted the syrup and hastened evaporation; rather than a pneumatic machine, a system of continuous evaporation and condensation created the vacuum. It worked at 62°C, but had the disadvantage of a lack of continuity, since on completion of each batch the process had to be interrupted. Aizpurúa brought one of these devices to Cuba and had negative results.[273]

In the 1830s the French firm of Derosne-Cail worked on the first complete sugar-processing system. It started with a three-roller horizontal mill, then a cane carrier, and proceeded through defecators, carbon filters, and vacuum evaporators. The first of these to reach the Antilles was installed in Guadaloupe and worked extraordinarily well.

When vacuum apparatuses began to revolutionize the sugar industry, the Junta de Fomento sent Alejandro Oliván to study them in Europe. He returned to announce that vacuum pans were a flop and that, for Cuba, the ideal was two trains of seven different-sized kettles and special treatment of the sugar with bone-black filters and dried blood. He also recommended ox rather than steam power. Both observations showed that he inhabited another world, outside the progress of the day.[274] On their first test at La Ninfa, the devices brought by Oliván failed completely; they were moved over to the Marquis de Villalta's San José sugarmill, where the results were equally disastrous. After being offered free to anyone who would install them according to Oliván's instructions, they finally had to be offered for sale as scrap. The kettles, however, were taken by the Count de O'Reilly, who installed them in the usual island fashion; José Arritola bought the filters but could never use them. Other implements were still in the Real Consulado's possession in 1845, with no buyers at any price.

We have lingered on this period because the introduction of Jamaica trains and rational furnace systems to Cuba has been attributed to Oliván. He was in fact a charlatan of the first order: he knew nothing whatever about sugar and the Junta de Fomento spent over $25,000 on a trip which benefited nobody. Cuban producers refrained from unmasking him because he was their paid employee, used in the Spanish Cortes as a shock-trooper against slaver interests.[275]

The vacuum pan spurned by Oliván was in fact the one possible solution for large-scale sugar production. Top hacendados soon perceived this, and in 1841 Villa-Urrutia bought the first one for his La Mella plantation at Limonar. To do so he borrowed $9,000 from the Junta de Fomento—and at that he only acquired part of the apparatus. He set up an incomplete system of evaporating and de-scumming in an old-style train and passing the syrup into the vacuum concentration apparatus. The French factory —which saw a fabulous market for its sugar implements opening up in Cuba—acted like any big modern enterprise: it gave Villa-Urrutia the rest of the machinery as a present and, since Cuba lacked the necessary technical resources, M. Derosne himself arrived in Havana to supervise its installation.[276] Cuba did not have to wait long to see the results. La

111

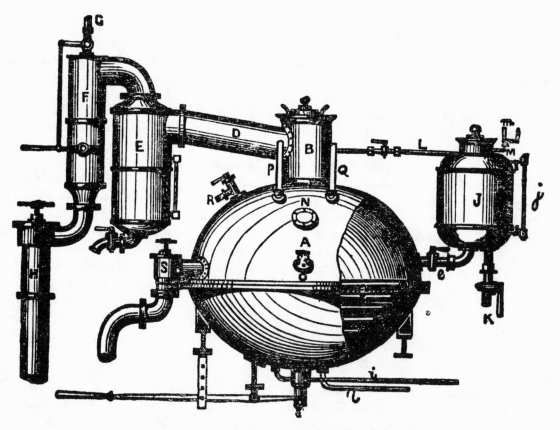

A TYPICAL VACUUM EVAPORATOR (1850)

Typical vacuum evaporators included: (A) A Howard-type closed boiler; (B) a top opening, hermetically sealed, for cleaning and internal repairs; (C) a heating surface consisting of coils through which steam circulated; (D) an outlet for cane-juice fumes; (E) a safety column to prevent passage of rapidly boiling syrup into the condenser; (F) a condenser; (G) a cold-water pipe for the condenser; (H) a connection to the pneumatic pump; (I) a steam supply to boiler; (i) and (i') outlets for condensed water from coil steam; (J) a juice measure; (j) glass leveling gauge; (K) a juice entrance point.

Mella's normal yield had hardly ever reached 4 percent of cane weight, but in the 1843 season it was 5.91 percent.

The most important effect was on the labor system. The new apparatus was too complicated for slaves, and Derosne trained free workers to operate it. Thus what had previously happened with the grinding mill now happened with the vacuum apparatus: another free-labor cell emerged within the sugarmill's slave establishment. The slave neither ran Derosne's apparatus nor tested its temperatures nor watched the safety valves. He continued his old routine, operating the whole process up to the machine and after the machine, while that particular sector of the production line was barred to him. Producers now felt the urgent need of labor which would be cheap but of a minimal technical level unattainable by slaves. The Industrial Revolution meant the changeover to the wage-worker. An intermediate solution was found in Chinese laborers —this is one reason why Cuba's Chinese colony began in the years when the sugarmills were mechanizing. The Chinese made possible the first steps in sugar industrialization.

Many European firms quickly started manufacturing the new vacuum apparatus; apart from those mentioned, the most important were E. Pontifex, J. Wood, and Benson & Day. In Cuba, however, Derosne-Cail almost monopolized the market. Casaseca, director of Havana's Instituto de Investigaciones Químicas and a notable chemist with first-class training, had been brought to Cuba to realize Arango's old dream of chemistry at the service of sugar. He did a fine job, and the prestige of Derosne-Cail apparatus in Cuba is largely attributable to him, although they were in fact no better than the Benson, Pontifex, and Rillieux machines. Casaseca had the privilege of being the technical brains of what he himself called the "Cuban industrial revolution." When at the age of seventy he ceased to be indispensable, the sugarocracy threw him out of Cuba like an old shoe, and his last years were tragic. He lived in Barcelona on a tiny pension which sometimes arrived four or five months late and from which 35 percent was deducted. The millionaire José Sama, to whom Casaseca had contributed great technical services, refused to help the old man with a few pesos. The only reliable source of help in his last years was his disciple Reynoso, who himself would come to the same wise, poverty-struck, and humiliating end.[277]

The installation of the vacuum apparatus meant the transformation of the whole production system. It meant doubling yields at one stroke. Casaseca realized that the small sugarmills could no longer compete with the big ones and were doomed to disappear. As a stout bourgeois he said this would be all to the good, for it "would stimulate the spirit of association among *hacendados,* and their joint capital would form big sugarmill companies which would yield high dividends to investors."[278] But this was not how it turned out. The big new factories were brought face to face with the stumbling block of labor and the need for lavish capital investment, and only men with previous capital accumulation and the possibility of acquiring Chinese could compete. All the large mechanized mills were based on Chinese labor, and the germ of today's sugar *central* was the doubling of yields by mechanization. It was no accident that the first mention of the big *central,* in Guadeloupe, followed the installation of a Derosne vacuum pan.

The small sugarmen could not industrialize themselves; vacuum apparatuses signaled the total ruin of Cuba's old producing class. Thousands of small sugarmills remained as before. At the dawn of the 1860s, as we have seen, the island only had 64 mechanized mills as against 1,248 animal-powered and semi-mechanized ones. Although the big ones equipped with vacuum pans only produced 8.3 percent of the total yield, the sugarmill working with open kettles and obsolete Jamaica trains was in retreat before the inevitable industrial advance. The new sugarmills not only obtained higher yields but got sugar of a quality the traditional trains could not

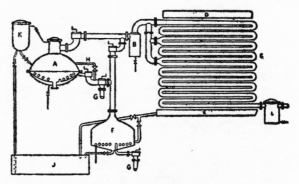

A DEROSNE TRAIN

Like all great inventions, this was the sum of previously known elements. The essential features were those of the previous illustration: (A) A closed Howard boiler, and (B) a safety column. The condenser (C), however, is of the Clark type. It served at the same time as a pre-heater of the juice, which was situated in the distributor (D), which fell into the deposit (E) at foot of the condenser. Because of this latter function, Derosne, in a play on words, called it a condenser-evaporator. In (F) it had an additional boiler.

match. Sugar quotations soon featured a new price—the highest—for "Derosne train white." The old quality was an also-ran, and Jamaica trains began turning out semi-refined muscovado.

With the introduction of the vacuum pan, the small producer's despair reached its depth: blinded to the slave system and without investment capital, he hunted everywhere for freak solutions. The industrial process always had its opportunists, its miracle salts and occult formulae, a mixture of bad alchemy and scientific principles. In these years they appeared as never before. There was, for instance, lead acetate, a product patented in England as a marvelous method for producing white sugar and spread around by an English charlatan, Dr. Scoffern, who left several publications about sugar.[279] The English capitalized on the fact that it was highly poisonous and used in refining in a campaign against Cuban sugar. The few Cuban producers who had tried it out, and the United States company which used it in a Havana refinery, quickly stopped. Other products appearing in a nimbus of mystery, and promising whiter-than-white sugar with the old slave system, included Dr. Stolle's Arcanum,[280] and Cayetano Aguilera and Fernández de Hita peddled "secret" salts. As director of the Instituto de Investigaciones Químicas, Casaseca had the job of testing and reporting on these

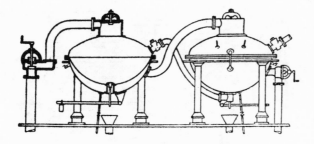

THE FIRST RILLIEUX EVAPORATOR

This was the first Rillieux patent, which consisted of two connected vacuum boilers. It did not add anything to the Derosne system, but did contain the seeds of the multiple effect system, which Rillieux built three years later. In spite of great intelligence, Rillieux, the son of a New Orleans mulatto woman, was so victimized by racial prejudice that he abandoned the city of his birth and lived out his life in Paris.

products. The touted Arcanum turned out to be a double alumina-ammonia salt; Aguilera and Hita, however, kept their nostrums so secret that they could not be analyzed. They took them, concealed in pouches, to the San Francisco sugarmill where a test of sugar-making with the wonder salts was carried out in a ceremony worthy of the theater. Predictably it all came to nothing, but the Junta de Fomento's on-the-spot report indicates the anguish of the search for something that would work with the obsolete Jamaica train, the only one slaves could operate.[281]

Of all the "mysteries" which exploded like soap bubbles, the most noteworthy was that of Dr. Louis-Henri-Frédéric Melsens. In Paris and Brussels it was proclaimed almost in unison that the doctor would make some experiments which would transform sugar production throughout the world. The journalistic build-up created a tense climate of anticipation. The Havana sugarocracy showed how lively they still were by hurrying to ensure that no one should get to the discovery ahead of them. European news clips which reached Havana pictured the sensational rise in productivity and the reduction of costs and of processing time which the invention would bring about: it would economize on labor, improve quality, and simplify the whole operation. The Junta de Fomento alerted the Spanish consuls in Europe and opened negotiations to obtain the fabulous secret. The Havana firm of Urtegui, Robertson & Co. served as intermediary. Amid great

expectations Havana's *El Faro Industrial* published on separate pages the world's first translation of Dr. Melsens' methods. The translation had been made directly from the French, from a copy acquired on the day of its publication in Paris and immediately rushed to Havana. In a display of incredible efficiency, two different translations—the one in the *Faro Industrial* and another in the *Diario de la Marina*—appeared on the day after the document's arrival. The secret unveiled was: bisulphite of lime.

All the *hacendados* had to do was to find out what bisulphite of lime was and how one could get it. Next day Casaseca showed his chemical expertise by describing it as a very easily obtainable salt: one mounted a Woolf apparatus and subjected the milk of recently slaked lime to the action of a continuous current of sulphuric acid. By way of further simplification, the front page of the Havana *Gaceta* two days later carried the complete explanation of the method, with a diagram of the Woolf apparatus. Matanzas *hacendados* Pedro Hernández Morejón and Tomás de Jaura y Soler, who had anxiously followed the proceedings, got a German pharmacist, Friedrich Helberg, to make them two bottles of the stuff. On December 1, 1849, they sent them to a friend with a letter which began: "We have triumphed, and you will have in your possession two trophies of the victory, consisting of two bottles of bisulphite of lime."

The sugar world was still at high pitch when, at the end of December, the first sad tidings came from Europe. The Spanish legation in Belgium reported that Dr. Melsens was unhappy about the results: the bisulphite gave sugar a horrible flavor. Finally, on January 20, 1850, Cuban tests were made on a grand scale in slave-trader Manuel Pastor's mill. Casaseca summed up the result: "With Jamaica trains, using the new proposed ingredients, a step forward has not in fact been made. The normal method with lime alone, practiced by a good sugarmaster, still seems preferable." [282]

It was impossible to advance with the old system: the Jamaica train belonged to a past to which there was no return, the vacuum apparatus to a boundless future. When the sugarmill changed its basic equipment, the system of production was turned upside down. This had not happened with the grinding mill or with the steam engine—secondary equipment both. From the 1840s until the crisis of 1880–1885, a

114

grim internal struggle was the reality of the Cuban sugar scene. Statistical jugglery has hidden most of this from historians and economists. Without a grasp of the technical facts, the position of the Count de Pozos Dulces, and the *El Siglo* reformists can never be understood. Havana's once-proud sugarocracy fell into step-by-step retreat. In 1867 Dau—a pioneer of his class, the translator in 1832 of the work of Richardson Porter, the champion of the slaveless sugarmill in 1837—published his *Manual para la elaboración del azúcar.*[283] At a time when extraordinary technical developments already existed, he retreated further back than his earlier works and pleaded for little Jamaica-train mills producing nothing but muscovado. In 1871 another industrial revolutionary of the 1830s, José de Arritola, insisted on a "new and marvelous" train which only differed from the Jamaica in that its kettles were square.[284] It was backwardness and defeat, the only road there was for slavery.

Technical controls. We have seen how eighteenth-century mills carried out the alkalization process with "lye," or a mixture which was given that name. In 1798, new-type mills began using powdered quicklime,[285] and alkalization control became one of the sugarmill's key technical problems. It had always required the strictest care because when there is too little lime the juice decants slowly and clarifies with difficulty, while when there is too much the impurities precipitate fast and the juice decants with less delay, but the lime acts on the glucose—especially at the high temperatures of the Jamaica train—to form lime salts from the organic acids; these take on a dark color and are transformed into acid substances which produce the inversion of the sugar.

The old sugarmasters, ignorant as they were of the problem's theoretical core, knew from experience the consequences of incorrect alkalization. Pizarro y Gardín, one of many who tried to formulate standardized rules, published some rules on the subject in 1847.[286] But juices varied from canefield to canefield and from year to year, making fixed rules impossible. Practice established a series of routines, and in the period under study alkalization was controlled by smell; this generally resulted in an excess of lime and was another reason for low yields. The great discovery by some sugarmasters was the use of litmus paper. When that was scarce paper dyed with turmeric, with sunflower, or with *palo de*

J. CAIL

Derosne's associate in the famous firm of Derosne & Cail. When Degrand got a French court order removing Derosne's name from all vacuum apparatuses sold by the firm, the name was changed and it was thenceforth known as Cail & Cie.

Campeche tree extract was used. This control method emerged in the second decade of the nineteenth century.[287] By mid-century Maigroth's "calciometer" and Belot's "calimeter" were being sold in Havana. Félix C. Belot, inventor of the latter, was the Havana-born son of French physician Félix Belot.[288]

There were few controls on the purity of the lime, which was usually imported from the United States. Large mills, especially, bought a "marble lime" which was simply a highly pure calcium oxide. Among the many subsidiary sugar businesses there then appeared that of "native lime," mined by Alejandro Bauzán and recognized by Casaseca as an almost completely pure lime carbonate.[289] Apart from lime, acid was used to control excess alkalization—an unusual practice which was abandoned—as was the albumen of the white prickly pear, *hibiscus esculentus, pitahaya,* and *maguey* cactuses, or of the *guácima* tree. Very rarely, egg white was used.

Although progressive producers constantly talked of Baumé degrees, the concentration of the syrup was always judged by eye. Calculation in Brix degrees was unknown till the 1880s.[290] The hydrometer was a much-mentioned but little-used device[291]—in Cuba it was called an "aerometer," or a "sugarometer," but the latter name can cause confusion. The sugarometer was usually a copper hydrometer graded in such a way that at 24° Baumé it was totally submerged.

However, in 1817 Alejo Lanier presented to the Real Sociedad Económica another type of sugarometer, "designed to determine the point to which sugar should be cooked for perfect crystallization." This sugarometer was really a simple modified-quadrant pyrometer, a rudimentary metal thermometer.[292] As in so many cases, we meet the same word used for different things.

The grade of purity of the sugar was also normally calculated by eye—hence the complicated classifications discussed later in this chapter. Although Jean-Baptiste Biot (1774–1862) first applied polarization of light to the analysis of saccharine substances, industrial use of his discovery was a post-1845 phenomenon and the first Cuban mention of polarization occurs in April 1849, when Eduardo Finlay—father of Carlos Finlay—brought home the famous Soleil polarimeter from Paris. With scientific seriousness Finlay explained to the Junta de Fomento how this "saccharimeter" (as it was first called) had resolved the problem of measuring sugar purity. It may have been Finlay who late in 1849 translated the Melsens document published by the *Faro Industrial*, in which an ample explanatory note on polarimetry appears.[293]

Technical controls in the period were indeed small and deficient, but even those few were rejected in the mills. Sugar had always depended on the eye of a good sugarmaster, and hydrometers, polarimeters, calciometers, and litmus paper were laboratory curiosities, not things to work with. Touch, hearing, and smell ruled the operation, and knowing when concentrate had reached the *"huevo"* (egg) or *"chicharrón"* (pork crackling) point was all that was needed.

The draining room. The last stage of sugar manufacture was a complicated crystallizing and draining process. When the syrup in the last kettle reached an optimal concentration point—"sugar," *huevo, chicharrón*—prompt and precise action was called for. The sugarmaster would always be on hand, presiding over the more trusted slaves. In Jamaica trains, the temperature was controlled by yells from the black kettle-minder to the furnaceman to add or remove firewood. Since under this system the sugar could easily be burned by excessive heat, it had to be transferred immediately to the coolers. This operation was performed with the *bombón*, although some more technified mills had a movable

teache system enabling the contents to be poured out quickly.

The coolers were simple wooden troughs where the syrup was "beaten" with wooden bats, or with the *bombón* itself, to speed crystallization by cooling. Later, curing began in molds. The first part of the curing was done in the boiling room, where the molds were filled and placed on a draining rack until the sugar was completely cool. A day or two later the bung was removed and the fluids allowed to drain out. The molds were then taken to the curing house for final draining.

Initially the molds were of clay; starting in the 1830s the industrial process led to large-scale manufacture of metal molds. José Baró, one of the century's most powerful *hacendados* and slavers, substantially controlled the subsidiary business of making and repairing molds. His big workshop on Havana's Calle Consulado, across from the old jail, was run by the proficient Spanish mechanic Ramón Rodríguez. Molds of tin, iron, and zinc were made there. The business also included repairs on deteriorated molds, either in the shop itself or at the mill.

Changes were few between 1800 and 1860. The one perceptible variant was the reduction of the applications of clay to sugar in the molds to two. From the 1840s on, iron tracks were commonly laid from boiling room to curing house, over which slaves hauled the molds on little hand cars. Some big mills installed artificial driers, but the basic system of airing, drying, and selecting sugars remained as in

A DRAINING ROOM
The interior of a draining room in one of the large mid-nineteenth-century Cuban mills.

the eighteenth century and the whole draining process did not really evolve after the sixteenth. Losses of crystallizable sugar were so great that many producers would "re-boil" the molasses to get more sugar.[294] In some cases there were two re-boilings, and in 1851 La Amistad mill was wrestling with the problem of a third—that is, a fourth cooking of the juice.[295] The quality obtained was, of course, lower in each cooking. La Amistad was estimated at the time to be obtaining direct from the cane a yield of 3 percent, another 1 percent from the first re-boiling, and 0.3 percent from the second—for a total yield of 4.3 percent.[296]

An exterior view of a draining room. The low-roofed extension on the left was the packing department.

The centrifugal revolutionized all this. The first one was brought to Cuba for La Amistad by Joaquín de Aristaraín in 1849; it was French and made by Cail.[297] In 1850 the English-U.S. house of Benson & Day exhibited another in Regla, and they soon came into general use even in Jamaica-train sugarmills. Curing was the sugarmill's last sector to be industrialized, and it is interesting to note how the whole process of mechanization chronologically followed the production line: grinding mill, boiling room, curing house. A Real Consulado document says that Dr. Eduardo Finlay got a 3,000-peso loan in 1840 "to plan a vacuum machine for draining sugar molds by suction."[298] The pneumatic curing operation had been patented by Vaughan in 1809, Hague had improved it in 1816, and it had been used in British Guiana since 1832 and in Mauritius since 1838. When Finlay began to study it, however, the

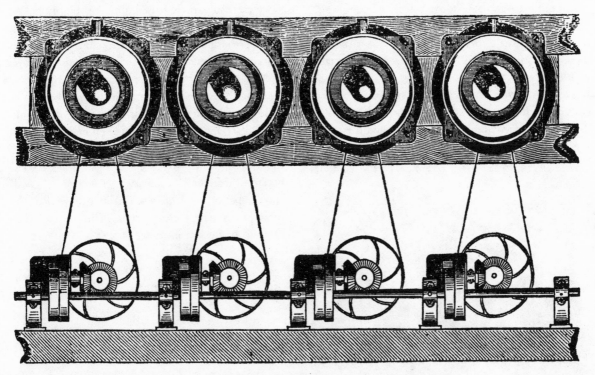

THE CENTRIFUGAL

A set of four centrifugals manufactured by the English firm Manlove, Alliot & Co., and acquired by Cuban mills after 1855. Although the Cail firm was the first to sell centrifugals to Cuba, Manlove & Alliot practically cornered the Cuban market up to the 1880s.

centrifugal had been invented and in a few years it replaced all former systems of separating sugar crystals from molasses.

The whole painful business of curing was avoided by sugarmills producing muscovado, which was taken directly from the coolers and packed in hogsheads of about 1,200-pound capacity. After some days a bung at the bottom of the hogshead was removed and the molasses run out; every hogshead was then refilled with the contents of other drained hogsheads and was ready for shipment. Other mills drained muscovado in large iron trays and then packed it in the hogsheads.

The curing house was the mill's critical point, the main bottleneck after mill equipment and boilers were mechanized. On the average one clay mold was used for each three arrobas (75 pounds) of the sugarmill's annual production, or for 15 arrobas if the molds were iron or tin. The big problem was labor. The curing house employed some 10 percent of a mill's labor force, and as slaves rose in price, *hacendados* sought to eliminate it and thus reduce the investment in buildings and molds as well.[299] This was one factor behind the growing tendency to produce muscovado almost exclusively, although not the main one. From the end of the 1860s the centrifugal virtually did away with curing, although there were still small mills continuing the old system in 1880.

Drying, selection & packing. At the end of the curing operation, which could last from thirty to fifty days, the molds were placed in the sun and the sugar was extracted some hours later. This was called "airing" the "loaves" of sugar. In typical sugarmill

PACKING REFINED SUGAR IN BOXES

account books there was always a column headed "loaves aired." The loaves were placed on shelf-shaped wooden trays to be dried by the action of air and sun. Once aired, the tips were cut off and stored separately. This procedure was constantly threatened by tropical downpours, although the harvest was always undertaken in the dry season. The one purgery advance in the sixty years under study was the artificial dryer, or *estufa* (stove), which was installed in some big mills.

Then came the most personal operation in the mill—the selection of sugars. Modern technicians, producing only one quality measured by polariscope, find it difficult to imagine this selection process by eye, the division of the loaf at precise spots to separate the first-quality white, the ordinary white, the first- and second-quality yellow, and the tips (brown). The usual order was to remove the tips and then arrange the white on higher trays and the yellow on lower. In harvest and grinding seasons lasting six months, canes of different maturities gave juices which differed in ease of defecation, and the quality of the sugar processed varied from month to month. Quality likewise varied from mill to mill, since each sugarmaster used different, highly personalized techniques, ranging from extreme care to the crudest routine. Thus when the sugar reached the market there was a final selection: that of the buyer.

The sugars known in the eighteenth century were raspadura, muscovado, *cucurucho* or *cogucho*, brown, yellow, and white—the last two being subdivided into "first" and "second." Sugar that ended up in the refinery was known as "refined." The names got more complicated with time: "first" and "second" became "inferior," "ordinary," "standard," "good," and "superior," and a new quality was added, that produced by the Derosne train. Thus Cuban sugar came to be quoted in these classes:

1. Derosne-train white
2. Superior white
3. Good white
4. Standard white
5. Ordinary white
6. Inferior or bad white
7. Derosne-train yellow
8. Superior or *florete* yellow
9. Good yellow
10. Standard yellow
11. Ordinary yellow

12. Inferior or bad yellow
13. Good brown
14. Standard brown
15. Good muscovado
16. Standard muscovado

These were the gradings of the Colegio de Corredores in 1850.[300] Before that the categories were fewer, and after 1860 they were again reduced until by the end of that decade muscovado and "centrifugal" were almost the only kinds.

Since it was difficult to deal with so many varieties, one was taken as a base: that is, a solution was sought similar to today's arrangement with pol. 96 commercial sugar.* Internationally, the French classifications predominated, with eight varieties in the 1830s:

1. *Clairce*
2. *Deuxième ordinaire*
3. *Belle troisième*
4. *Bonne troisième*
5. *Fine quatrième*
6. *Belle quatrième*
7. *Bonne quatrième*
8. *Quatrième bonne ordinaire*

The top French quality corresponded to good Havana white; the others were in descending scale down to our bad tips. In the second half of the century the French added two new types:

9. *Quatrième ordinaire*
10. *Basse quatrième*

Faced with this chaos, and as a first step toward standardization, the so-called Dutch Treaty fixed internationally accepted classifications after 1850. In Cuba, when sugars were quoted on the basis of this agreement, "TH" (*Tipo Holandés* or Dutch Standard) was added after the quotation. The international gradings had a short life, for in their first years the polariscope, which definitively replaced color with sucrose-content as a classification, came into wide industrial use. From the 1870s on, only three qualities were processed industrially in Cuba—centrifugal, muscovado, and concentrated. The last was massecuite that came from the pans without undergoing the curing, draining, or centrifugal process.

By chain reaction the centrifugal produced a radical change in packing—but only after the 1860s;

until then the old system of boxes and hogsheads was retained. From the beginning of the eighteenth century refined sugar was packed in big wooden boxes with a 16 to 22 arroba capacity. Saco and Pezuela, and all later historians who copied them, insisted that small boxes continued in use till the mid-eighteenth century, a lie they invented to square with Arango's faked statistics. Nothing could be less true: there is ample documentary proof that the average *caja* (box) from the early eighteenth century —and even in the last decades of the seventeenth— weighed from 16 to 18 arrobas. The only mention of smaller ones is a reference in 1759 to *caxitas* (little boxes) which contained 5 to 6 arrobas and were always referred to in the diminutive.[301] There was another kind, holding 10 to 15 arrobas, always described as *estuches*. We should also note that in the nineteenth century only empty boxes were called *envases* (containers); when full they were always *cajas*.

Muscovado, with its quantity of suspended molasses, was packed in barrels; the most-used type from the early nineteenth century was the *bocoy*, a hogshead with 40 to 60 arroba capacity. We know of no eighteenth-century reference to Cuban muscovado; the first specific nineteenth-century reference is in 1804, and our first production figures are La Ninfa's in 1808—604 hogsheads and 1,715 barrels.[302] The average capacity of the barrels seems to have been 9 arrobas and of the hogsheads, 40. In 1813 we find muscovado being packed in 16-arroba *tercerolas* (medium-sized barrels). By mid-century sizes had been comparatively standardized and Rebello gives the average capacity of hogsheads as 54 arrobas (Trinidad and Cárdenas), 60 (Cienfuegos), 58 (Remedios), and 56 elsewhere. The *tercerola* had by then been standardized at 20 to 30 arrobas and barrels at 10 to 12. These sizes should not be confused with those used for other products. *Bocoyes, tercerolas, cuarterolas,* and barrels were made in different sizes for muscovado, molasses, and rum.

Large wooden containers created a new and flourishing subsidiary industry. The island's labor shortage made it cheaper to buy lumber in the North than to cut it in our rich forests, and box and hogshead "pieces"—sawed and planed ready for nailing together in Cuba—were imported after the end of the eighteenth century. This is the first instance we know of the use of prefabricated materials in the colony. The vast importation of

* Pol. 96 is the equivalent of 96° sugar. (Trans.)

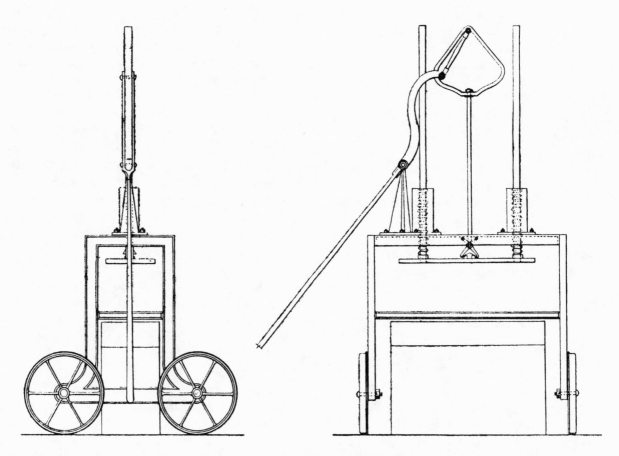

A SUGAR-PACKING MACHINE

A belated attempt to semi-mechanize the packing of sugar in boxes. The drawing hardly needs explanation. The machine moved on wheels along the line of crates. Marcos Cabrera patented the invention in Havana in 1865. In fact, it was a semi-automated press.

timber just when hundreds of caballerías of forests were being burned annually was one of the sugar industry's many contradictions. In the first fifteen years of the nineteenth century, over 9 million pesos' worth of sugar-box board were brought from the United States.[303] This was justified by the kind of wood used. Odorless, tasteless, light-weight, tough, and easily nailed wood was needed for packing sugar, and Cuba's *acana,* mahogany, *sabicú, chicharrón,* etc., did not fill the bill. Thus pine and cypress were preferred among foreign woods, *jobo* among Cuban woods. Cedar was used with some frequency, but when the contents got damp its color and bitter flavor were absorbed. Around 1811 José de Arango tried to make a big business of *jobo*-box manufacture, using a steam saw that then existed in Havana. The Marquis de Arcos packed the product of several harvests in *jobo* boxes, but finally returned to buying boxes abroad. Each time the price of containers rose,

for political reasons or because of commercial speculation, some Creole manufacturer would offer a national solution of the problem. The last official petition in this matter was signed by the Count de Mopox and José Guerrero.[304]

No problem was more discussed in the sugar world. In the late eighteenth century there was such a scarcity of boxes that sugar was packed in empty flour barrels. The price of containers rose from 7 to 8 reales to 26. In the nineteenth century their price fluctuated as much as that of sugar itself. Rich *hacendados* would buy them well ahead of need while others bought when they could, raising their production costs.

The packing system was very simple. The sugar and the containers were first dried in the sun, then each container was weighed, numbered, and tared. The sugar was thrown in in layers, each one stamped down by slaves. Finally, the top was nailed on and the corners reinforced with ox-leather strips. The system inevitably produced great variations in the weight of the boxes. By the middle of the nineteenth century sizes had been more or less standardized at five spans long x two high x three wide. But the weight of the box and its contents was a merchant's nightmare. A lawsuit to standardize weights was begun in the late eighteenth century and decided on September 27, 1860. The problem was the difference between the real weight and what was marked on the box. In 1830 the issue became explosive when the Real Consulado of Cádiz complained that sugar boxes always weighed eight to twelve pounds above the marked amount, and called it "a fraud." Many other illegalities committed by *hacendados* and merchants promptly came to light, and the protests of the Malaga, Coruña, and Valencia consulados were added to that of Cádiz. By then the fraud had become an international scandal, and the Real Consulado of Havana—since its top members were involved—tried to dodge it for seven years. When that became impossible, the buck was passed to General Tacón, with the sole recommendation that the producer's name should be marked along with the tare on every box so that the swindler would be identified. Too clever to get involved in such a problem, Tacón returned the file, pointing out that such economic matters were within the Junta's province and that it "could not and should not beg off." The Junta, pushed up against the wall, met on July 5, 1837, and agreed "that the problem must be studied."

On the international level there were no fixed rules either. The custom in the trade with respect to Cuban sugars was as follows (in 1836): Antwerp, Bordeaux, and Marseilles discounted 14 percent of the gross weight; Amsterdam 18 percent; the United States 15 percent; and Hamburg discounted 65 German pounds or 67.5 Spanish pounds. Thus they showed their total mistrust of the tares marked on the boxes. When the fraud reached its height the King intervened with a Real Orden of October 24, 1838, requiring information on the regulation of tares. Havana's Real Consulado could not fake the answer and replied with lofty bourgeois principles: "Resolution of the disputed points should be based less on the legal aspect than on that of the public interest; and this suggests that the government should eschew interference in transactions by businessmen, leaving to their own vigilance the precau-

STACKING SUGAR BOXES
The only drawing known of the interior of the Santa Catalina sugar warehouse in Regla. Constructed on a cast-iron frame and designed by the great U.S. engineer J. Bogardus, it was one of the world's most remarkable buildings of its type. Like many more exceptional architectural achievements in Cuba, it was senselessly destroyed.

tionary methods that their interests dictate to avoid falling victims to speculators of bad faith." With this formulation, made in the session of February 29, 1839, the matter was once more swept under the rug.[305]

Linked to the problem of a lack of standards was a morass of speculation. Cooperage and box manufacture became a multi-million-peso business in each grinding season and a further factor in the merchants' control over the *hacendado*. Only those well supplied in advance with boxes and hogsheads could be assured of their product's immediate arrival on the market. Refusal to sell boxes was a typical form of commercial reprisal and coercion. The merchant-moneylender speculated to the utmost, and extortion continued in transport and warehousing. In the last stage of production the extortion took two forms: charging exorbitant prices for warehousing, and garnering profits from the drained-off molasses. White sugar hardly diminished in weight with time, but yellow and especially brown and muscovado—with very low polarization and hence a large amount of suspended molasses—leaked out between imperfectly closed boards and staves. Beneath the warehouse there were troughs and boilers to recover this molasses and raise the warehouseman's profits. Amid all this speculation the Junta declined to confront the problem of standards.

For their part, the producers joined forces in building cooperages and box factories, as well as warehouses at embarkation ports. The pioneer in this was Eduardo Fesser, who owned the Regla warehouses. After him came the Depósito de Hacendados and San José warehouses, and those of Aldama and Alfonso in Matanzas. The picture began to change a little after the 1860s: the centrifugal and the modern mill replaced boxes with sacks, and big industry did away with small-time plunder, placing commercial robbery on a higher plane.

Cane by-products: molasses and rum. The importance of by-products did not escape the remarkable mind of Arango y Parreño—especially when, after the United States won its independence and began trading massively with Cuba, run-off molasses became an important sugarmill item.

There were two possibilities for the molasses: convert it into *aguardiente* or rum, or sell it direct to the United States, whose distilleries for many years used molasses from the Lesser Antilles and then switched to bringing it from Cuba.[306] When the sale was made, the big question was warehousing and transport. From the late eighteenth century on, animal transport of molasses became a healthy subsidiary business. Here arose the same interminable conflicts about the capacity of containers. A Real Consulado dispute which began on December 1, 1795, only ended—without a solution—in 1842 when the railroad resolved it.[307] Its essence was that the muleteers had one size of barrel to buy and another smaller capacity one to sell. The average beast's load was four barrels, which meant mobilizing 2,500 beast-journeys to move a mill's average production of 10,000 arrobas to the embarkation point. In the early nineteenth century animal-back transport of molasses was replaced by carts transporting big pipes and hogsheads.

These confused operations can be summed up thus: United States businessmen, almost exclusive buyers of molasses in the first half of the nineteenth century, made deals at so much per hogshead (110 gallons). Traders acting as intermediaries with the *hacendado* bought in 7-gallon barrels and delivered to buyers in 5.5-gallon barrels. This was denounced countless times as a swindle. The traders, however,

explained it as a normal discount for losses suffered in decanting the product. Another murky angle was the annual sale of thousands of hogsheads of muscovado described as molasses, thus avoiding the payment of duty.* The Spanish government fixed duties so high that by 1825 it was estimated that three voyages of a molasses ship paid as much in taxes as the ship was worth. When the price of molasses fell below 2½ reales in the crisis of 1825, some five hundred persons involved in its sale and transport were unemployed in Matanzas alone. The surplus of molasses was such that mills far from seaports threw it into the river or accumulated it in large pools.[308] Finally around 1840 big distilleries competing with U.S. ones were started in Havana, Matanzas, and Cárdenas.

High-production sugarmills set up their own distilleries as a sideline business after the end of the eighteenth century—an attempt to develop a native industry which was rich in possibilities. Until the Las Casas administration (1790–1796) Cuban rum had been taxed to protect the Spanish product, but the sugarocracy got this legal hurdle removed and built production into a big business. The English policy of giving liquor rations to soldiers of the empire was profitably followed. The only technical problem was that cane liquor had an unpleasantly musty taste and smell. In 1841 Casaseca put in for a Real Consulado award for having discovered an infallible remedy for this,[309] but it soon emerged that Casaseca's method had been published in 1817 in *L'Art du destillateur* and that it produced an even worse taste. By 1850 a rum of today's taste and quality was produced for the first time, opening up the big liquor industry development of the second half of the century.

In one form or another molasses and rum contributed to the sugarmill's revenues and lowered production costs.

---

* With regard to these frauds, to which Puerto Príncipe sugarmen were especially addicted, see "Report of the Secretary of the Treasury . . . in relation to frauds upon the Treasury in introducing sugar into the United States in the form of syrup" (May 2, 1832: 22nd Congress, 1st Session, Senate Doc. No. 139). The fraud nevertheless continued and on July 31, 1846, there was another "Report from the Secretary of the Treasury . . . relative to frauds in recent importations of syrups and molasses from the West India islands, and the measures necessary to be adopted to prevent their recurrence" (29th Congress, 1st session, Senate Doc. No. 467)

Yields

In 1843 Villa-Urrutia produced several pages on industrial yields, the first report known to us treating this subject in modern terms.[310] The whole question of yields in nineteenth-century Cuban mills is hard to analyze for want of a minimum of indispensable information. Not that the producers lacked analytical indices, but these indices were different from today's and there are no standards of comparison. It is easy to copy the figures of the period—as they were calculated—but they are no help to the modern investigator since they do not permit the determination of proper ratios.

First let us analyze calculations made during the 1800–1860 period, when it was customary to express the ratio between sugar produced and area of land. In 1796 *hacendados* considered that average land should yield 2,000 arrobas of sugar per caballería. Based on contemporary calculations, Baron de Humboldt estimated that a caballería of ordinary land gave 1,500 arrobas and fertile land could easily yield 3,000 to 4,000—half white and half yellow. Much later the French technician Dumont talked of average production of 2,000 per caballería, but set a maximum of 6,000 in recently cleared Matanzas land. To conclude what could be interminable quotes, we have Sagra's calculations, using Rebello as a source:[311] *

	Arrobas per caballería
All Cuban mills	2,211
Western area	2,123
Eastern area	2,773
With Jamaica trains	2,023
With vacuum pans	2,815
With Derosne vacuum pans	2,801
With Rillieux vacuum pans	2,842
With ox-powered grinding mills	2,373

Sagra then lists twenty-one sugarmills with the highest sugar-per-caballería yields:

1. San Martín	5,400
2. Las Cañas	5,300
3. San Joaquín	4,917
4. Flor de Cuba	4,471
5. Belén	4,252
6. Porvenir	4,030
7. Aguica	3,808
8. Arco Iris	3,786
9. Vizcaya	3,623
10. Santa Rita	3,468
11. Luisa	3,456
12. Jesús Nazareno	3,433
13. Habana	3,404
14. Santa Elena	3,362
15. Concepción	3,336
16. Petrona	3,306
17. Santa Susana	3,258
18. Asunción	3,254
19. Santa Gertrudis	3,187
20. Andrea	3,129
21. Santa Lutgarda	3,076

These calculations suffer from these fundamental errors:

1. They are not comparable. The various sugarmills produced various types of sugar, and we would have to compare, for example, the big Derosne multiple-effect producers of white sugar with animal-powered sugarmills producing only muscovado. Since these are totally different products, the same index cannot be applied to both.

2. Agricultural productivity is not taken into account but is considered as a constant; it is really a variable subject to great fluctuations. Hence in analyzing yields we do not know if the differences are due to the agricultural or the industrial sector.

3. Specifically with respect to Sagra, his calculations are based on caballerías harvested, not on cane actually cut and processed in the mill. The margin of error is so substantial as to make his efforts worthless.

Here the inevitable question arises: If these indices reflect elementary statistical errors which could not have passed unnoticed by the awakened economic mentality of the period, why were they advanced? They were slave-system indices. Villa-Urrutia provides the key: they express the sugar production of a given land area planted with cane, "because in reality, other conditions being equal, the larger or smaller extension of cultivated land represents a larger or smaller quantity of hands working on them, and consequently the respective costs of our industry's agricultural sector." The explanation could not be clearer: producers only cultivated lands of a determined agricultural productivity, and thus at the

* See note for conversions to tons per hectare and pounds per acre.

123

end of the harvest obtained the calculated quantity of cane per caballería. They also had reasonably correct estimates of the labor force required per caballería. And since labor was the mill's costliest item, reduction to caballerías was more or less a reduction to men/sugar.

In 1843 Villa-Urrutia presented the first series of yields based on quantity of sugar per given weight of cane processed—a great technical advance. His figures were taken from his own La Mella mill in Limonar and covered the years 1830–1843, with the exception of the 1841 and 1842 harvests. These yields have a special interest for us since they reflect the evolution of a sugarmill in the process of modernization. The first years correspond with the ox-powered grinding mill and Jamaica train system; the second with the steam-powered grinding mill and Jamaica train; and 1843 with the steam-powered grinding mill and a mixed system, defecating and clarifying with open kettles and evaporating with vacuum pans. The figures are:

Ox-powered grinding mill and Jamaica train:

1830	3.02
1831	3.97
1832	3.33
1833	3.26
1834	3.72
1835	4.51
1836	4.02

Steam-powered grinding mill and Jamaica train:

1837	3.94
1838	3.31
1839	3.03
1840	3.56

Steam-powered mill and mixed evaporation system:

1843	5.91

Casaseca's extensive figures in his study of industrial yields in 1851 were based on the old sugar/caballería concept, although he came up with some industrial statistics.[312] According to him, semi-mechanized sugarmills (steam grinding mill, Jamaica train) produced 4 arrobas of clayed dry sugar per 100 arrobas of cane. This is understandable when there is no processing of molasses, but a second re-boiling with the Mourgue apparatus could raise the yield to 5.2, and in highly mechanized sugarmills (steam grinding mill, complete vacuum evaporation process) an industrial yield of 6 percent could be obtained.

The Casaseca figures have been much used and discussed, but in fact lack all validity. He started out from figures offered *a priori* by Pedro Diago, and at no point used concrete production measurements. Only some additional data in his work make it of any interest.

More important was Sagra's analysis in 1860 of five big mills in Banagüises and a small grinding mill in Sagua la Grande.[313] Beginning with the most backward (oxen and Jamaica train), we find in the Delta mill an average 4.5 yield, with a 7.25 maximum in a particular month. Delta produced only muscovado. An example of a big semi-mechanized mill with steam grinding mill, Jamaica train, Mourgue apparatus, and six centrifugals is Conchita, which had a total yield of 3.9 in 1859, including processed molasses. This, with many other yield calculations taken directly from harvest reports, makes nonsense of Casaseca's figures.

As for mechanized mills, Sagra took data from four giants of the period—Ponina, San Martín, Flor de Cuba, and Las Cañas. Ponina, with a mixed system of open kettles and Derosne and Pontifex vacuum pans, obtained a 3.8 clayed-sugar yield in the 1859 harvest. With re-boilings of molasses to produce muscovado, the total yield of the two types of sugar was 5.2. We know that San Martín produced a 4.2 clayed-sugar yield in 1859, but it did not report on molasses processing. The Flor de Cuba data are more precise. In 1858–1859 this mill, one of the period's most modern, produced:

Cane processed	33,300 cartloads
Clayed sugar	8,375 boxes
Muscovado	1,032 hogsheads

The equivalences of the period were:

1 cartload	=	120 arrobas
1 box	=	17 arrobas net
1 hogshead	=	54 arrobas net

Thus, converting production figures to arrobas, we have:

Cane processed	3,996,000	arrobas
Clayed sugar	142,375	"
Muscovado	55,728	"

Based on these figures, Flor de Cuba's yield was:

Clayed sugar	3.5
Total sugar	4.9

Juan Poey's Las Cañas was for thirty years a real model of its type. It was already Cuba's most modern mill in 1850, and up to 1880 it kept adding new machinery in a continuous process of renovation. When Sagra visited it in 1860 it had 300 active slaves, 55 Chinese immigrants, and a good number of wage-workers. Its grinding mill was the best in the island, with rollers 7 feet long and 34 inches in diameter, and it had a smaller auxiliary one. The boiling-room equipment included 8 defecators, 2 coil clarifiers, 1 molasses cooker, 2 skimming vats, 14 Dumont filters, 4 Taylor filters, 2 Rillieux multiple effects, and 5 centrifugals. Overall fuel consumption was 500 tasks of firewood plus bagasse. Its figures for the 1859 grinding were:

Cane processed	3,312,840	arrobas
Clayed sugar	151,290	"
Muscovado	38,005	"

The muscovado was obtained from successive re-boilings of the molasses. This type of sugar was known from the 1860s on as "molasses sugar," to distinguish it from that obtained direct from the juice, which was called "juice sugar." A simple calculation of yields from these figures gives us:

Clayed sugar yield	4.5
Molasses sugar yield	1.2
Total	5.7

Chosen as a model in 1873, Las Cañas' figures were submitted to the Vienna International Exhibition; for this, Fermín Rosillo y Alquier published a detailed description and claimed a sugar/cane yield of up to 8 percent. We do not believe this figure. It might possibly have been obtained at one particular time, but it was not the average yield of a whole season. Proof of this is in the excellent sugar manual, published in 1881, by Las Cañas sugarmaster E. Pimienta, one of Cuba's most capable technicians of that century. He speaks of maximum 7 percent yields, including molasses sugar.[314] Thus Rosillo y Alquier's figures must be discounted.

The first scientific analyses appeared in mid-century, using the polarimeter to judge sugars in their richness in sucrose rather than their color. This movement began in France and was the first serious attempt to standardize quality. Clerget's pamphlet on the analysis of saccharin substances served as a basis for the industrial use of Soleil's saccharimeter.[315] A French ministerial commission was named in 1851 to sit down with outstanding scientists and seek a solution to the sugar problem. The use of decolorization agents in sugar-beet factories and the introduction of these methods into Antillean mills made the old color classifications obsolete. Sugars of different richness looked the same to the eye of a customs expert. Soleil's saccharimeter and Clerget's statistical tables seemed to resolve the problem, but soon the commission ran into new and insuperable difficulties. The polarimeter was not sufficiently perfected to permit its general use. Its inventor, Biot, himself firmly opposed its industrial use: it was, he said, a laboratory instrument which if improperly used by non-experts would give false results and thus redound against scientific progress. It was the optician Duboscq who in fact perfected the saccharimeter (thenceforward called Soleil-Duboscq), making it an industrial instrument for general use. However, French factories had started using it long before: the Grar refinery was the first to set up a special sugar-analysis laboratory under the physicist Pesier.[316]

Records of the first polariscopic analysis of Cuban sugar enable us to study industrial yields in a modern way. While all such analyses before Sidersky contained a certain amount of error, we believe it was small enough not to invalidate our conclusions.[317] Summing up the few calculations made in the period, analyzing mill reports still available to us, and taking as base the polarizations of Clerget, Dubrunfaut, Sidersky, Delteil, and others, we can conclude:[318]

1. The yield of an animal-powered grinding mill producing only muscovado was 3 to 4 percent of the weight of the cane. The lower figure emerges in mills with vertical ox-driven grinding mills processing Creole cane, the higher one where horizontal iron grinding mills ground yellow Otaheite cane. An exact figure and a general comparative index are hard to arrive at, the first difficulty being the different intensity of the curing. Many mills hardly extracted any molasses from the muscovado, which then ended up with the same characteristics as the massecuite in the *teache:* in such cases muscovado was almost the same as so-called "concentrate sugar." Other mills drained carefully by sedimentation in big iron pans or in the hogsheads themselves. Such diverse methods produced muscovados of very different richness in sucrose.

Numerous measurings show us that the sucrose content of the muscovado was approximately pol. 80. An analysis by Delteil gives pol. 72.2,[319] and a later one by R. E. Doolittle gives pol. 83.1.[320] The variations are normal if we remember that until 1870 nearly all muscovado was drained by hogshead sedimentation and that after this it was done with centrifugals. There are over 8 points of difference in purity between the two procedures.

Attempting to establish an index comparable with our own times, we believe we can fix at 2.25 to 3 percent of cane weight the average yield of an animal-powered mill producing only muscovado between 1800–1860.

2. The production of semi-mechanized Jamaica-train sugarmills normally processing clayed sugar varied through those sixty years. The normal procedure throughout the eighteenth century was to produce "half white, half yellow." To achieve such a balance intensive draining was necessary, lasting no less than forty-five days during which three clay washes were applied—the *bollo, barrillo,* and *aguaje.* There was an economic reason for this long process: white sugar was in great demand and maintained a high market price. To assure sale of the yellow, *hacendados* offered the two kinds of sugar in combined lots—a system known as "half and half"—and the would-be buyers of white had to buy the same amount of yellow. But U.S. preeminence in the market for Cuban sugar changed the situation. Soon protectionist laws covering U.S. refineries dictated a bigger sale of yellow than of white; producers continued the half-and-half system, but now to assure sale of the white.[321] The new tendency was to produce more and more inferior sugars and less white. Many mills, especially after 1846, confined themselves to muscovado,[322] although the general ratio of white to yellow to brown was 3.5:7.5:2.5.

On the basis of the above proportions, which prevailed from the 1820s on, these mills' yields in purged sugar were from 2.5 to 3.5, and up to 4 where sugarmasters were of the finest and the owner exceptionally attentive, as in Villa-Urrutia's La Mella. A case typical of conditions at the time is that of the Río Abajo plantation, which averaged 35,000 to 45,000 arrobas per season. Its yields from 1840 to 1847 were:[323]

1840	2.59
1841	2.63
1842	2.71
1843	2.70
1844	3.30
1845	2.87
1846	3.20
1847	3.05

According to Delteil, the best white sugars from the biggest Havana mills contained pol. 96.75 sucrose; thus the so-called whites of the semi-mechanized sugarmills, processed with the Jamaica train, must have been of lower polarization. The analyses made by Clerget, Maumené, Basset, Delteil, Sidersky, etc., show that these clayed Cuban sugars fluctuated between 87.5 for *bonne ordinaire* and 95.5 for *terre blond.* The yellow, according to quality, varied between 83 and 87.5, and the brown more or less ranked with muscovado firsts, with an average of 83. Reducing all this to an index comparable with modern mills, we can say that yields fluctuated between 2.00 and 2.80. When these semi-mechanized sugarmills concentrated on muscovado production they obtained a 2.50 to 3.25 yield.

3. Mid-century mechanized sugarmills had considerably higher yields, not only in production totals but in quality. In the 1859 grinding season Las Cañas managed to produce 57 percent prime white (decolorized by sulfitation) with polarization above 97, similar to the famous French *sucre clairce,* which ranked first in that country and was generally considered semi-refined. Production of brown was down to 2 percent. Apart from this, Las Cañas turned out a good quantity of muscovado, processing the molasses and curing it in centrifugals.[324] The average of the five highly mechanized sugarmills for which we have concrete data between 1855 and 1865 gives us these sugar production percentages for each 100 arrobas:

Muscovado	19.5 percent
Prime white	45.8 ”
Prime yellow	19.4 ”
Yellow seconds	13.6 ”
Brown	1.7 ”

These figures apply exclusively to Las Cañas, San Martín, Flor de Cuba, Alava, and Progreso in the 1858–1861 grindings. We do not know if they are applicable to all the highly mechanized sugarmills.[325] On the basis of this type of production, these mills' sugar yields fluctuated between 5 and 6 percent of cane weight. Enough data to calculate polarization is lacking, but we believe that with a small margin of error the yield, in figures comparable with modern mills, must have fluctuated between 4 and 5 percent.

To sum up: each of the three types of mill analyzed at the beginning of this study had a yield in accordance with its industrial installations, the amount of cane processed, the final type of product, and its work system. Reduced to a pol. 96 base to obtain figures comparable with today's mills, these yields were:

Animal-powered sugarmills with low-pressure vertical or horizontal mill, producing only muscovado	2.25 to 3.00
Semi-mechanized sugarmills, with good horizontal grinding mills and Jamaica trains, producing muscovado	2.50 to 3.25
Semi-mechanized sugarmills, as above, producing clayed sugar	2.00 to 2.80
Mechanized sugarmills, with big horizontal mills, Derosne, Pontifex or other similar vacuum pans	4.00 to 5.00

These yields do not include re-boilings of molasses.[326] The loss in producing clayed sugar is caused by the absurd system of molds which left a molasses with more than 50 percent crystallizable sugar.

All our figures are derived from an analysis of sugarmill records and various other surviving data—extremely tricky material due to the typical inaccuracy of the period. Thus they cannot be taken as definitive, only as a minimal attempt to arrive at indices which can guide us through this dark and confusing sugar world. Later research will no doubt correct the errors.

More illustrative than technical indices is an economic one which can show the value of the sugar at market price for a fixed amount of cane processed. On this basis we can obtain a clear view of the sugarmill situation in our period from the figures for 1859, the year on which we have the most data. Average prices in that year, according to the Colegio de Corredores, were:[327]

	Reales per arroba
Derosne evaporator white	14½
Good white	12
Derosne evaporator yellow	10
Good yellow	9
Good brown	7

Good to superior muscovado	7
Standard muscovado	6

Applying these prices to the yields indicated above, we get the following values (in reales) of sugar produced for each 1,000 arrobas of cane:

Animal-powered sugarmills, producing muscovado	135 to 180
Semi-mechanized sugarmills, producing muscovado	150 to 195
Semi-mechanized sugarmills, producing clayed sugar	188 to 264
Mechanized sugarmills	446 to 557

In semi-mechanized sugarmills we find this phenomenon: producing clayed sugar, a 30 percent higher gross value in processed sugar was obtained. But an additional investment of roughly 32 percent was needed to produce clayed sugar. Thus the real profit—that is, in relation to capital invested—was much lower in semi-mechanized sugarmills producing clayed sugar than in the same mills producing only muscovado. Furthermore, Cuban white sugar produced and drained by slaves was of much inferior quality to the European product made with modern industrial techniques. And we must note the highly developed countries' protectionist policies with respect to refined sugar—which finally subjugated Cuban sugar.

We can now understand why production of clayed white was abandoned by mid-century and why all except the mechanized sugarmills concentrated on muscovado. This was the great change in the Cuban production structure. Arango's and Echegoyen's words had come true: by and large Cuba had ended as a muscovado producer. Arango had sought to avoid this in 1817. Now, in 1860, the best business for those who could not industrialize was to fall behind—and, if possible, not even to drain the muscovado but to sell "concentrate sugar" (massecuite) for curing and refining in the United States. At the beginning of the nineteenth century Cuba was a Spanish colony, but it was making its own sugar laws: to that extent it was an economic metropolis. By 1860 it was still a colony politically and was also one as a producer, merely supplying semi-refined products to the industrialized countries. The tree of slavery had borne its fruits.

5
THE WORK
(1780–1860)

"Thus there came into being a sort of practical code of absurd principles, in which the farm worker's stupidity became the guarantee of the farm's security, physical force the sole motive power, routine the only agricultural law . . ."

—Ramón de la Sagra

HANDS FOR SALE

From the end of the eighteenth century on, a peculiar mixture of wage and slave labor existed in the Cuban sugarmill. There was no succession of one form by the other, but a simultaneous juxtaposition of both. There was even a third type not classifiable as either pure form: the hired slave, perhaps from the economic standpoint nearer to the wage- than to the slave-worker. Furthermore, sugar plantation slavery did not correspond with the theoretical scheme of a slave system. The slave as such, and the trade in blacks, were typically capitalist phenomena. The Cuban slave's function was almost exclusively to produce merchandise for the world market. What we had was a slave system with a "Factory Act," with specific labor-task regulations that often did more good for the slave than did English laws for the wage-worker.[328] Many mills, for instance, recognized minimal property rights for the slave, who cultivated the ground and traded his products with the master.

In all this there was, of course, no common criterion. Labor conditions varied from mill to mill, from region to region, and also from period to period. In the late eighteenth century slavery was the fundamental solution for Havana's sugar expansion, but this does not mean that wage-workers were lacking; in that same period the mills absorbed all the free labor available. We have seen that the violent expulsion of the tobacco growers from San Julián de los Güines had, among other aims, the incorporation of peasants into the mill. Account books of the period show that clearing forests, carting firewood, and even much cane cutting and hauling was done by free hands. In the sugarmill's

manufacturing sector there were likewise white and black wage-workers working beside slaves. But the labor market was small. Hands were scarce on the deserted island, and its few free workers maintained a system of privileges that permitted them to obtain far higher pay than was then current in Europe. The capitalist law of labor supply and demand did not operate under these conditions.

To think that our sugar producers were slavers because their mental attitude was opposed to progress would be absurd. We have seen how Havana's sugarocracy awoke to the capitalist world with a profound bourgeois awareness. Production for the world market imposed on them the essential laws of the capitalist system. They were slavers because they lacked wage-workers, because only slavery could make the initial sugar expansion possible. In Cuba, as in all colonies, there was a passionate desire for cheap and submissive labor, of a type to which our nascent capitalists could dictate conditions rather than have to submit to those labor imposed.[329] The worker who arrived in Cuba quickly became a farmer or artisan, or took advantage of the special conditions existing to demand wages well above the cost of slave labor. By 1805 Arango was estimating that for the same work a Havana producer paid $200 a year within the slave system and $400 when he used a wage-worker. Arango includes in his $200 the slave's maintenance and the annual average amortization on capital invested.

The Cuban sugarocracy very soon perceived the disadvantages of slavery and tried to form a class of cheap wage-workers: the so-called colonization projects were nothing more than this. The pluses and minuses of the two labor systems were already being analyzed in the first half of the eighteenth century. In 1754 José Martín Félix de Arrate compared slaves and wage-workers in pages as economically enlightened as, for example, the study by Zachary Macauley in 1802.[330] Arrate described his experience in New Spain, where the pauperized Indian masses sold themselves to mine owners for less than the cost of a slave's labor. In 1798 the Marquis de Cárdenas de Monte-Hermoso frankly confessed that the entire Cuban labor force had been absorbed and was insufficient to fill the big production vacuum.[331] A year later Pedro Diago complained of the Cuban sugarmills' technical inferiority due to the negative influence of slavery.[332] During the nineteenth century the theme would be repeated in a thousand forms in our economic literature.

The whole discussion reveals how the economic contradictions of sugar production awoke the consciousness of our producers. The slavers themselves, with their interest in maintaining the anti-economic slavery system, joined in the polemic with rationales for the continued importing of blacks. The barbarous exploitation of wage-workers by the English in the first half of the nineteenth century was a potent argument for slavery. No reader of Engels' pitiful descriptions of the Irish in Great Britain, of the "white slaves" in England, can hold the Cuban slave traders to have been entirely in the wrong.[333] Not because Cuban slavery was a kindly servitude, but because the same barbarism, the same lust for wealth, gripped men of both worlds as they sought to extract the last ounce of labor. Since the island lacked a broad labor market and the price of slaves kept soaring through the century, slave-masters had to give their men a minimum of good treatment to avoid exhausting in a few years the substantial capital invested. The death of a worker represented a reduction of fixed capital. We cannot say to what extent it was propaganda or to what extent objective reality, but we find many Cuban and European references to the superior conditions of the American slave compared to those of the worker in the Old World. Cuban producers were already making this point in 1790, proclaiming that their slaves lived better than free workers in New Spain's mines or than Spanish olive-oil workers.[334] In 1819 Juan Bernardo O'Gavan published a pamphlet wholly

dedicated to this theme.[335] We cannot take this odious document seriously—it has the author's contemporary Anastasio Orozco y Carrillo exclaiming: "You scoundrel! I hope you turn black so you can really pay for your sins."[336] However, with regard to Spain O'Gavan's pamphlet brought out such obvious truths that Spanish liberals had to recognize his accuracy.

We have said that although slave and wage labor always coexisted in the sugarmill, the primary quantitative solution was slavery. In the eighteenth century Wakefield called it the sole natural basis of colonial wealth. Marx quoted him and commented that without workers—that is, without slavery—capital would have perished, or at least been reduced "to that small amount which each individual could employ with his own hands." In other words, it would have stopped being capital, for capital only exists where there is a coincidence of the conditions necessary for the means of production to function as means of exploitation and enslavement of the worker.[337] Capitalism had furthermore organized the broad system of trading in Africans with incredible efficiency. Cuban sugarmen initiated large-scale production by using existing channels to fill their mills with slaves, which meant that one objective condition of sugar production did not depend on the Cubans themselves. But the producers quickly realized that they could not depend on foreigners to solve their labor problems. Cuban sugar needed a Cuban slave trade; they had to have their own suppliers of hands, and so was born the Hispano-Cuban organization of the slave trade as a subsidiary business. At the prompting of Arango, the Real Consulado feverishly created a system of economic stimuli and tax exemptions for men who plunged into the black flesh market. Actually, no more than the fat profits of the business was needed. The first successful expedition garnered 156 percent profit in a mere six months. Although the enormous demand for hands made slaving an exceptionally lucrative enterprise, successes were few in the late eighteenth and early nineteenth centuries. In Africa the Spaniards had to fight the English authorities in the pay of Liverpool slavers, and anyhow they were amateurs in this complicated business.

Long on improvisation and short on big-business technique, the Hispano-Cuban slave trade had a certain spice of adventure up to 1805. All the sugarocrats and merchants, plentifully endowed with cash from sugar's first dance of the millions, attempted expeditions to the African coasts. Arango tried it a few times himself, and other times dealt through Richard Tunno or his frontman, Jáuregui.[338] Soon the trade entered the higher stage of large-scale enterprise. There was the same approach to acquiring know-how from foreigners that we have seen in sugar, with study trips abroad and the importation of foreign experts. The firm of Cuesta y Manzanal, for example, started an intensive personnel-training program. Its first major expeditions with the ships "Ciudad de Zaragoza" and "Junta Central" used experienced Englishmen, while young Spaniards sailed with them to learn the details of the business.[339] By 1809–1810 Cuban and Spanish merchants were sufficiently expert to mount some thirty successful expeditions. These could hardly satisfy the pressing demand of the mills, but were a long step forward in training Hispano-Cuban slave-trade personnel. When Spain suppressed legal trade in 1819, twenty-two big Havana merchants had almost completely replaced the old foreign elements; furthermore, several important U.S. slave traders had moved their offices to Cuba.[340] The apprenticeship had been fast and productive. Imports of blacks rose every year. After the Anglo-Spanish abolition agreement, contrabanding slaves became one of the world's most gainful pursuits. Spurred by profits often reaching 200 to 300 percent, expeditions followed on each other's heels and at least up until 1830 enough blacks were available in sugar-port barracoons, at relatively low prices, to meet the needs of booming production. But in the 1830s the old conflict between sugar producers and slave merchants arose again. The great cholera epidemic of 1831–1833 wiped out thousands of Africans and suddenly there was a labor shortage. The price of men soared upward and sugar began raiding coffee plantations for slaves.

Without going into the details of the trade, two points must be clearly made. It started as a subsidiary of sugar and was stimulated, facilitated, and partially organized in Cuba by the producers. Since nearly all the big merchants with accumulated capital were Spaniards, these took the ascendancy in the new business. This control over the labor supply had a decisive influence on sugar production. The merchant was already a moneylender, the middleman in sugar sales, the warehouser of sugar and molasses, the supplier of equipment—lumber for boxes, food and clothing for blacks; now he also dominated the labor force. All these businesses carried on by the merchant were more or less subsidiary to sugar, each being smaller than sugar production itself; but between the beginning and end of the nineteenth century, the sum of all these subsidiaries became equal, and finally superior, in importance to the main business. Making long-term deals with comfortable security margins, the merchants were untouched by big price fluctuations and ended by profiting from them. Little by little the producer was edged into the background and the merchant emerged as king. This displacement inevitably brought the producer into social and political affairs. He was a man of bourgeois consciousness and thus a revolutionary element within his world. His survival and success were only possible by constant renovation of the means of production. His role was to fight for lower costs, better quality, and the steady growth of his enterprise's productive capacity. The usurer and usury exploit a given system of production, they do not create it: their role is to preserve it for continued exploitation while continually aggravating its plight.[341] The producer had to solve the labor problem: he was a slaver by necessity, not for profit. Black Africans were his solution from the outset, and he helped foster the slave trade. But with the passage of time slaves became a regressive force paralyzing productive development and tying the producer to the merchant. At that point he began to think of the overriding need to establish mills on the basis of free labor and therefore to abolish the slave trade.[342]

As always, Arango realized all this thirty years ahead of his contemporaries. We have seen that at the end of the eighteenth and beginning of the nineteenth centuries he was among the major organizers of the trade; but death would find him writing and translating studies of slavery and its abolition. Superficially he liked to see this deep change of ideas as a matter of personal repentance; that is, he attached moral significance to something that was purely economic. Such an interpretation— whether politically motivated or simply ingenuous— cannot be applied to a man like Arango, a robust representative of his class who had one of America's finest bourgeois minds and a complete awareness of his acts. His belated abolitionism was a manifestation of the class struggle. Slavery was a condition of life and death. It retarded bourgeois development and removed the sugarocracy's political potential, yet its suppression meant economic ruin and thus the class's disappearance. Arango saw the problem clearly: slavery had to be abolished to stop the growth of merchant power, but at the same time there had to be created a big labor market which would make abolition a benefit to the producers.

Arango's cynicism never reached such heights as in this abolitionist period. In 1832 he had been a mill owner for thirty-four years and knew sugar production better than anyone in the Americas; but in that year he discovered that slaves were worked too hard, were cruelly punished, and had wretched food, clothing, and medical care; they had no time to cultivate their plots or tend their livestock; their companions and children, the only consolations in their woeful life, were taken from them; they had no conception of religion and lacked all protection from the barbarians who ruled over them.[343] He discovered all that he had seen daily in his La Ninfa mill and had been denying for forty years. He proposed a series of measures he knew to be useless—moral declamations about Christian doctrine and the marriage sacrament—leading up to what really interested him: "That rural slaves be declared *glebae adicti,* not to be sold even to pay the government." [344]

But more important than this was Arango's project for a great labor market in Cuba. Since 1816 he had envisioned an island of 8 million inhabitants, just as twenty-five years earlier he had envisioned an island of 600,000 slaves: millions of people in a Cuba without state or unoccupied lands, all having to sell their labor—a way of eliminating physical slavery and substituting wage slavery, of obtaining a wage-worker who would be cheaper than a slave, whereupon slavery would die a natural death. A basic obstacle was the stigma attached to sugarmill work as "strictly for blacks," so Arango proposed to "wipe out or destroy the concern about color." As usual, this has been interpreted idyllically. The careful reader can see that Arango's one concern was to put whites to work alongside of blacks: to wipe out prejudice as the one way to form a proletariat, a working mass forced to sell their labor to the producers. The project had all the earmarks of a cattlefarm-proletariat system. He spoke of setting up colonies in suitable places which would be half workers direct from Europe and half black women.

The idea was not crossing black men with white women, but white men with black women, in conformity with a simple demographic calculation: the white woman must not obstruct the island's "whitening" process by having mulatto children; the black woman, on the other hand, would procreate mulattos and thereby hasten the process.[345] The situation in which this would leave black men was not mentioned. Years later the idea was brought up again by Saco.[346]

These artificial devices to make a proletariat for the mills could not, of course, be implemented. As the years went by the *hacendados'* situation grew steadily more intolerable. With the slave trade suppressed, contraband followed, raising the price of blacks. The cholera epidemics dealt many mills a heavy blow, leaving them suddenly with a 20 to 50 percent labor deficit. The cruel treatment of blacks ended all possibility of natural reproduction and in the 1830s and 1840s the need for hands became desperate.

Even more serious was the visible crisis in the labor system itself. The steam engine and vacuum pan, which were being experimented with in Europe in 1812, started a sugar-industry revolution which left Cuba no alternative but to establish a cell of wage-workers within the mill's slave corps. While sugar-beet factories made daily progress in Europe, Cuban mills stagnated or went backward. Everyone agreed that industrialization with slaves was impossible. It was not a question of lowering costs: free workers were a matter of survival, the only way to make the leap from manufacture to big industry. Slaves showed their innate rebelliousness by slowing down on the job, doing it badly, or simply sneaking off. As machines began to be the only solution, the negativeness of slave labor made itself painfully obvious. Slaves worked badly and grudgingly, beat the animals, ruined the tools—a trend against which handbooks and regulations were as futile as punishment. All this was reflected in the instruments of production: enormously thick and heavy machetes, spades and hoes any free peasant would have refused to work with, iron *jans* of vast size.[347] If the change of implements slowed down the high incidence of breakage and damage, it also made slave labor slower and less productive. So much slovenly work resulted that in the end only the simplest physical tasks were assigned to slaves. And, as a final and insurmountable obstacle, year after year the system germinated violent rebellions. *Hacendados* now only felt secure when they had slaves degraded and demoralized by the most ruthless exploitation.

Thus, according to Sagra, "there came into being a sort of practical code of absurd principles, in which the farm worker's stupidity became the guarantee of the farm's security, physical force the sole motive power, routine the only agricultural law." [348] Ahead of all Cuban or Spanish economists, he pointed out the impossibility of farming rationally, introducing machines and better techniques, under a work system in which the more stupid workers were, the more useful they were considered. The railroad experience showed that when certain kinds of work were introduced, wage-workers had to be imported. Introduction of vacuum pans confirmed the pressing need for change, and along with these new machines groups of free workers entered the mills. It was more than clear that sugar could not continue along the road of history without an effective labor market from which to supply itself.

The solution was called "colonization." The whole Hispano-Cuban colonizing theory was based on importing cheap labor into the colonies, and importing whites was a business not much more humane than the slave trade. Cristóbal Madán, who had a great interest in it, could not but see it as "a trade in men for the big entrepreneurs' profit and the industrious native's loss." [349] Juan Agustín Ferrety and José María de la Torre were among the first in the trade,[350] but their enterprises did not meet the producers' pressing needs and failed. The same fate befell Dau, who published his famous pamphlet entitled *Ingenios sin esclavos* (Sugarmills without slaves) in 1837. His project would have made the colonists into proprietors, while what interested the producer class was just the opposite: a dispossessed proletariat obliged to sell its labor to survive. By 1838 the results of the importation of whites—both Spaniards and foreigners—began to be felt. Cuba needed technical personnel to run the sugarmill steam engines, and every mechanized grinding mill had its United States or English mechanic. In a report compiled for the Sociedad Económica, Francisco de Paula Serrano pointed to the benefits of this, not only in increasing the white population, but as the dawn of a new form of work within the old mill structure.[351] The owner of the Sucrerie mill started

official negotiations for the shipment from Old Castile of thirty to forty peasants to plant cane for a small wage, but the plan was thwarted by the attitude of the Old Castilian peasants, who had not sunk so low as to work with slaves.[352]

The first really fruitful attempt from the bourgeois standpoint was the importation of Canary Island and Irish workers to build the Güines railroad—a purely sugar-industry project, as we have seen. The business arrangements were linked with London and so Irishmen, who constituted the lowest and most miserable of the working class in Great Britain, came along with the machinery and equipment. They had emigrated to British factory centers and become a morally and physically degraded lumpenproletariat. Carlyle describes how they lived in filthy hovels, sleeping on straw and old rags, throwing their excrement out the door, raising pigs under the same roof and sometimes sleeping with them. In the first industrial phase of unrestricted exploitation the migrant mass from Ireland competed with English workers and lowered even further the "minimal human needs" of factory personnel. Psychologically, drink was an important element in the lives of these people. As the cheapest workers available in Europe who knew enough to lay rails, they were brought to Cuba by the railroad contractors to be submitted to a slavery similar to the Negro's. When their contracts ran out many became human scrap: they were often found dying in the Havana streets, and the police would throw them in jail until the Real Consulado finally fulfilled its written obligation to repatriate them.

Canary Islanders were big business for the Cuban-Catalan firm of González y Torstall, importers of dried meat and men. They were brought in under contract for a fixed 9-peso-a-month wage, but out of this they had to pay for their passports and passage, the company's expenses, and monthly fees for a clinic which would attend to them when ill. It was estimated that after a year's work a Canary Islander had a cash total of between 12 and 18 pesos; the rest was absorbed by the man-importing firm which, in addition, garnered a due percentage for selling the contracts to the railroad-building concern. Standard Cuban wages for free white, mulatto, or black workers were from 12 to 25 pesos, so the Canary Islanders and Irishmen represented almost a 50 percent saving in railroad labor. To keep them from quitting the contracted job for something better paid, they were imported under army law; non-appearance at work was treated as desertion, punishable by prison or in some cases shooting.[353]

Nevertheless, work conditions were so appalling that constant rebellions occurred on the railroad project. As in the sugarmill, the workers lost all hope. It was almost impossible to get away. A petition to the Real Consulado in 1838 by the mother of thirteen-year-old Francisco Rufino to return him to the Canaries was denied. According to the file the boy had worked for six months and still owed the contractors 40 pesos: that is, he had to work five and one-half months more without getting a penny.[354] Some months later the name of Francisco Rufino appears in a list of workers who died on the exhausting job. Another cause of friction was the food. In January 1837 the Canary Islanders' rations were so bad that the scandal reached the office of the Capitán General. Miguel Tacón told the Junta de Fomento that its food contractors were starving the workers to increase their profits. The Junta, as evidence of how well the workers were really treated, pointed out that when they were sick they got the same diet as inmates of the Havana jail. In February 1837 Canary Islanders working in Bejucal, instead of eating their rations, took them to the mayor and asked that the municipal notary draw up a deposition. The food, according to this document, consisted of "a box full of raw plantains, sweet potatoes, and twenty-three bits of bone, mostly stripped clean, all of a blackish color and so unpleasant looking that eating them as rations was impossible." The protest landed the workers in jail, and later they were taken back to the railroad, this time as forced labor without contracts. A lawsuit was initiated against the mayor of Bejucal.[355]

The Güines sugar railroad, like sugar itself, was made with blood. Hunger and the sixteen-hour work day left their grim toll of dead. In El Cerro parish alone, burial rights were paid for 340 slaves who died on the first stretch of the line;[356] others breathed their last in Bejucal, Melena, Quivicán, and Güines parishes. There were as many Canary Island and Irish dead as there were blacks—perhaps more, for dead Canary Islanders and Irishmen represented no loss of invested capital. Barracks were built along the line and were called hospitals; the first was near Puentes Grandes, at the spot known as Los Filtros; the second was in El Retiro. We can get a glimpse of

these hospitals in the reply of Antonio María Escobedo and Miguel de Herrera to General Tacón in 1837, a document praising the fine conditions for the workers: seventy-seven were hospitalized at Los Filtros and in El Retiro eighteen Canary Islanders died during August and September; the writers were filled with optimism by the fact that, thus far in October, only six had died.[357]

The experiences of the Canary Islanders and Irishmen were hardly encouraging to other European workers, but hunger in Spain made it easy to continue the traffic in men. Between 1840 and 1845 the so-called colonization system was tried out on a grand scale. Three forces operated on the producers: the high cost of slave labor, the need for wage-workers to mind the machines, and the black rebellions, which had created a climate of terror. Under O'Donnell's chairmanship the Junta de Fomento began encouraging the trade in whites, as forty years earlier it had stimulated the trade in blacks. For newly mechanized mills—Villa-Urrutia's was one— five hundred farm workers were requested on the basis of free passage, plus 8 pesos for clothing suitable to the Cuban climate and free lodging for a month. The month's free lodging was known to physicians at the time as "acclimatization." There was an obligation to pay on arrival a wage approximately half the going rate for equal work in Cuba. Artisans "with guarantees of health, morality, and suitability" were also welcome.

Other projects were more directly aimed at the sugar industry: prizes were offered for the mill which could exhibit on its lands twenty-five white families dedicated to planting cane. There was a fabulous 20,000-peso prize for anyone setting up a mill in which cane was cultivated by thirty white families and sugar vacuum-pan processed without employing any man of color.[358]

Without winning any prizes Puerto Príncipe's La Colonia mill made the first spectacular experiment in 1840–1841: the big harvesting job was begun by a group of Catalans contracted by the trafficker in whites, Miguel Estorch. Betancourt Cisneros ("El Lugareño") displayed clear bourgeois perceptions in an enthusiastic letter about it to José de la Luz y Caballero dated January 3 1841:

Estorch's Catalans are doing splendidly. In one week they have cleared a caballería and a half of ground and they are full of zeal to plant and reap the fruits. No need to persuade or whip them; they scramble for jobs and elect their own team leaders. As workers they choose the one who works best—it is a real republic, a temple of security and peace and industriousness. What an example for the slavers! These blacks, you know, are more brutish than the brutes—they're used to blood and nothing stirs them up but the crack of a whip. In that department it's a pity that this farm isn't run by a Mola or a Rodríguez—the Estorches and company are men of theology, law and learning.[359]

The Estorch plan was a total fiasco for a number of reasons.[360] For one thing, the Catalans found much better-paid work in Puerto Príncipe and became artisans or farmers on their own account. Estorch ended by winding up the white-labor experiment and selling the contracts. Getting whites to work eighteen hours a day like the slaves in the harvest and grinding season was a real problem, and he cynically confessed it. On the maintenance side, the Catalans as a group consumed 465 pesos more a month than would have been given to an equal number of blacks. He could not make them accept inferior conditions since they had not come, as had the Canary Islanders and Irishmen, under the military law which prevented desertion.[361] Cuba now faced a phenomenon that English economists had noted in the eighteenth century as being typical of the depopulated colonies. Wakefield, master of Merivale, tells how a Dr. Peel brought to Swan River in New Amsterdam maintenance and production supplies along with three thousand English workers; the workers promptly took off for one or another of the many opportunities which the virgin land opened up to them. Many years later Karl Marx commented ironically: "Unhappy Mr. Peel who provided for everything except the export of English modes of production to Swan River!"[362] The words might have been spoken for Cuba. Only one thing marred the perfection of Estorch's experiment: there was no coercive machinery to keep the Catalans like slaves; no dispossessed proletarian mass, with all doors to life closed, which could make them continue selling their labor cheap to La Colonia.

Almost simultaneous with Estorch's Catalans was Aldama y Alfonso's attempt to set up a big mill with Spanish workers from Vizcaya—Aldama lent the project a certain slave flavor by calling them "my Vizcayans." But since Vizcaya was one of Spain's less poor provinces, its inhabitants could not easily be drawn into the market in hands.[363] Galicia was another story: pauperized by hunger and the latifun-

dio, it was the richest source of white merchandise. Vázquez Queipo refers in his fiscal report to peasants bought for 80 pesos a head and sold in the República de la Plata. Here, under the name of "colonization," the business of selling white hands to Cuban mills was organized by the Cortes deputy for Orense province, Urbano Feijóo Sotomayor.[364] When the business was ready to roll, in 1853, conditions for shipping out Galicians were presented to the Capitán General's office. A "patriotico-mercantile corporation" was formed, which undertook to pay the migrants' passage and give them an outfit of three shirts, one pair of trousers, one blouse, one palm-leaf hat, and one pair of shoes twice a year. The company was also obligated to find them work at no less than 6 pesos a month for a period of not more than five years,[365] and then to send them back home. Political as well as economic advantages were envisaged. Politically, the plan would ensure a staunchly Spanish population able to defend the colonial structure and to fight, from inside Cuba's production centers, against any attempt at independence. General Pezuela was well aware of the importance of having the material at hand to raise an armed militia against the buds of Cuban rebellion—the volunteer corps of 1868 and 1895 would amply bear this out. Economically, the colonists would come under coercive laws that blocked their escape from their sugarmill duties; and at a 6-peso wage they would be much cheaper than hired blacks—for whom the prevailing rate was 20 to 25 pesos.[366] The idea, in a word, was to submit a free man to a condition worse than a slave's.

The first contingent of five hundred Galicians, whose contracts Feijóo Sotomayor hoped to sell for 200 pesos, reached Cuban shores in 1854. The slavers, together with others whose motives are somewhat obscure, promptly mobilized against this competition. The result was a rising of the Galicians who had been installed in "acclimatization" barracoons. Many of them lost no time in taking illegal jobs in business and small industry. The Capitán General issued a circular on October 7, 1854, calling this rebellion "insubordination of colonists brought to the island." Since there were no available *rancheadores,* the army was mobilized to "capture the escaped Spanish colonists and restore them to their places of work or acclimatization."[367]

Although the project had partially failed, Sotomayor sold enough Galicians to producers to recoup his expenses. Others managed to get out of the contract and stayed in the cities or found sugarmill employment on their own: for example, the Dos Mercedes mill in Matanzas had several of these immigrants on its payroll.[368] Many years later, in the 1880s, Sotomayor's methods of recruiting Galicians in Spain began to be revealed. First Emilio Saco y Breig, and then Conrado y Asper, left colorful descriptions of "this horrible trade in human flesh, similar to the trade in blacks."[369]

By the 1860s, when an unbridgeable abyss had already opened between Cubans and Spaniards, colonization to gain free labor was the ruined producers' only hope. The well-defined economic basis and clear political motivation of the problem had not changed. It was true that the importation of whites—if they were Spaniards—provided a shock force for the colonial government; but it also liquidated the plantation system that was ruining the Cubans. This was the period when the cry for "white hands" was loudest—a racial connotation painted political tints on economic need. The reformist group, those we have classified as spokesmen for the afflicted producers, cried out desperately for colonization. Fermín Figuera demanded freedom for anyone to set up a man-importing company;[370] one of these was formed in Havana as the "Free Labor Importers," and its shareholders included some of the top mid-century producers.[371] The arguments of the old sugarocrat maestro Arango—still useful to his class even in the grave—were brought up again; Saco revived his plea for the production of mulattos to whiten the island,[372] and Porfirio Valiente wanted the laws against racial intermarriage abolished.[373] The slavers, for their part, presented a united front against white immigration and the freeing of the slaves.

At least until the 1870s white colonization could not be achieved by any of these means. Added to the slavers' powerful opposition was the lack of enthusiasm of the colonial government. The budget appropriation was 48,063 pesos in 1861–1862, although collections under various headings to raise this amount far exceeded estimates and the Treasury ended with an 84,000-peso surplus for this item. But while there was no serious effort at colonization in Cuba, 1,028,132 pesos of the Cuban budget were spent on the colonization of the Spanish colony of Fernando Po.[374]

The other—and decisive—problem was the ex-

pense. From a purely economic standpoint wage labor was cheaper than slave labor, especially in a seasonal industry like sugar: that is beyond dispute. But Pezuela, for one, could never understand how the greatest economists had supported a principle which did not hold true in Cuba. "For the time being," he wrote, "we cannot find more economical labor than that of our slaves . . ."[375] The simple fact was that slaves who existed could not be compared with wage-workers who did not. There was no labor market. To replace the 200,000-odd slaves working in the mills, the island needed a great wage-working mass that was not there. So minimally was the demand satisfied by the few colonists brought in that existing conditions were unaffected; furthermore, these exceptional immigrants enjoyed exceptional conditions. To make them cheaper than slaves they had to be treated as slaves, given an outfit like slaves, and then submitted to an eighteen-hour day without any chance to leave the mill; they had to be obtained without any payment and employed only when they were needed. Quite naturally, the colonist preferred to remain in the cities. In Havana and Matanzas, where there was in fact an important labor market, he displaced free blacks and ended by displacing house slaves, offering his labor for less than the cost of theirs.[376]

Parallel with white "colonization" and the continuing slave trade, effective systems were evolved to expropriate independent workers and peasants. While seeking hands abroad, the producers indulged in internal plunder. We have earlier noted the two basic aims of burning tobacco lands in the late eighteenth century: to get lands for cane and tobacco growers for the mills. The peasants resisted this invasion as well as they could, but events in the big Mayabeque valley repeated the capitalist depredations of Lincolnshire and Hertfordshire on a small and colonial, but none the less tragic, scale. As in England, many farmers went into the factories or took refuge in the cities.[377] A new social structure emerged in the countryside and the city. The rebel peasant, who would neither work in a factory nor join the city lumpen, became a highwayman and did his best business stealing blacks. The Cuban back country had always been a good refuge for bandits and fugitives, but all nineteenth-century documents attest to the fact that the rise of sugar lent the phenomenon a new form. In its session of August 8,

1816, the Havana Cabildo recognized the tremendous effects of the demoralization of slavery upon the free population, and saw that the plunder of men and lands had resulted in these groups marauding the countryside. The admission was wrapped in euphemisms—such as that "lack of charity" was partly responsible—but more frightening was the phrasing of the commission set up to study the matter: "The calamitous period of blood and iron which began in 1789 . . ."—precisely the year that the brutal expulsions of tobacco growers began under the Las Casas administration.[378]

Havana's always large floating population was swelled by people taking refuge in the slums which huddled under or overflowed the city walls. In all the sugar-terminal cities the large number of lumpen got steadily larger. The producers investigated and began to consider how they might turn these people into a potential labor market. Police records and sugarmill reports of the period fulminate with indignation against this mass of people without known occupation, living off gambling or prostitution or as petty hangers-on or middlemen, always flatly refusing to bury themselves eighteen hours a day in the sugarmill. This accounts for all the measures against vagrancy, measures which invariably proved ineffectual. Every institution studied the problem and the ideal form of coercion was sought: Saco produced, for the conferences called by the Sociedad Patriotica, his famous *Memoria sobre la vagancia* (Memorandum on vagrancy). Like all this author's work, the *Memoria* correctly identified many of the causes of the phenomenon, but offered no solution. Its chapter on how vagrants should be employed was absurd and unworkable. Justo Reyes wrote a *Memoria* equal or superior to Saco's, but neither author pointed out the decisive influence of slavery on the white man's so-called vagrancy.[379]

The recommendations were always the same: make the vagrants work in the mills. In mid-century there were sporadic requisitionings of men without known employment for forced labor on special colonial government projects. In a report to the Capitán General's office, the Junta de Fomento made two concrete proposals: first, that non-slaves over eighteen, of whatever color and having no property or apprenticeship, must contract themselves to *hacendados*; second, that persons considered to be vagrants must deliver themselves to *hacendados* or farmers for a fixed term and proportionate wage. The Junta described this veiled form of slavery as "extracting all possible utility from the existing population."[380]

The Junta's proposals were simply an expression of the producers' yearning for cheap and submissive labor, for a class upon which they could impose their conditions. Cristóbal Madán was clamoring for Asians, Yucatecans, Polynesians, or any sort of worker who could be had for less than 300 pesos on an eight-year contract at 4 to 6 pesos a month.[381] He also gave thought to the human material available in the cities. As a first step he proposed police laws to requisition free city blacks and make them work for wages in the mills. He also proposed an abolition system under which manumitted slaves would stay on at a wage fixed by the master. In sum, he wanted all the advantages of slavery with none of the disadvantages, without any obligation to maintain the slaves in the dead season, old age, or ill health. Eduardo Machado, another typical sugarocrat spokesman, confirmed that these were class sentiments when he echoed Madán's views. Machado's idea of emancipating slaves was that they should be obliged to work seven more years for the master who freed them and then remain under contract for another five. Blacks who were already free should, he thought, also be compelled to work in the mills; otherwise police laws should be applied, either by jailing them so they could be put to forced labor, or by expelling them from Cuba.[382]

Another way of obtaining hands was the violent business of the *rancheadores*—the pursuers of fugitive slaves. In the absence of any tested method to prevent their flight from the mills, the sugar boom filled Havana province with slaves. Since there was at the same time a rise of banditry, there were reciprocal influences. Many displaced peasants became bandits and organized gangs which stole blacks from one mill and sold them to another, or dedicated themselves to the furious pursuit of fugitive slaves. They sold them at the market price and earned handsome profits. The producers wondered how best to deal with this. On the one hand, they wanted to encourage the pursuit of fugitives; on the other, they needed to know that a slave, once captured, would be returned to his owner, but without being excessively punished by his captors, since this often resulted in the slave becoming useless for work. Arango, with

139

his soaring visions of the future, undertook to organize a system of hunting fugitives to return them where they belonged. In this, too, he was a pioneer of his class. On December 20, 1796, the King approved the "New Regulations and Tariffs Governing the Capture of Fugitive Slaves," [383] a formidable code drawn up by Arango to ensure a fugitive's imprisonment and return to the mill at a low cost. Seeking to restore order in the Havana countryside, which according to reports of the period was flooded with *rancheadores,* the regulations were the fruit of prolonged study and were aimed at stimulating the *rancheador*'s activity and at the same time curbing his avarice. Arango's report, used as the introduction to the project, contained this sentence: "The producers have been clamoring with great vehemence in the name of humanity (that is, in their own interests) . . ." [384] The parenthesis—Arango's own—is a conscious revelation of what the producers meant when they spoke in the name of humanity.

The producers' final inspiration for rounding up available hands was the exploitation of freedmen. Under the Anglo-Spanish treaty of September 23, 1817, blacks found on any illegal ship were to be guaranteed immediate liberty by the government. These so-called *emancipados,* for whom the Capitán General's office was responsible, were supposed to get a minimal preparation for living in the island or to be returned to Africa. In fact, *emancipados* were exploited even more than slaves. The so-called "deposits" for fugitive slaves had been fully organized by this time, and were also used for *emancipados.* The theory was that the Capitán General would hand them over to a responsible person, who had to indoctrinate them in Christianity and teach them a job to rehabilitate them in the future; after five years they would be given full liberty.

Like all the others, the regulations were ignored. Through the slaver Francisco Marty Torrens, Tacón sold into slavery not only *emancipados* but men who had already fulfilled the five years necessary to win freedom. The price of an *emancipado* varied from 6 to 9 ounces of gold. Sales were conducted so brazenly that on November 18, 1834, the Count de Casa Barrieto wrote asking Tacón to let him have twenty-five of them "at the price Your Excellency has set." [385] Although Tacón replied that he was in error, the incident is symptomatic. "Dead" *emancipados* came into fashion early: they were hired out to

sugarmills and when a slave died—recall the annual 10 percent loss of blacks—the *emancipado* was recorded as having died. According to Porfirio Valiente, many producers did not even bother with this formality, but simply paid the standard bribe to the priest and rural judge for the necessary certificates. It was a kind of Cuban version of *Dead Souls.* Such was the need for labor that the deposits for *emancipados* and fugitives became another big business. The slave deposit in Havana was rented by the Real Consulado, which used its inmates for railroad building. Later, in 1845, the Real Consulado sublet it and the sublessee in turn hired out the inmates. Everyone in the business did well. [386]

The slave trade, white colonization, violent efforts to submit city freemen to wage slavery, and finally the exploitation of *emancipados* and fugitives—none of these could solve the problem of cheap sugar labor. By mid-century new ideas of trading in men were being tried. There were projects to bring immigrants from Polynesia, Tonkin and Cochin China (parts of Vietnam), China, and Yucatán— South American Indians, Indian Indians, and so-called "free Africans." Only the Chinese and Yucatecan projects came off. Torrens' initial business trips to Yucatán were as successful as his previous deals in black slaves and *emancipados.* His new line of man-traffic inspired Pezuela to describe him as "an intelligent speculator." General Santa Ana, after surrendering part of his Mexican fatherland to United States expansionism, assisted Cuba's Indian-traders in this lush business, selling Yucatecans for some years at 40 pesos a head. There are no precise figures of the number of Yucatecans delivered to our mills. The business was killed by the violent reactions of the Mexican government and the English fleet, but there were various attempts to revive it, and as late as 1870 we find approved applications to import Yucatecans under conditions similar to the Chinese. The 1862 census—a fraud like all Cuban censuses—lists 786 Yucatecans in the sugarmills. There were many more.

José Zorrilla, author of *Don Juan Tenorio,* lent a poetic touch to the trade in Indians in 1859 when he launched an ambitious Yucatecan-selling project in partnership with Cipriano de las Cagigas. Having closed a deal with Mexican agents, both men went to Havana to make contacts and to study the market closely. Yellow fever wiped out Cagigas and the business; only a few romantic passages in a travel book remain for posterity. In Havana Capitán General José de la Concha heaped attentions on Zorrilla, and his frustrated partner Manuel Calvo lodged him splendidly at his tranquil coffee plantation. His day done as a merchant of men, Zorrilla returned to his former pursuit of poetry.[387]

When Aldama failed in the business of importing Vizcayans for his mills, he wrote to Delmonte: "Many *hacendados* have made up their minds to bring in colonists, and if we must go to Siberia for them we have to get them." They went even further away: the labor problem was solved with Chinese, the traffic arranged with the help of English and French veterans in the human flesh trade. The sugarocrat-dominated Junta de Fomento rushed the initial paperwork and in 1847 the first cargo of 315 Asiatics arrived on the *Duke of Argyle*. As usual, the first frauds showed up in the Junta. There is a big file—with references to blots, crossings-out, torn-out pages, and even lost books—about one attempt to bring contract account-books to light. The small rumpus, lasting eight months and involving Villa-Urrutia, the Arrieta brothers, and other top sugarocrats, was finally settled by general agreement.[388] From the outset the traffic in Chinese was clearly a more productive and less dangerous business than slaving, and naturally everyone wanted to control it. Slavers fought against it with outcries about the mixed-race threat to Cuba. But the Junta flatly denied the need for any concern about the possible results of introducing a new race. The problem was economic: "Territorial production and the agricultural industry need hands; those which the introduction of Asiatics promise to supply fill a small part of the need, as results will show."[389] By now Cuba's bourgeoisie had shed the figleaves hiding its economic pudenda.

Contracts for Chinese bodies sold at first for 60 pesos and were up to 300 by 1860. Chinese became a big business and special regulations became necessary in the mills. Feijóo y Sotomayor proposed the following:[390]

1. They should not be allowed off the farms.
2. They should get the same food as black slaves.
3. Wages should not be paid them when they were ill, sickness being a natural accident under the contract.
4. Masters should have jurisdictional power over them.
5. They should not be allowed to obtain freedom until the end of the contract, or to leave the farm after the contract if still in debt.

6. Marriage with white women should not be allowed.
7. There should be political equality with the free mulatto.
8. There should be fifteen hours' work a day.

These, more or less, were the conditions actually imposed. In 1854 a labor code similar to that for the slaves was promulgated for Chinese and Yucatecans.[391] Poey, who had many Chinese working for him in Las Cañas mill, admitted that the harvest season work day was eighteen hours.[392] One understands why the Matanzas mayor's office began a report with the words: "Free Asiatics, as everyone is pleased to call them, live on our farms exactly as do slaves."[393]

Although it seemed the same, it was not. The Chinese colonist was a miserably paid wage-worker—precisely the one our producers wanted, cheaper than the slave and capable of making the mechanized mill a viable proposition and launching the great sugar transformation. Many masters tried to submit him to slave conditions, thereby wiping out the advantages of wage-labor, but the highly mechanized mills avoided that mistake. In one of his letters Sagra wrote: "I think I am justified in saying that the introduction of Asiatics has been most beneficial: without it, who knows how the advances already made would have been possible?"[394] All the highly mechanized mills filled their boiling rooms with Chinese. The Progreso mill's Benson and Day vacuum apparatuses were run by a French boiler-master and 40 Chinese; Las Cañas had over 100, Flor de Cuba 170, Alava 130. The enlightened bourgeois Sagra gazed enthusiastically upon the free Asiatics' contribution to the productive giants of the day—Angelita, San Pelayo, Santa Susana, Conchita, Flor de Cuba, San Martín, La Ponina. He saw this as the gearing of labor to industrial operations—the steady pounding of the piston, the tension of the steam, the fixed level of the thermometer; quick-moving men, like a transmission belt, operating with the mathematical regularity of a pendulum.

Sagra's enthusiasm should not be interpreted as mere racism: he was one of the Negro's staunchest defenders. He was not talking about differences between Africans and Asiatics, but about the deep gulf between wage- and slave-workers.

The Chinese were the first major solution to the labor problem because they made it possible to begin industrializing sugar, to make the jump from manufacture to big industry. But for small Jamaica-train producers he was no solution; he merely prolonged their lives. Asiatics working Jamaica-train mills under the same old slave conditions functioned as routinely as did the blacks. The exploitation system had not stopped, but a historic step forward had been made; wage-worker exploitation replaced slave exploitation.

LIFE IN THE MILL

The conditions of life in the sugarmill describe a curve beginning with the semi-patriarchal regime of the early eighteenth-century factories, arching through the super-barbarity of the first half of the nineteenth century, and ending in the 1860s and 1870s with what hacendados called "good treatment of the slave." Economic determinants were the variables of the slaves' treatment, and these were, primarily, the volume of labor available, the price of slaves, production techniques, and market conditions. In this aspect, as in all that we are studying, there is no unity of time and place: the slave's fate was subject to the period and to the type of mill in which he worked. We can, however, make a general survey valid for most mills at a given moment.

The first fact about conditions in the mills is that the natural reproduction of slave crews was impossible. This problem became serious in the late eighteenth century and continued through most of the nineteenth. In the economic terminology of the day, hacendados of 1790 described the concept of births compensating for deaths as "always retaining the principal set up by our first purchases." [395] Natural replacement, in other words, would prevent a Negro's death from being an irreparable loss to his purchaser. In fact, however, from the late eighteenth century until the 1840s mill crews were only maintained by new purchases. Madán was still talking in 1854 of the small number of births in the mills and calculating the decrease by death at 4 percent a year; Delmonte put the figure at 5 percent, and other writers at 8, 9, and 10 percent. [396]

The producers had figured the costs of natural reproduction, and Arango cynically set them forth in his 1811 Representación to the Cortes. A pregnant female was useless or low-yielding for some months, and this raised the mill's production costs. Costs were also raised by even minimal care of the mother and new baby. On balance, Arango found that "the black born on the estate has cost more, by the time he can work, than one of the same age bought in the public market." The hacendado's ideal would have been a great human cattle herd, constantly multiplying and daily offering new hands. But the hurdles were insurmountable. Of the many circumstances limiting sex life in the mill, the first was the great disequilibrium between the sexes. Sugarmen imported only males; very few mills had any females because, according to early nineteenth-century hacendado logic, as low-yield animals it made no sense to buy them. It was ruinous to bring too many in since production did not measure up to investment, while too few made them the foci of constant quarrels between the males. Some hacendados made the pious excuse that they bought no females to avoid the sin of sexual contact between unmarried persons. To this, Padre Caballero made the apt reply that the sin would be worse if all slaves were masturbators, sodomites, and practiced abominations. [397] Arango, as usual perceiving sugarmill problems ahead of his fellows, managed to spur the importation of black women: at his instigation special taxes were proposed on mills having less than 33 percent females in their crews. Early in the nineteenth century a Real Cédula required masters of all-male mills to buy as many women as were needed for slaves wishing to marry. It was completely ignored by the mill masters.

The sexual disequilibrium made the slave's wretched life even grimmer. But as slave prices rose the smaller hacendados bought some women, figuring that, although they yielded less, they also cost enough less to compensate. Thus, again for economic reasons, the sexual problem was reduced, and experience soon showed that the low yield of females was a myth—they worked the sixteen to eighteen hour day alongside their men. We have seen that La Ninfa's 1827 harvest was cut by women who met their daily 400-arroba quota. Anselmo Suárez y Romero wrote of them:

They rest neither on Sundays nor saints' days; they seem to be made of iron. What with only five hours' sleep in the grinding season; rising before dawn has even begun to display its splendors; toiling in the canefields without let-up save for the short noon break to come in and eat; cutting cane in the melting tropical sun interspersed by torrents of rain; in winter suffering cold which penetrates to the bones of an African; and then, on Sundays and saints' days, nursing the baby, washing and mending the clothes, cooking the food—well, I just don't know how they stand up to it! Yet with it all, my friend, would you believe it? They always look happy—smiling faces, never that heavy expression that the males have—and it is quite rare for them to get desperate and hang themselves. So the overseers say they have more resistance and work more conscientiously than the males, and attribute this to their physical nature giving them a better character; but of course overseers can't penetrate into the heart of things.[398]

Such experiences gradually brought more black women into the mills, although in 1865 the Matanzas mayor's office still saw the sex disproportion as alarming and listed several mills lacking a single female. On the other hand, breeding became a business: one of the first to discover it, José Suárez Argudín, set up a stud farm near Bacuranao beach; and Tomás Terry went into the business in Cienfuegos. The most shameless of such establishments was Esteban Cruz de Oviedo's one at the Trinidad mill of which Justo Cantero wrote: "Attached to this farm, and served by its female blacks, is a stud farm which is the apple of the proprietor's eye. It yields him an increase of some thirty blacks a year, while losses of mature ones are figured at no more than ten over the same period."[399] This is what the Real Consulado in 1854 called "a system of conservation and reproduction."

Apart from the sex imbalance there was the females' natural repugnance at producing slave children to suffer the same exploitation and misery. On this Francisco Barrera, our first slave doctor, made some somber observations;[400] and later Bernardo de Chateausalins, who had under his care the big slave crew of Drake's coffee plantations and sugarmills, vividly described the black woman's activities.[401] Both said that female slaves so detested pregnancy that they used certain bitter herbs to produce abortions—a pathetic demonstration of rebelliousness. But even where there was no conscious attempt to abort, the same result was produced by the heavy tasks required of pregnant slaves. Chateausalins writes of miscarriages by women who, in the ninth month of pregnancy, had to cut 400 arrobas a day like the men. On other occasions the loss of the child was the normal result of a flogging with a manatee-hide whip. Steele describes pregnant black women being condemned to flogging on the belly.

If the child was born, its chance of growing up was remote. First, it ran the serious risk of "seven-day sickness"—tetanus—which was generally caused by the custom of using cobwebs to heal the navel and tying the umbilical cord with candlewick.[402] Our first important bacteriologist, Juan N. Dávalos, showed that candlewick was an ideal nest for tetanus bacilli. The babies were then wrapped in old, seldom-changed rags and, according to the doctors, spent most of their time in their own excrement. On the second or third day after giving birth, the mother returned to her work cutting cane or in the curing house, and the infant stayed with the mill's other babies under the minimal care of some old slave woman who was past doing any production job. The sugarmill's infant mortality reached incredible proportions: Chateausalins wrote of hacendados who did not achieve a single surviving slavelet over many years. The figures ranged from very high for slaves to lower among free blacks to much lower among whites—that is, in direct relation to exploitation and misery. Death rates were especially high in December, January, and February, the season of harvesting and cold. If born alive and avoiding infant's tetanus, the child had a hard struggle ahead, without either the care of the mother or the concern of the master. Many slave women paid little attention to their babies and even let them die—an attitude due, Chateausalins thought, to "natural dislike for bearing them to see them become slaves, destined to toil all their lives for the master's enrichment." If a child reached five or six he then began his career in the mill since, by slave development, he was old enough to be incorporated in the production crew. But, as we have said, crews never reproduced themselves naturally. The mills were like huge grinders which chewed up blacks like cane. Growing old was a privilege as rare as it was sad, especially in the super-barbaric stage of slavery.

The black man's life was directly related to production costs. As long as a dead worker could be quickly replaced by a live one, the mill went on its way devouring men: to replace was cheaper than to care. This was expressed in economic terms by sugarocrat Madan: "The more a slave costs, the more he is cared for." Hacendados admitted that when a man cost $300 or $400 there was no corner of the estate for attending the sick, the allegedly low-yield woman was not purchased, and the child was not attended to—for no one was interested in long-term investments. Economic motives, not moral rules, determined the slave's treatment; everything was calculated by productivity and cost. In the early nineteenth century Baron Humboldt observed with astonishment an economic discussion on the alternatives of imposing intensive labor on slaves—thus reducing their useful life—or lightening their work and delaying their death. In modern mathematical terms, the optimal yield-point was sought as a function of two variables: daily work-hours and the number of years in which these could be endured. Poey defined the alternative in one sentence: "Whether it pays better to sacrifice the slave to the work or the work to the slave." [403]

Mechanization brought great changes in the slave's life. From earliest times there was, in the manufacturing process, a conscious desire to cut the work-time necessary for production. The specific machine in this process was the slave himself—the black man as collective worker. Specialization gradually developed, depending on the greater or lesser complexity of the job and the physical effort needed to perform it: thus, there came to be a hierarchy of labor. The introduction of highly perfected iron horizontal grinding mills, followed by steam power and other modern advances, produced a functional disequilibrium between the mill's mechanized departments and the surviving manual ones. The first big conflict arose when man was coupled to machine: collective labor working to the rhythm of steam. In our analysis of the mill's technical aspects we saw how this arose and was resolved. In the beginning, all labor, from planting cane to packing sugar, was basically manual: the grinding mill was the only machine and even that was animal-powered. We also noted that mills in the first stage were called trapiches, identifying all production with the one true machine. The grinding mill was perfected and new machines began to perform some operations, while others remained manual. Mechanization took place first in the elaboration tasks, producing radical differences between two once closely united phases, the agricultural and the manufacturing. In manufacturing, machines were introduced side by side with manual techniques, and the latter made big bottlenecks which were resolved by adding Negroes, intensifying the work, and lengthening the work day. This partial mechanization increased the traditional barbarism of the mill by demanding synchronization of manual work with mechanical processes. Thus, too, the machine at first meant the growth of slavery,

since more manual workers were needed to keep up with the tasks the machine could perform.

But by way of grim contradiction, the machine that brought more slaves into the mill needed a wage-worker to run it. This is the root of the insoluble production conflicts that ruined many Cuban *hacendados*. Slavery's darkest years, from 1820 to 1850, were characterized by the quantitative but deformed growth of the semi-mechanized mill. With the installation of the efficient iron grinding mill— later to be powered by steam—the boiling room had to expand and accelerate with only the antediluvian Jamaica train. Total mechanization was impossible for most producers, and the ungainly semi-mechanized mill could not achieve any stability of production. To take full advantage of the machine, the utmost had to be extracted from the slave's useful time. This was not a purely Cuban phenomenon: it occurred wherever there was a profound industrial transformation. Cuban producers followed the only possible course: in the unmechanizable phases of their operations the work had to be rationalized. They took as their own Franklin's classic bourgeois slogan, "Time is money." The atoms of time were the creative elements of profit. Cuban mills evolved their own kind of speed-up system, a rationalization process designed solely to wring the last drop of work from the slave. From the end of the eighteenth century, tasks were measured with watch in hand, and systems for gaining seconds in manual labor were studied. [404]

Some of today's economists have the mistaken notion that sugarmill tasks in the past century were carried out without specific controls, and describe as "modern" the cost and production reports and careful standards which enable daily labor distribution and efficiency to be analyzed. But even in 1783, on the basis of a study of records kept by Santo Domingo producers, Dutrone had worked out a practical set of standards; and big Cuban mills such as La Ninfa, La Nueva Holanda, El Cangre, Anfitrite, etc., soon picked up the idea. The registers they kept in the first decade of the nineteenth century show the remarkable standards by which they followed the production flow and controlled every detail of manufacturing and agricultural activities. Arango in Havana knew from week to week the exact situation in each of his mill's eighteen departments. He was completely familiar with the labor picture by distri-

NEGROS CAMPESTRES.

Varones.....

Hembras.....

TOTAL.....

SON LOS MISMOS

Parvolr. Huiles. Enformos. Havana. Regin. Comon. Cafetal. Sitio de viands. Mayabeque. S. Pedro.= Texar. Carpintería. Herreria. Auxilio Alambique. Recua. Tiro de mión. Casa de vivienda del Ingenio. Idem del mayoral. Para el servicio del Ingenio.

DISTRIBUCION DE LOS DEL SERVICIO DEL INGENIO.

Observaciones del .....administrador.

Observaciones del administrador.........

En trabajos de Molienda.	Vs.	Hs.
Cuidando bueyes..........		
Cortando leña..........		
Tirandola..........		
Cortando caña..........		
Poniendola en las carretas..		
Conduciendo estas al molino..		
En el mismo molino........		
Sacando bagazo..........		
Llevandolo á la casa de calder.		
En el servicio de. esta....		
En el de la casa de purga...		
En el de los secaderos y almac.		

En otros que realmte. no lo son.	Vs.	Hs.
Sembrando caña..........		
Limpiandola..........		
Abriendo canales..........		
Desaguandolos, ó reparando-los..........		
Con los arbañiles..........		
En la pedrera..........		
Tirando piedra..........		

Bueyes.
Su número.
Su distribucion.
- En Camoa..........
- En San Pedro..........
- En el cafetal..........
- En el texar..........
- En el ingenio.......... Los mismos.

Caballos de carga.
Su número.
Su distribucion.
- En Camoa..........
- En el cafetal..........
- En el Ingenio..........
- En San Pedro..........
- De volante.
- En la Havana..........
- En Camoa..........
- En el cafetal..........
- En el Ingenio..........
- En San Pedro..........

Mulos de recua.
Su número.
Su distribucion.
- En Camoa..........
- En el Ingenio..........
- En San Pedro..........
- En el cafetal..........
- De volante.
- En la Havana..........
- En Camoa..........
- En el cafetal..........
- En el Ingenio..........
- En San Pedro..........

Carretas.
Su número.
Su distribucion.
- En Camoa..........
- En San Pedro..........
- En el Cafetal..........
- En el Ingenio.......... Las mismas.

REGISTER OF LA NINFA SUGARMILL

This first page, in use from the first 1801 harvest, shows under various headings what La Ninfa's male and female slaves ("*Varones*," "*Hembras*"), oxen, horses, mules, and carts were doing and where on a given date.

145

ESTADO DEL INGENIO LA NINFA

en la semana que empezó dia   y concluye hoy   de   de 180

Número 1.	Número 2.	Número 3.
Molino.	**Casa de Calderas.**	**Casa de Purga.**
Carretadas de caña cortadas desde el principio de la Molienda............. En esta semana........ Nombre de los cañaberales de que proceden...... Carretas en exercicio..... Dias que ha molido el trapiche...............	Clarificadoras cogidas.... Panes que produxeron....	Panes hechos desde el principio de molienda...... E traidos para el Secadero. Quedan en casa de purga. Hechos de miel de purga.. Extraidos para el Secadero. Quedan en la casa...... Desde el principio han entrado de cucurucho...... Se han extraido......... Quedan de esta clase.....

Número 4.	Número 5.	Número 6.
Secadero.	**Almacen de azucar.**	**Almacen de miel.**
Panes existentes de la 1. clase............... Idem de la segunda..... Idem de la tercera......	Caxas de blanco embasadas desde el principio de molienda............... Idem de quebrado..... En todas............. Peso de las primeras..... Peso de las segundas.... De miel de purga....... Su peso............. Remitidas á la Hav. de bco. Su peso............. Idem de quebrado....... Su peso............. Idem de miel de purga... Su peso.............	Barriles extraidos para hacer azucar............ Idem para el alambique.. Idem para vender.......

Número 7.	Número 8.	Número 9.
Alambique.	**Sierra.**	**Carpinteria.**
Cargas de agte. comun destilados desde el princ.de moliend. Remitidas á la Havana desde entonces.............. Destilados en la semana... Existentes en el alambique.. Barriles de Rom destilados desde principio de moliendas Remitidas á la Havana desde la misma epoca........ Destiladas en la semana.... Existentes en el alambique.. Barriles de miel consumida. desde el principio de moliend. Idem en la presente semana.	Tozas de cedro aserradas.. Tablas que produxeron.... Tozas de caoba......... Tablas que produxeron... Tozas de pino......... Tablas que produxeron... Tozas de jobo......... Tablas que produxeron...	En que se ha ocupado Que obra se ha hecho Quanta madera ha recibido Quanta ha consumido

REGISTER OF LA NINFA SUGARMILL

These second and third pages are production reports for the various departments of the enterprise, with figures for the past week and for the entire harvest to date. The first 13 columns list the production from canefields, boiling room, curing

Número 10.	Número 11.	Número 12.
Herreria.	Molino de maíz y arroz.	Carnicería.
En que se ha ocupado	Fanegas de maíz recibidas desde principio de año..	Reses muertas..........
	Idem en la semana......	Arrobas que produxeron..
	En todo............	Huesamentas..........
	Arrobas de maíz molidas desde principio de año---	
Que obra se ha hecho	Idem en la semana-----	
	En todo----------	
	Vendidas desde princ. de año	
	Consumidas desde entonces.	
	Idem en la semama- --	
	Existentes - - - - - ---	
	Arroz.	
Quanto fierro y asero ha recibido	Arrobas de arroz en cascara recibidas desde el principio······	
	Idem en la semana···········	
	Total·············	
	Descascaradas desde el principio··	
	Idem en la semana···········	
	Total·············	
Quanto ha consumido	Vendidas·············	
	Consumidas·············	
	Existentes··········	

Número 13.	Número 14.	Número 15.
Texar.	Negros.	Negras.
Hormas hechas desde principio del año	Recioidos............	Recibidas............
Idem en la semana......	Recien nacidos..........	Recien nacidas.........
Idem quemadas en la semana............	Enfermos............	Enfermas............
Existentes de ambas clases.	Muertos............	Muertas............
Texas hechas desde principio del año..........	Huidos............	Huidas............
Idem en la semana......	Aprendidos............	Aprendidas............
Idem quemadas.........	Con prisiones..........	Con prisiones..........
Existentes de ambas clases.		
Ladrillos hechos desde principio de año..........	Nombres de los huidos.	Nombres de las huidas.
Idem quemados..........		
Existentes de ambas clases.		

Número 16.	Número 17.	Número 18.
Boyada.	Caballos, mulos y mulas.	Almacen general.
Comprados.............	Caballos comprados.......	Efectos recibidos en la semana.
Vendidos.............	Sus nombres..........	
Muertos aprovechados.....	Idem vendidos..........	
Arrobas que pesaron.....	Sus nombres.........	
Muertos sin aprovechar...	Idem muertos..........	
	Sus nombres.........	
Nombres de los muertos.	Mulos comprados.......	
	Sus nombres.........	
	Idem vendidos..........	Idem extraidos en la semana.
	Sus nombres...........	
	Idem muertos..........	
	Sus nombres.........	
	Mulas compradas.......	
	Sus. nombres.........	
	Idem vendidas..........	Idem existentes en el dia.
	Sus nombres.........	
	Idem muertas.........	
	Sus nombres.........	

house, distillery, sawmill, etc.; columns 14 to 17 show the production and loss, of male and female, of slaves, oxen, horses, and male and female mules. The slave crew is broken down into males and females "Received," "New born," "Sick," "Dead," "Escaped," "Captured," and "Jailed," with a space for "Names of the escaped." Column 17 keeps separate records for horses, male mules, and female mules: "Bought," "Their names," "Sold," "Their names," "Dead," "Their names."

bution, sex, age, and type of work assigned. He received a daily harvest and grinding report which noted the number of cane-cartloads ground, kettles refilled, sugarloaves made and aired, containers packed under five headings, and so on, to the number of blacks entering and leaving the infirmary, escaped or dead. All important mills kept records reflecting the minutiae of daily activity in astonishing detail, and many have survived for us to study.

There is some justification for saying that modern sugarmill controls have added little to the system established long ago. Rationalization of labor was the only way to lower costs, and the producers went about it efficiently. The slave's life was governed second by second: the master's or administrator's economic ideas dictated how long he could survive. As long as high production at a large cost in lives was the supreme law of sugar, blacks died in shoals. In that sense Cuban mills were the most barbaric in the world during part of the last century. English and French technicians, in their reports on Antillean sugar production, expressed amazement at the enormous output obtained with small crews. What made it possible was savage pressure on the Negro. In 1823 the sugarocracy's own spokesmen had to admit officially—in the *Memorias de la Sociedad Patriótica*—that there was hardly a mill without 25 percent of its labor force "useless, injured, and sick." [405] Deaths were officially reckoned at 7 percent, but the Sociedad recognized that they ran much higher. The labor distribution registers of the period show that an average of 20 percent of the blacks were always in the infirmary.

The slaves worked seven days a week. On Sundays the grinding mill rested but not they: they were cleaning troughs, scraping boilers, carting green bagasse, doing curing-house chores, cutting firewood and cane for the grinding which was resumed either on Sunday evening or at latest at dawn on Monday. Only technical trouble stopped work on weekdays, but such interruptions were almost never complete: when the big grinding mill broke down there was a small one, and when one Jamaica train failed the others carried on. Contrary to the *hacendados'* claims, grindings were never stopped on religious grounds during the nineteenth century. Mill reports show that, for the slaves, business continued as usual over Christmas, despite sugarocrat assurances that the Birth of Our Lord was an obligatory rest day. The

priest of San Julián de los Güines had the mills stopped in his parish on an important holy day and Arango sent the Consulado one of the most sizzling protests that ever came from his pen. When the Real Cédula of May 31 ordered sun-to-sun work hours with rest on Sundays and specific saints' days, the producers insisted that if they obeyed they would have to close their mills. [406]

The limit of a slave's work day was his physical capacity. He began to the nine chimes of the Ave Maria and ended to the nine chimes of Vespers. Another bell summoned him at noon to return to work until he heard the evening call to prayer, when he left the fields to cut hay for the animals and do other marginal jobs. The cart drivers, having already spent eight to ten hours in the fields, rotated with boiling-room blacks and continued working until dawn. The cutters became feeders of cane into the grinding mill and carters of dry and green bagasse. Boiling-room workers shifted to the curing house. Each group went off to sleep for three, four, or at the most five hours as this fantastic rotation system continued. Administrators and overseers saw to it that the process was meticulously carried out so that, alternating in the various jobs, the slaves worked a full day of seventeen, eighteen, or twenty hours. [407] As a mill was mechanized and some tasks called for more specialization, this routine was discontinued and slaves stayed in the same place, repeating a thousand times the same exhausting motions until the curfew tolled for them long after nightfall: "the signal," as sugarmen called it in their religious terminology, "for repose and retreat." [408]

Just how many work hours the various mills tolled out on their bells we do not know. The Reglamento de Valdés—our first great Factory Act, promulgated in 1843 to the producers' fierce objections—prescribed sixteen hours of work in the harvest and grinding season, two of rest, and six of sleep at night. [409] Madden writes of mills where work lasted twenty hours and four were considered enough for sleep. The bell marking the rhythm of the endless tasks was like a sacred and profane symbol of the sugarmill. Just as a church without a bell tower was inconceivable, so with mills and coffee plantations. The mill's bellringer did not need to learn the varied and complicated combinations of the city: he was generally an old Negro useless for production tasks, psychologically and physically unfit for flight, living his daily death beside the tower. The tower of the Manacas mill still stands, legend encrusted, in the fields near Trinidad. The niche at its top where the bell once hung is bare, but it is a mute reminder of canefield slave labor. There it stood—lookout, fortress, and bell tower—tolling out each day the sixteen, eighteen, or twenty hours of toil. It also served as a means of communication throughout the broad valley. There was a ring to call the oxherd, another for the administrator, another for the overseer; and from time to time a light, quick peal announced the departure of a slave for the mill cemetery.

In its greed for surplus labor, capital demolished not only moral, but purely physical, work-day barriers. Suárez y Romero, owner of the Surinam mill, described in a few words the work rhythm of his blacks:

Cutting cane if it is harvest time, in the full heat of the sun, feeding it into the grinding mill, minding molds and kettles, stoking the furnace, heaping up cane; loading it on the burro, carrying bagasse; at night doing these tasks in the cold and dew of the pre-dawn and dawn hours, dying of sleepiness since there are but five rest hours for each nineteen of toil; and after the harvest, planting cane and clearing the canefields—one of the mill's toughest jobs, for the body must be bent over, not permitting the machete, the implement regularly used, to be wielded freely; and all this time enduring the tremendous downpours of the rainy season, the mud underfoot; that, although seen from a great distance, is a picture of the kind of work which is done on these farms, and about which I will tell you more in another letter.[410]

This regime made sleep one of the mill's worst problems, especially in mills which, convinced that blacks could last twenty hours a day, put them to work in the boiling room at night after ten hours of cutting and loading cane in the sun. The extra work was politely called *faenas* (chores). Some mills made their slaves perform *faenas* and *contrafaenas,* which added to their regular job to make a twenty-two-hour day. As a reward they were allowed to sleep six hours the next day; then they resumed the same stint of twenty or twenty-two hours. José Ricardo O'Farrill noted in his 1792 *Cartilla* (Handbook) how many a black died or lost his arm when, overcome by sleep on the night shift, he kept his hand on the cane as it fed into the crushers. The fatalistic expression still heard in Cuba—"When sleep seizes you"—dates from this period. No one could discuss slave tasks without referring to sleep. It took possession of the exhausted crews under the hypnotic rhythm of movements endlessly repeated; in the monotony of canefield, grinding mill, and boiling room; through the interminable hours of days each like the other; under the threat of the whip and the desperate wait for the bell. Suárez y Romero, who left us the most truthful and detailed sugarmill descriptions, paraphrased in literary language the doleful, illiterate chant of a Negro in his mill: "That harvest-time shifts were more than they could stand; that sleep overcame them and that sleeping they skimmed the kettles, sleeping they removed the boilings, sleeping they beat the sugar in the coolers, sleeping they carried the molds to the draining racks, sleeping they spread the bagasse over the mill yard." [411]

The *hacendados* calculated, and expressed in pesos, the danger a slave ran when seized by sleep. A death through sleep reduced the mill's assets and was reflected in production costs. Furthermore, since a sleepy slave was a low-yield worker, a few cuts with the whip—especially on the night shift—were recommended to liven up the pace. In the second half of the century, when the price of slaves was very high, they were allowed to sleep one or two hours longer and received less punishment. Some masters even advised their overseers to ignore certain offenses, such as falling asleep in the harvest and grinding period.[412] At La Lima mill, under the Cidra administration, the unique experiment was tried of letting blacks sleep six hours a day—a measure described as "a philanthropic system with beneficent results." [413] That blacks should enjoy the physically necessary minimum of sleep was so newsworthy that it was featured in *La Aurora de Matanzas* and the Havana *Gaceta.*[414] It was a time when *hacendados* talked of some "good and happy" harvests in which nothing deplorable occurred except for "that little boy who fell asleep walking and died, trampled by the oxen." [415]

To conquer sleep and maintain discipline, a system of government was set up. The mill had a simple hierarchical structure. Big producers divided their personnel into two separate worlds, slaves and wage-workers. The top man, with total responsibility for the plant, was the *mayoral* (overseer) or *administrador.* From the 1820s on there was a definite tendency to limit his power, removing him from

DOTACION DE NEGROS

Del ingenio la Ninfa, el dia 18 del mes de Dic.re de 1829

Su distribucion.	Varones. 180	Hembras 180
Infantes sin ocupacion	26	32
Chapeando		
Limpiando zanjas	2	89
Corte de caña	90	
Carreteros de idem		
Carreteros de leña, miel y azùcar . . .	19	1
Idem de gabazo		
Idem de idem verde	10	2
Idem de gabazo seco.		9
Trapiche	2	6
Calderas	20	
Purgando secaderos de azùcar . . .	2	7
Cuidando bueyes	4	
Arando.		
Cortando leña		
Labrando madera		
Cortando arcos		
Arrieros	3	
En la carbonerìa	2	
En la herrerìa	2	
Arrancando piedra	1	
Aserradores		
En el alambique	6	3
Con el albañil . . , . . .	1	
Con el tonelero	1	
Con el carpintero	3	
En el tejar	6	
Canasteros.	1	
Talanquero y guardieros. . . .	6	
Sirvientes	1	9
Impedidos.	1	0
Enfermos	19	10
Huidos.	1	1

REGISTER OF LA NINFA SUGARMILL

The daily record of slave crew activities used in 1829. Note that the number of controls has been reduced: in this too there was regression.

Noticia de los trabajos, entradas y salidas que ha habido en este ingenio la Ninfa, en la semana que empezó el dia 7 y acabó el dia *Bdo* *de 1827*

Carretadas de caña molidas en esta semana. *808 liads*
Idem desde el principio de la zafra......
Calificadoras llenas en la semana.......... *109*
Idem desde el principio.................
Bocoyes llenos en la semana............
Idem desde el principio...............
Bocoyes remitidos en la semana.........
Idem desde el principio..............
Idem existentes....................
Panes de azúcar hechos en la semana.... *956*
Idem desde el principio..............
Idem aventados en la semana...........
Idem desde el principio..............
Existentes en los secaderos............
Idem en la casa de purga............. *956*
Cajas llenas en la semana.............
Idem desde el principio..............
Idem remitidas.....................
Idem existentes....................
Pipas de refino llenas en la semana....... *9 con 1890 galo*
Idem desde el principio .... *427 con 63665 gaas*
Idem remitidas..................... *293 pi y 1429 cas con 64693 gon*
Idem existentes.................... *42s pi cons*
Negros aumentados en la semana.........
Idem nacidos ....
Idem muertos.....................
Bueyes aumentados en la semana.........
Idem muertos...................... *1 buey*
Idem existentes.................... *118 existes*
Carretas aumentadas en la semana.........
Idem desechadas....................
Idem existentes.................... *93 nuevas y 27 carretts*
Carretadas de piedra recibidas en la semana. *mdas*
Idem desde el principio............... *622*
Tareas de leña cortadas en la semana......
Idem desde el principio............... *6201*
Tareas de leña conducidas en la semana.... *180*
Idem desde el principio.............. *1862*
Tierra arada.......................
Tierra sembrada de caña en la semana....
Idem desde el principio..............
Tierra sembrada de viandas en la semana..

administration and leaving him in exclusive charge of the practical work. At that point there appeared an *administrador* with executive functions in the mill's economy, responsible for the daily production reports and breakdowns. The *mayordomo* had charge of internal organization not directly connected with production: food, clothing, the infirmary, housing, warehousing, etc. The *boyero* was responsible for the carts and oxen. Depending on the size of the mill, there might be a second or third *boyero,* and further overseers known as "yard overseers," "orchard overseers," etc., according to their area of authority. The technical side was under the sugarmaster. If there were steam engines, the machinist and his assistants were in charge of them. Other minor wage-workers were the blacksmith, the brickmaker, the brazier, the infirmarian, the gasometer man (from 1845), carpenters and coopers, messengers, etc. To these must be added woodmen, quarriers, lime-kiln men, and others who worked by the job. The average semi-mechanized mill had a minimum of ten full-time wage-workers; the mechanized had at least forty or fifty since it needed special furnacemen and boilermen, a "mold master" (who replaced the old sugarmaster) and his two or three assistants, and not less than ten men for the vacuum apparatuses and centrifugals. As production increased, more second overseers, carpenters, brickmakers, and so on, were required; and when the personnel topped four hundred, a doctor moved into the mill instead of getting a stipend for periodic visits. From the 1840s on, there was also "a free Negro woman known as Black Mama." [416]

The slaves lived apart from this salaried world. If there were Chinese or Yucatecans, they were separate, forming a new division in the mill. Normally wage-workers dealt with the *administrador,* while the overseer managed the slaves, but there was no fixed rule on this. The overseer became one of the most typical figures in the colony. His very name (*mayoral*) endowed him with an aura of power and decision, and as such he passed into twentieth-century political literature. The owner did not figure in the mill's hierarchical structure since he rarely lived there. The custom was for him and members of his family to visit the place once or twice a year, lending a dash of feudalism to the big slave camp. During the week of the family's presence masses were said, slaves were baptized, punishments were remitted, and rewards were given for good conduct. Here is the basis of the romantic descriptions which have come down to us. But the exhausting life and work continued as usual, and when the family returned to the city, the overseer reassumed his omnipotence.

In the late eighteenth century the first known satire on the overseer appeared in Havana's *Papel Periódico*. It was a masterly profile of his cruelty, his need to impress his personality on the crew, his sadism, his sex life with the best black women.[417] In the nineteenth century this figure persisted in our best romantic literature. Juan Padrínez depicts him as having bushy side-whiskers, a whip, dogs, and a deeply rooted sadism. He is the outstanding character in the novels *Francisco* and *El Negro Francisco*, and is the Don Antonio described by Mauricio Quintero. There is no doubt that the overseer's calling was always fraught with danger and the need to find security by sowing fear made him hostile and brutal, like a man who had never assayed his own medium and functioned in it more or less blindly. The sadism was no more than a reflection of the fear that forever pursued him. His routine of managing slave crews desensitized him, and his constant efforts to implant a sense of inferiority in others made him an inferior being himself.

Overseers were always white, but there were black second overseers and rear overseers (*contramayorales*). The countryside is full of stories about blacks, but these men who managed slaves of their own blood are an especially long-standing tradition. Without trying to penetrate his psychological traumas, we may assert that the black assistant overseer must have been moved by deep ancestral fears. Above all, there was the fear of returning to the slave crew, fear of the overseer and the white master. Whipping others was insurance against being whipped himself, and also of slightly better rations, a little more clothing, and sexual satisfaction with some of the mill's few black women. And of a little more sleep.

The other employees remained relatively anonymous. Machinists lent the mill a certain exotic tinge since they were nearly always foreigners. The 1842 census counted fifteen hundred from the United States working in our sugarmills; later there were many Spaniards, especially Catalans, and machinists' and mill records show there were Frenchmen, Swedes, Prussians, and Russians. Political authorities tried to make capital out of these aliens as an alleged danger to society.

Most slandered of all workers was the sugarmaster. We have seen how this personage—upon whom, after all, the quality and quantity of production depended—threw the producers into despair; but he continued to be an institution in our mills. The old-time sugarmaster was in fact an expert in slave work who knew how to get the most out of Jamaica trains from many generations of experience. All his secrets were the result of long practice, obtained in daily contact with canefields and boiling rooms. He was basically an artisan, guided by judgment which years of living with sugar had acutely sensitized. Calculating everything by sight, smell, and taste, he knew if enough lime had been added, when clarification or defecation was completed, and when the conglomerate had reached the sugaring point. His eye measured the correct amount of beating and the moment to air the sugarloaves. The tragedy of the sugarmaster, his loss of supremacy, came when vacuum pans were introduced and his judgment was replaced by physical measuring apparatuses.[418]

NOTES

1. *Libro de cargo y data de las porciones de Azúcar que contribuien los Individuos dueños de Yngenio, por el Cinco por ciento correspondiente a S.M.; y en que se incluirán las Cantidades que produxen las ventas que se hicieren en este Puerto, que corre desde 6 de Octubre de mil setecientos cincuenta y nueve (que principió la contribución),* Miscelánea de Libros, no. 2646, Archivo Nacional. This is the only known document giving a detailed account of mills in the Havana area between 1759 and 1765, including their owners and production. It provides enough data for a rough estimate of the island's total production, and shows the falsity of all our historians' calculations based on traditional sources—those of Pezuela, Arango, Humboldt, etc.

2. "It is known that until 1763 only three or four ships came from Spain for our entire needs." (Arango, *Obras*, vol. II, p. 18.) Statements like this appear in Arango's *Discurso sobre la agricultura en La Habana* and are insistently repeated in most of his later political writings. Historians of the past century restated them because this suited their class interests. Considering the capacity of ships of the period, it is impossible that three or four of them could have carried the extraordinary sugar production mentioned above, plus tobacco, timber, and so on.

3. ". . . a war which will always be painful . . . but which may be said to have opened the true epoch of Havana's resurrection." (Arango, *Obras*, vol. I, p. 117.) ". . . with their blacks and their free trade, the English had done more in a year than we in sixty years . . ." (Ibid., p. 118.)

4. "From being the most humane among all European slave owners, the Spanish colonists have become the most barbarous and demoralized." (Merivale, *Lectures on Colonization*, pp. 40–41.)

5. Rosenda de Neyra was the daughter of Juan Gregorio de Neyra, considered to be Cuba's richest mulatto in the first half of the eighteenth century. His descendants achieved total whiteness in successive marriages, but in 1802 proceedings were begun to stop the marriage of one descendant, María Josefa de la Luz Hernández, on the grounds of tainted blood. That file provides us with the family's whole remarkable story, the honors won and wealth possessed. See: *Expediente promovido contra María Josefa de la Luz Hernández para evitar su casamiento*, Archivo General de Indias, section II (Cuba), leg. 1956.

The following verses, published at the time in Havana's *Papel Periódico*, may possibly have been aimed at the Neyra family:

> If a rich dark man
> confesses his grandpa was black,
> nothing wrong with that.
> But if he thinks his cash
> makes him a dark gentleman,
> it doesn't follow.

6. For a detailed account of this contraband, see: *Dictámen dado a S. E. por el Don Joseph de Abalos, de lo que es el Ramo de Comisos de la Isla de Cuba: la descripción que haze de las diferentes clases de contrabando; y los medios que le parecen oportunos para que pueda contenerse el comercio clandestino,* Archivo General de Indias, Santo Domingo, leg. 1156. Among many lesser references, see: Arango, *Obras*, vol. II, p. 37.

7. "Original sources seen by me show that in 1762 it sold for 16 and 12, $15\frac{1}{2}$ and $11\frac{1}{2}$. With small differences this continued until the French Revolution." (Arango, *Obras*, vol. I, p. 477, n. 27.) For year-by-year sugar prices for the thirteen Colonies up to independence, and afterwards for the United States, see *The North American and West Indian Gazetteer, 1760–1793*. The most complete information on prices in this period is in the chapter on prices in William

Reed's *History of Sugar and Sugar Yielding Plants* (1866).

8. English planters stressed this relation between the thirteen Colonies and the Sugar Islands, and also the influence of sugar on English manufacturing: ". . . that the Manufactures, traffick, treasure, and Power of Great Britain depend in great measure on the Fate of our Sugar Islands." (*A Supplement to the Second . . .*, 1744.) "The northern colonies supply the Sugar Islands, chiefly with lumber and provisions." (*Candid and Impartial Considerations, 1763.*)

9. The process in Cuba was the same as that observed by Cairnes and noted by Marx with respect to slavery in the United States: "Hence the negro labour in the Southern States of the American Union preserved something of a patriarchal character, so long as production was chiefly directed to immediate local consumption. But in proportion, as the export of cotton became of vital interest to these states, the over-working of the negro and sometimes the using up of his life in seven years of labour became a factor in a calculated and calculating system. It was no longer a question of obtaining from him a certain quantity of useful products. It was now a question of production of surplus-labour itself. So it was also with the *corvée*, e.g., in the Danubian Principalities." (Marx, *Capital*, vol. I [New York: International Publishers], p. 236.)
10. Ibid.

11. Ibid., p. 236.

12. Aguirre Beltrán, *La población negra de México*, p. 81.

13. Roig de Leuchsenring, "De cómo y por quénes se hacía en Cuba la trata de negros," *Revista Bimestre Cubana*, May–June 1929.

14. On September 19, 1798, at the request of José Ricardo O'Farrill, the Real Consulado's board of directors congratulated Beltrán Gonet on the occasion of the happy arrival from Senegal of a cargo of 123 blacks on his account and at his risk. See: *Espediente sobre el apoyo y protección ofrecidos por este Cuerpo a D. Luis Beltrán Gonet en sus espediciones de negros*, Real Consulado, leg. 72, no. 2778; *Espediente relativo a la solicitud de D. Luis Beltrán Gonet sobre rescate de dos barcos apresados por los ingleses*, Real Consulado, leg. 88, no. 3684.

15. *Copias de las cartas que se escriben por esta Administración de la Real Compañía de La Habana desde 21 de julio de 1763 a Don Diego José de la Cosa, Secretario de la Junta de Comisión por S. M. establecida en la Corte*, Miscelánea de Libros, no. 1435, Archivo Nacional, p. 5.

16. Ezpeleta's proclamation is to our knowledge the first legal move to regulate the traffic in men. Its six basic provisions highlight the sugarmills' critical labor shortage and indirectly give the lie to the so-called economic crisis of these years.

17. The legal process freeing and stimulating the Hispanic-American slave trade was as follows: All subjects, settlers, or residents were allowed to purchase blacks wherever they were obtainable—permission for two years (Real Consulado, 28/2/789). Same permission extended for six years (Real Consulado, 24/11/791). Period for sale in the ports was extended for Spanish slave ships to forty days (Real Orden, 3/1/793). Complete freedom for Spanish slave ships where half the crew and the captain were Spanish; exception for ships bought for the purpose (Real Orden, 24/1/793). The Viceroy of Buenos Aires was directed to help an expedition by an English ship (Real Orden, 14/1/794). Spaniards finding no blacks in foreign colonies were allowed to return with sugarmill utensils, machines, and tools (Real Orden, 19/3/794). Equipment of the port of Manzanillo for Spanish slave trading (Real Orden, 23/3/794). Trade in barrel hoops and staves was permitted (Real Orden, 14/12/794). Extension of permission for free trade in blacks to the Viceroyalty of Peru (Real Orden, 21/5/795). Tax for Morro lighthouse was not to be imposed on slave ships (Real Orden, 14/1/797). A two-year extension of permit to Buenos Aires, Peru, and Chile (Real Orden, 12/4/798). A twelve-year extension in Cuba for Spanish slavers, six for foreign (Real Cédula, 30/4/804). All this documentation is in: *Espediente sobre prórroga del término concedido por S. M. en Real Orden de 22 de abril de 1804 para traer negros de la costa de Africa*, Real Consulado, leg. 74, no. 2836.

18. The method used in these calculations is fully explained in Part 4. The only estimate of caballerías of cane in the period is in a fragment written by Padre Caballero in 1806. According to this there were in that year some 400 mills, and 15,000 to 16,000 caballerías of cane were under cultivation. See: Caballero, *Escritos varios*, vol. I, p. 153.

19. "The *Señores* enjoying the usufruct of herds and corrals or cattle farms retained only the agrarian base of European seigniory, while lacking the vassals who accompanied the latter to their wars and worked the land for them. To assure themselves of service they established the slavery of Indians and Africans and even a semi-slavery of whites." (Le Riverend, *La Habana*, p. 56.) It is strange how Cuba's historical process, seen so clearly by Le Riverend, has confused other students. To Juan Clemente Zamora, for example, the whole Cuban phenomenon—even the political disputes between Spaniards and Creoles—is a feudal form of conflict. See: Zamora, *El Proceso Historico*, p. 188.

20. Marx, *Capital*, vol. III, p. 617.

21. *Espediente sobre aclaración del dominio de las vegas naturales que la Real Junta de Factoría de tabacos arguye de realengas*, Real Consulado, leg. 94, no. 3954.

22. Arango, *Obras*, vol. I, p. 411.

23. The Marquis' report is in: *Espediente sobre abolición de días festivos en fomento de las labores del campo; y sobre facilitar a los capellanes de los ingenios para que puedan decir misa en ellos aún en los días esceptuados; administrar los sacramentos y sepultar los cadáveres en cementerios hechos al propósito*, Real Consulado, leg. 93, no. 3938.

24. *Para los pregones, posturas y remate de la Renta Decimal del Ramo de Ingenios y Haciendas del Partido de Güines, cuyo arrendamiento se hace por tiempo de quatro años que empezaron a correr de 1º de Henero de 1785 y terminaron en 31 de diciembre de 1788*, Intendencia General de Hacienda, leg. 504, no. 7.

25. *Espediente, sobre el entredicho puesto por la Real Junta de Factoría de tabacos a las tierras de la vega de Güines*, Real Consulado, leg. 85, no. 3489.

26. Arango, *Obras*, vol. I, p. 442. In note 75 in his *Informe sobre el tabaco* (*Obras*, vol. I, p. 487), Arango again insists: "Coca says that in 1792 he abandoned tobacco growing after having marked with an 'N' and put to the flames all the fifty-two loads he brought to the Factoría, although he pointed out that there was a buyer for it and that, in a year of hurricane and misery, it was his entire production."

It is astonishing that a historian as alert as Ramiro Guerra should have fallen into this sugarman's trap. In the year that Arango called one of "hurricane and misery," sugar production figures were the highest to date in Cuban history. Six years later, José de Coca y Aguilar had finished developing the Nuestra Señora de las Mercedes, alias El Barbudo, sugarmill, which was appraised at 200,000 pesos—an extraordinary amount for the period—and which became one of Cuba's production giants in the nineteenth century.

27. The first denunciation against this mill was made in 1807 by Rafael Gómez Roubaud. Arango, lying as usual, tried to depict the "Respectable Don Luis de Las Casas" as innocent of accepting the bribe, writing that: "This mill started on four caballerías of land and was initially set up when D. Luis de Las Casas was not yet Capitán-General of this island." (Arango, *Obras*, vol. I, p. 391.) However, on Las Casas' death the true date of its foundation and the Governor's personal activity in the sugar business came to light. The frontman was Joaquín de Aristarán, whose son would change the name to Ayestarán. For the undercover deals in connection with this mill, see: *Incidente de la testamentaría de Luis de Las Casas promovido por Tomás Gimbal*, Escribanía de Guerra, leg. 965, exp. 14,407.

28. Padre José Agustín Caballero writes: "He himself joined the delegation sent to observe a French artisan's experiment with the new machine to grind cane without the cost and trouble of oxen; and there he was in Mr. Lafage's [sic] hut, just like one of us, feeling the springs of the machine, calculating its power, taking lessons in mechanics, and interesting himself in the performance of a device which looked as simple and practical as one could desire."

This idyllic picture of Las Casas' interest in the invention is far from the reality. Enough documents have survived to reveal the whole murky, multi-million-peso transaction hinging on the success of La Faye's experiment. To exploit it there was a corporation whose first two shareholders were Las Casas and Calvo; the third, naturally, was Arango. For details of the transaction see Arango's papers in leg. 19 of the Fondo Pérez Beato in the Biblioteca Nacional; and *Copia de los papeles que en oficio de 19 de agosto de 1795 incluyó el Dr. Don Carlos del Rey a quien se devolvieron*, Archivo de la Sociedad Económica de Amigos del País, leg. 57, no. 1, Biblioteca Nacional.

29. There is copious documentation on the arrangements between Arango and Valiente in the Fondo Pérez Beato, leg. 15, Biblioteca Nacional. The co-ownership of La Ninfa, for many years Cuba's largest mill, came to public knowledge because Arango was drawing his profits from Valiente through commercial firms. However, this was only revealed, to our knowledge, in an anonymous pamphlet in 1838. The pamphlet, one of the most interesting in the colony's records, was undoubtedly written by an economic higher-up with detailed knowledge of official dirty deals. We have been able to document the truth of nearly all its scandalous statements. With regard to Valiente, I wrote earlier: ". . . of D. Pablo Valiente, top official of the public treasury at the time, it was notorious that in contravention of law he acquired the famous La Ninfa mill . . ." (*Estado actual de la Isla de Cuba*, p. 42.)

30. *Informe de la Comisión nombrada en 1820, por la Junta de Fomento para el estudio de las vegas naturales*, Real Consulado, leg. 94, no. 3954.

31. *Informe de Nicolás Calvo al Real Consulado, 6 de noviembre de 1797*, Real Consulado, leg. 85, no. 3489.

32. Arango, *Obras*, vol. I, p. 410.

33. Ibid., p. 393.

34. *Informe del Intendente de Hacienda en 15 de septiembre de 1817*, Real Consulado, leg. 94, no. 3954.

35. *Espediente instruído a virtud de informe del Contador de glosa de las cuentas presentadas por la Administración General correspondiente al año de 1792, sobre que se remitan de la Intendencia de Ejército las diligencias generales seguidas por dicha Administración para que se diese cumplimiento al artículo 14 del Reglamento de Alcabalas y a la Real Cédula de 14 de octubre de 1767 preventiva de que se presenten por los propietarios de ingenios las relaciones de sus cosechas*, Intendencia General de Hacienda, leg. 7, no. 14.

36. Arango, *Obras*, vol. I, pp. 118–120.

37. Maldonado's mill was called San Diego, had twenty-six slaves, and was located in the area now known as El Cerro. (See *Reforma Social*, vol. VII, no. 1, pp. 40–42.) "There is no doubt about the general proficiency in 'borrowing' other people's money to promote businesses and haciendas. Until well into the eighteenth century, funds from local or state tax collections could be counted on to disappear almost completely, although these were certainly of some magnitude." (Le Riverend, *La Habana*, p. 58.)

38. "Out of the cheap molasses of the French Islands, she [New England] made the rum which was chief source of her wealth." (Woodrow Wilson, *History of the American People*, cited by Taussig, *Some Notes on Sugar and Molasses* [1940], p. 52.)

39. A book on sugar and annexation needs writing. Annexationist ambitions were born with the rise of sugar just as United States investments in Cuba began after U.S. independence. The notion that before 1900 there were hardly any Yankee investments in the island is absurd. The late-eighteenth-century sugar boom was largely financed by U.S. firms which, having got into deep water when their trade with the British Antilles was shut off, transferred their mercantile activity to Cuba. In 1799 the delegation named by the Consulado to study the auctions project of Santiago Drake, reported: ". . . bearing in mind that most of the houses now dealing with foreigners in this city are directed and administered by these neutrals themselves . . ." (*Espediente promovido por Don Agustín Rodríguez y Don Santiago Drake sobre establecimiento de una venduta en esta plaza*, Real Consulado, leg. 72, no. 2783.)

For a small idea of these budding U.S. plutocrats' economic and financial activity, see the letter copybook of one of the important commercial firms established in Havana between 1782 and 1787: *Copy of letters from the 4th January until the 25th January 1787*, *Miscelánea de Libros*, no. 1369, Archivo Nacional.

40. Arango, *Obras*, vol. I, pp. 121–122.

41. Ibid., p. 134.

42. *Memoria sobre la restauración de la cosecha de la caña dulce y de los ingenios de azúcar en este Reyno, presentado a la Sociedad Económica y publicada en 1793*, Valencia, B. Monfort, 1845.

43. ". . . i zuccheri di Sicilia sostennero per due secoli circa una ventaggiosa concorrenza con i prodotti americani; segno univoco, che le spese, la mano d'opera, la influenza del clima e del terreno, poco o nulla alteravano i resultati d'un beneficio commerciale." (B. V. e P. [Gaspare Vascari] Sul Richiamo della canna zuccherina in Sicilia e sulle ragioni che lo esiggono di G. V. e P; Palermo, Presso La Tipografia di F. Solli, 1825.) Tommasi, *Della maniera di far lo zucchero coll'uva* (Firenze, 1798).

44. Converted to tons of sugar, these figures are:

1761	43	
1792	58	
1804	136	
San José de los Dolores		471
San Miguel		372
La Asunción		334
La Ninfa		336
San Cristóbal de Baracoa		301

45. Report of Diego José Sedano to the Real Consulado in 1807, in *Espediente sobre calificar la estrema decadencia que sufre la agricultura y comercio de esta Isla, particularmente en el ramo de azúcar*, Real Consulado, leg. 93, no. 3953.

46. *Cuaderno mandado a formar por separado, con los documentos designados por José Antonio Bosques, relativo a sus negocios con Bonifacio González Larrinaga*, Tribunal de Comercio, leg. 28, no. 2.

47. Marx, *Capital*, vol. III, pp. 609–610.

48. *Espediente promovido por Don Felipe Alwood, solicitando que esta corporación represente a S. M. recomendándole para que no se le expulse de esta Isla, por ser extranjero*, Real Consulado, leg. 201, no. 8913.

49. All the information on big moneylenders is based on: Real Consulado, leg. 93, no. 3953.

50. Nearly all historians interpret superficially and make frequent mention of the French immigrants' influence as an exclusive phenomenon of Cuba's eastern zone. When they speak of the big coffee plantations, they refer only to those whose imposing remains still stand in the Sierra Maestra foothills. They forget or don't know that:

1. Cuba's biggest coffee plantations were started not in Oriente but in the western Havana-Matanzas area. The biggest of all, with over three hundred slaves and quasi-Asiatic luxury, was near Madruga and the remains of it and its huge cemetery can still be seen. With the expulsion of the French it passed into the hands of the millionaire Drake. It had been started by French immigrants, and the French doctor Bernard de Chateausalins came to Cuba to look after its slaves. What happened to the western coffee plantations is that sugar expansion wiped them off the map, especially after 1832. The eastern coffee plantations, on the contrary, survived sugar.

2. Coffee plantations were important, but second to sugar. In only four of the first thirty-two years of the nineteenth century did the coffee harvest surpass that of sugar. However, French immigrants working in Havana-Matanzas sugar, though they left no visible traces, were more important economically than those in coffee. To appraise this influence one must bear in mind:

—The giant sugarmills of the first decades of the eighteenth century, and the last decades of the nineteenth, were built by Frenchmen. The Güines valley plants—La

Ninfa, El Cangre, La Nueva Holanda, Anfitrite, etc.—owed their bumper production to technicians from Haiti. Of the ten biggest mills grinding the 1804 harvest, Frenchmen built eight.

—French technicians were responsible for the introduction of the perfected water-driven grinding mill, the cane turner, the new transmission systems applied to the grinding mill, the French (later known as Jamaica) train, the increased use of the hydrometer, the first experiments with horizontal grinding mills, the mass production of clay molds and flat tiles, the use of litmus paper, and the use of lime instead of lye.

—The western road system, one of the basic necessities of sugar expansion, was largely directed and organized by French technicians. We owe to La Faye the best study of roads written in Cuba. Jean Lage directed the Los Güines road project, with its great movement of earth. Julian Lardière was to an extent the technician of the frustrated Los Güines canal, presented in the name of the Count de Macuriges.

Under these men's far from disinterested contribution, Cuban sugar made its big leap into the world market and Cuba became the first big producer. Enriched and protected by the *hacendados,* few of them were touched by the expulsions of 1808, and in the 1820s we find Dumont, Lardière, Lage, and La Faye owning mills. A final note: Frenchmen expelled from Cuba gave a big push to sugar in Louisiana.

51. In his *History of Sugar* (1949), Noel Deerr has documented the first sugar experiment with a steam engine: it occurred in Jamaica between 1768 and 1770 and used the famous John Stewart machine mentioned again elsewhere in this book. Two copies survive of a pamphlet Stewart published concerning this machine. One, consulted by Deerr, is in the New York Public Library; the other, of which we have a photocopy, is in the Library of Congress. Arango knew of the pamphlet's existence—it was in Calvo's library—and mentioned the Stewart experiment in his *Discurso sobre fomento de la agricultura.* Deerr, however, commits an error of interpretation in suggesting that the first successful application of steam to the grinding mill occurred in Cuba. His evidence for this is a quotation from Baron von Humboldt, who spoke of twenty-five trapiches grinding with steam engines. The small error in Deerr's excellent study stems from his ignorance of the fact that Humboldt did not base his work on data obtained on his first Cuban visit: thus he refers to steam trapiches grinding in the 1820s. What was truly remarkable in Cuba was the continuous experimenting with machinery until success was achieved in 1817. We should point out in conclusion that the Cuban error was not in the machines but in the grinding mills. When the grinding mills were perfected, the steam engine could be successfully applied.

52. Arango, *Obras,* vol. I, pp. 225–239.

53. Arango's first observation on refined sugar appears in his *Discurso.* Later he wrote a report entitled *Resultan grandes perjuicios de que en Europa se haga la fabricación de refino* (in *Obras,* ibid.), ending with an expert description of Mr. Nash's refinery in London. Thanks to this pioneer work, permission was obtained by Real Orden of February 23, 1796, to establish refineries throughout the island. In 1813 Arango's original position on refining was unchanged. According to Echegoyen, he said in private conversations that "If it was in his hands, he would allow no unrefined sugar to leave the island." Echegoyen felt that Arango's idea stemmed from his desire to take the profit of the second operation from foreigners and keep it in the country. (Echegoyen, *Fabricación de azúcar* [1827], p. 44.)

54. Dutrone de la Couture, *Précis sur la canne et sur les moyens d'en extraire le sel essentiel* (1790); Corbeaux, *Essai sur l'art de cultiver la canne et d'en extraire le sucre* (1785).

55. *The Art of Making Sugar* (1752) was practically copied from Père Labat's chapter on sugar, "Du sucre et de tout ce qui regarde sa fabrique et ses différentes espèces," in *Nouveau Voyage aux Isles de l'Amérique* (1724), p. 224.

56. *Memoria sobre el cultivo de la caña dulce y extracción del azúcar* (1766); *Origen de las cañas de azúcar, modo de prepararlas y beneficiarlas* (1719).

57. The school of chemistry was ardently promoted by Nicolás Calvo, an almost unknown figure in Cuban history but assuredly one of the most brilliant minds Cuba had produced. According to José Agustín Caballero, Calvo played the harpsichord, knew Latin, Greek, Italian, English, and French, specialized in mathematics, and was always to be found in his home studying the camera obscura, electrical and pneumatic machinery, and celestial and terrestrial objects; he had a fine chemical laboratory, a valuable botanical collection, a microscope, a telescope, and many other instruments of an extraordinary kind for the Cuba of those days. A man of well-defined bourgeois ideas, he was the only intellectual peer of Arango in the last decade of the eighteenth century. With his capitalist understanding he saw "the school of sugarmasters, which should more properly be called the school of chemistry," as the indispensable basis for technifying sugar. Referring to the botanical school, he wrote of the "exact science for the knowledge and good cultivation of sugar." Arango took up his ideas and made them a reality in the 1820s. See: *Discurso de don Nicolás Calvo promoviendo el establecimiento de una escuela de clínica y botánica, Memorias de la Real Sociedad Patriótica,* vol. I, pp. 147–160. On p. 17 of the same *Memorias* appears this paragraph: "Of all the sciences encompassing these truths, none is more analogous and to the point than chemistry. Invented for the

analysis and comparison of different substances which combine in the formation of bodies, its principles are peculiarly applicable to the elaboration of juices expressed from cane, forming what should properly be called the Art of Making Sugar."

For the only small biography in existence, see: *Elogio del señor Nicolás Calvo y O'Farrill* in Caballero, *Escritos varios*, vol. I, pp. 179–196. Calvo was a sugar-chemistry pioneer who expressed in Cuba, in 1793, the same ideas that French experts would enunciate in Paris in 1810. In 1812 France established its Ecoles de Chimie et des Fabriques Impériales pour l'Extraction du Sucre de la Betterave; see: Dureau, *De la fabrication du sucre de la betterave* (1858).

58. *Exposición que D. Joseph Ricardo O'Farrill hace a la sociedad del método observado en la isla de Cuba, en el cultivo de la caña dulce y la elaboración de su jugo*, Memorias de la Real Sociedad Patriótica (1793), pp. 119–147.

59. Martínez de Campos, *Memoria sobre el mejor modo de fabricar el azúcar, que en junta celebrada por la Sociedad Patriótica de la Habana* (1797).

60. Morejón y Gato, *Discurso sobre las buenas propiedades de la tierra bermeja para cultura de la caña de azúcar* (1797).

61. In accordance with literary customs of the period, the Sociedad Patriótica's dissertations were apt to be inspired by classical models. Campomanes, the organizer of these societies, suggested Tacitus as an example. Yet in all of Arango's copious work not one quote from the old classics appears—not because he did not know them but because he was intentionally trying to introduce a new approach to problems. In this too Arango was an innovator, using the clearest and most "modern" prose in America. This conscious effort is seen in the following paragraph of a speech he delivered to the Sociedad Patriótica around 1795. The manuscript offers no clue as to the occasion and precise day of the speech:

"Heaven did not endow me with the gift of words, and however great my efforts I have not been able to penetrate those respectable spheres in which admiration and applause greet the orator. Sadly remote as I am from the tribune, and from the sublime complacency of dominating men by the enchantment of my phrases, I would not presume to speak before this assembly if its constitution were different; but constituted as it is to be a school of patriotism, and to base its work if possible purely on that sentiment, it cannot hold me to account for the scarcity of figures of speech and agreeable epigrams in my speeches. On the contrary, I think we are responsible to the Fatherland for all the moments which we rob from its service and use for our own glorification. I submit that it is our duty to declare formally that we will speak here only in the simple language of the ordinary farmer and that, dispensing with preambles and idle digressions, we

will look straight at the facts and analyze them with no other company than good logic and precise reasoning."

62. José Ricardo O'Farrill, *Exposición*, p. 137.

63. The first mill to plant and process Otaheite cane was Tomás de Jáuregui's Nuestra Señora del Rosario in 1789. In the Real Consulado file covering the introduction of Otaheite cane to Cuba, the fact that it was already known and planted in the Barlovento district is recognized. See: *Espediente sobre introducción de la caña de Otahití en esta Isla*, Real Consulado, leg. 92, no. 3930.

64. "Ingenios de nueva planta. Representación en que se da cuenta de las novedades introducidas en el ramo de Ingenios a beneficio de los esfuerzos de esta Junta de Agricultura y de los vecinos más ilustrados. 8 de agosto de 1798." In: *Espediente, promovido por varios dueños de ingenios situados en tierras de Guanabacoa para que este Cuerpo manifieste a S.M. los perjuicios que les causaría el cumplimiento de la provisión del Real y Supremo Consejo de las Indias que dispone se restituyan las tierras a los naturales de Guanabacoa*, Real Consulado, leg. 92, no. 3933.

65. The first mention known to us of iron bases is in the 1766 inventory of Nuestra Señora de Regla, alias El Retiro, mill. See: Fondo Pérez Beato, leg. 14, Biblioteca Nacional. According to José Ricardo O'Farrill, iron rollers were introduced in Cuba around 1783. All these metal parts were in general use by the turn of the century. In 1803 Juan Steegers had a workshop in Havana making bronze bearings and axles. See: *Instancia de D. Juan Steegers sobre la máquina que ha inventado para facilitar el movimiento de los trapiches de ingenios con menos bueyes que los que se usan*, Archivo de la Sociedad Económica de Amigos del País, leg. 15, no. 10, Biblioteca Nacional.

66. The *volvedora* is first mentioned in the contract signed by La Faye in 1793, which says: "The machine itself, without other help, will oblige the cane to pass once more between the first and the superior roller, without going askew either to right or left." (Archivo de la Sociedad Económica de Amigos del País, leg. 57, no. 1, Biblioteca Nacional.) *Volvedoras* began to be installed in new-type mills after 1793. In a report by O'Farrill, José Manuel López, and Juan José Patrón, dated Havana, August 8, 1798, they are described as one of the chief technical improvements introduced in Cuba. See: Real Consulado, leg. 92, no. 3933.

67. *Informe de la Diputación encargada de examinar las proposiciones de D. Guillermo Duncan, sobre establecer en esta Isla la máquina de un molino de viento o de agua, para moler caña*, Memorias de la Real Sociedad Patriótica, vol. I, pp. 107–118.

68. *Espediente relativo a la edificación del primer trapiche de viento instalado por el Sr. D. Pedro Diago*, Real Consulado, leg. 93, no. 3943.

69. "But it was not enough to improve the grinding mill as such: the power of water as a motive force had to be harnessed too. Posterity will be startled to hear that until these times our agriculturists did not take this question seriously. At the end of the last century Havana had several water-trapiche mills on the nearby Río La Chorrera, but agriculture was in such bad shape that they were soon abandoned—either because, not knowing how to save fuel with reverberators, they were compelled by a firewood shortage to demolish such haciendas, or because the rise in land values with the growth of population made it more profitable to subdivide lands than to continue reaping from them such meager fruits. The economization on oxen needed for animal-powered tra-piches—their maintenance during the six non-grinding months when they could not be fed bagasse, and the men required to care for them—was not a weighty enough consideration. Neither the example of neighboring colonies, nor the secure profits clearly obtainable, could induce them to adopt this machine; and before they would include it in their plans the colony had to rise to its present high level. The first trial was ill-fated, as Your Excellency will see below. But finally two water-trapiches have been grinding in this harvest, and others are being installed in areas favored by nature for the purpose." (Real Consulado, leg. 92, no. 3933.)

70. According to the description available, La Faye's horizontal grinding mill differed from the horizontal type on a single axis described by Père Labat. The three rollers, while at different levels, were arranged in a scalene triangle. The typical horizontal grinding mill after 1800 placed each axis at a vertex of an isosceles triangle. The *Informe de los amigos diputados para el reconocimiento de la máquina del señor La Faye* tells us that: ". . . the machine was ingenious, its parts well executed, and above all the horizontal position of its cylinders very advantageous for grinding cane. It was proposed to Sr. La Faye that, in the event of facilities and enough time being unavailable to complete his machine as called for in the agreement, its main components be incorporated in a model, so as to produce a better and more durable trapiche than those we have, even though two yokes of oxen be necessary for its regulated movement and a reasonable product; by which no small economy would be achieved." (*Memorias de la Real Sociedad Económica*, vol. I, p. 106.) La Faye accepted the proposal to improve his horizontal grinding mill and on March 30, 1795, it was first tested, with Governor Luis de Las Casas checking its operation, watch in hand. See: Fondo de la Real Sociedad Económica de Amigos del País, leg. 57, no. 10, Biblioteca Nacional.

71. Real Consulado, leg. 92, no. 3933. This was the first steam engine tried out in Cuba. For the transactions in connection with its purchase, see: Fondo Pérez Beato, leg. 12, Biblioteca Nacional. However, the first specific mention of a steam engine applied to the grinding mill is in 1795. It was offered by an Englishman whose name we do not know. Francisco Lemaour refers to it in a document of October 31, 1795, in which he shows a good knowledge of physics and a familiarity with European machinery. He concludes: ". . . the general use made of it in England . . . proves without much argument its many advantages and few disadvantages: if until now it has not been installed to move grinding mills in our country, this is because none of those who could afford it has persuaded the others of its virtues." (*Proyecto sobre mejorar la máquina de exprimir caña*, Fondo de la Sociedad Económica de Amigos del País, leg. 15, no. 21.)

In 1799 John Steegers offered a steam engine to move grinding mills, and it was first tried out in the Paula Coliseum on September 16, 1800. It consisted of a simple pump which lifted water into a big deposit about 30 feet above the grinding mill; the falling water moved a hydraulic mill of the current type. Thus it was not a steam engine to move the mill but to pump water. See: *Informe de la diputación nombrada para examinar la máquina propuesta por D. Juan Steegers*, Fondo de la Sociedad Económica de Amigos del País, leg. 15, no. 11, Biblioteca Nacional; *Copia del informe dado al Sr. Governador sobre el arquitecto Steegers, quien se ofreció a la construcción de una máquina para moler caña por medio de una bomba de vapor*, Fondo de la Sociedad Económica de Amigos del País, leg. 15, no. 9, Biblioteca Nacional.

72. Real Consulado, leg. 92, no. 3933.

73. As the rest of the same paragraph shows, *hacendados* of the period thought that keeping the workers in a semi-barbaric state was a long-run advantage against possible rebellion: ". . . to accept new inventions, for we know from experience that even the simplest old ones are not used with the practical intelligence they require. Although this ignorance seems at first sight—and indeed is—disadvantageous, it could bring incalculable benefits; but it is not relevant to enter into this discussion." (Real Consulado, leg. 92, no. 3933.)

74. Real Consulado, leg. 93, no. 3943.

75. Sierra, *Método teórico práctico de elaborar azúcar* (1857), p. 4.

76. Pizarro, *Instrucción para el uso y administración de la cal en la elaboración del azúcar* (1847).

77. Montalvo y Castillo, *Tratado general de escuela teórico-práctico para el gobierno de los ingenios de la isla de Cuba en todos sus ramos* (1856).

78. For complete information on this inflationary process, see: Real Consulado, leg. 93, no. 3953.

79. Ramiro Guerra also speaks of the 1796 depression,

invented by the sugarmen. He bases himself on the legal withdrawal of Cuba's right to trade with foreign countries, ignoring the fact that these laws were never observed. He writes: "The almost total paralysis that was produced, together with the fall in sugar prices, caused a painful economic depression to begin in the last year of the Las Casas administration." (Guerra y Sánchez, *Manual de historia de Cuba*, p. 207.) In the so-called "depression," sugar fetched extraordinarily high prices, from 27 and 23 reales up to 31 and 27, and shipments from the port of Havana reached 2,039,609 arrobas, higher than at any previous time. See: *Espediente en que consta la estracción de azúcar en este puerto*, Real Consulado, leg. 71, no. 2764.

80. For detailed "official" reports of maritime traffic out of Havana between 1796 and 1801, with nationality, class, port of origin, cargo, entry, and sailing dates of ships, see: *Espediente sobre la gracia concedida por S.M. al Sr. Conde de Mopox y Jaruco para extraer al Norte de América 900 pipas de aguardiente e introducir en esta Isla su valor en harinas de aquella procedencia*, Real Consulado, leg. 71, no. 2767; *Espediente promovido por D. Antonio Paula en solicitud de permiso para establecer una lonja en esta capital*, Real Consulado, leg. 72, no. 2773; *Espediente sobre tráfico de neutrales en Santiago de Cuba*, Real Consulado, leg. 72, no. 2774; *Espediente promovido por Don Agustín Rodríguez y Santiago Drake sobre establecimiento de una venduta en esta plaza*, Real Consulado, leg. 72, no. 2789; *Espediente sobre fijar las reglas que deben observarse en los protestos de las letras giradas desde esta plaza a la península*, Real Consulado, leg. 72, no. 2794; *Espediente sobre los perjuicios que sufrirá la población y el comercio si se suspende el tráfico con neutrales en Matanzas*, Real Consulado, leg. 72, no. 2792.

81. *Espediente relativo a la oposición profesada por el Consulado de Veracruz a todo cuanto se ha obrado por este de La Habana tanto sobre el comercio con neutrales como sobre la remisión de caudales y frutos preciosos*, Real Consulado, leg. 72, no. 2788.

82. Escribanía de Guerra, leg. 965, exp. 14407.

83. For full documentation on the shady flour business, see: Fondo Pérez Beato, leg. 19, Biblioteca Nacional. The following are particularly significant: *Preguntas que en 29 de agosto de 1798 hubo de hacer el Sr. Don Ignacio Pallares al Sr. Conde de Santa Cruz de Mopox, con las respuestas que a cada pregunta contesta; Correspondencia entre José María Iznardi y Francisco de Arango y Parreño; Cuenta de José María Iznardi con Francisco de Arango y Parreño en La Habana 10 de octubre de 1798; Cuenta de venta, Gastos y Líquidos de 3,200 barriles de harina, recibidos en los buques que expresaremos, por la cuenta del Sr. Conde de Mopox. La Habana, 23 de agosto de 1797. Santa María y Cuesta; Cartas de José María Enrile a Francisco de Arango y Parreño. desde Filadelfia, a 3-3-97; 18-9-97; 3-1-98; 9-1-98; 18-1-98; Contrato entre José María Iznardi y Luis de Noailles, en 19-9-97; Correspondencia entre Arango y Parreño y Carlos Martínez de Irujo. 30-4-97.*

162

84. *Espediente sobre examinar si convendría pedir a S.M. la abolición del Reglamento que prohibe la venta de géneros y efectos por las calles, formado a consecuencia de una solicitud de D. María de los Dolores Fernández Valiente.*

85. See the report in: *Espediente sobre cumplimiento de la Real Orden derogatoria de la providencia general de 18 de noviembre de 1797 acerca del comercio de neutrales*, Real Consulado, leg. 72, no. 2781.

86. Barrera y Domingo, *Reflexiones histórico físico naturales médico quirúrgicas* (1798), p. 138.

87. "As presently organized the Sociedades Patrióticas cannot bring the blessings of which they are susceptible: lacking authority, funds, and stimuli to make their members work, they exert the meagerest influence on the common good: if those which exist in the Peninsula hardly serve to reconstruct, how should we persuade ourselves that the one to be established in Havana can construct such intricate edifices from the ground up? This is not to suggest that their establishment is harmful; but toward the proposed ends it contributes very little or nothing. At best it can serve as an auxiliary to another body to be created with greater deference to the public, moved by more resilient springs; in a word, which would be capable of quickly creating and propagating, by itself or through its agents, the knowledge of physics, chemistry, botany, etc., which we now lack." (Arango, *Obras*, vol. I, pp. 137–138.) For other, even more robust, critiques see ibid., pp. 198 ff.

88. "The Consulados, in my view, were organized very faultily from the outset—that is, without fulfilling the purposes of their establishment—and for this reason have degenerated so much . . ." (Arango, *Obras*, vol. I, p. 209.)

89. The irresponsibility with which Cuba's history has been written is a real disgrace. Historians have proclaimed almost in unison that the Real Consulado was set up at the instance of Arango instead of—as the record shows—in spite of him. This error is forgivable in Friedlaender, who was after all a foreigner—arriving without knowledge of our language, yet leaving us a good manual of economic history full of serious suggestions; but not in those who were born and raised here. If they had merely given close study to Arango's *Obras* (first edition, 1862), they would have had to reach the contrary conclusion. It is clear that he was really proposing to liquidate the Consulado from *Reflexiones sobre la mejor organización del Consulado de La Habana, considerado como Tribunal* (*Obras*, vol. I, pp. 207–221). He wanted to abort the Consulado and the Sociedad Patriótica before they were born: ". . . for in the matter of establishing a Sociedad Patriótica and Consulado, I wanted my Junta to perform the functions of both." (*Obras*, vol. I, p. 198.)

90. See Marx, *Capital*, vol. III.

91. Friedlaender, *Economic History of Cuba.*

92. Arango, *Obras*, vol. I, pp. 162 and 178.

93. *Incidente al Concurso de la Sra. Marquesa la. viuda del Real Socorro, promovido para que se separe de sus bienes el quinto perteneciente al señor su esposo*, Escribanía de Guerra, leg. 806, no. 12282.

94. *Copia sin autorizar del espediente relativo a que los cosecheros de azúcares paguen la alcabala de las partidas menores de dicho fruto que se vendan para el consumo dando la relación jurada de todas las ventas que se verifiquen de la manera que les prescriba la administración de Reales Generales. La Habana, año de 1789*, Intendencia General de Hacienda, leg. 907, no. 16.

95. In view of the high offices he filled, Arango always needed a frontman through whom to conduct his unmentionable deals, and Andrés de Jáuregui filled this role. For example, during the Anglo-Spanish war (1807) Arango and Valiente, both in top official jobs, maintained their commercial relations with the English. The London house that looked after their business was Tunno & Loughercan. Direct trade being impossible, they worked through the United States, where Thomas Tunno, brother of the London firm's director, was installed. The middleman in Havana was Drake, Crawford & Co., and the signer of the agreements with Drake was Jáuregui. The transactions came to light when Arango reneged on his promises to Tunno, and Tunno sent him an explosive letter through Drake, who translated it into Spanish. Tunno wrote: "I protest that had you then told me Mr. Jáuregui or anyone else in Havana was interested in this, not one crate of sugar would have been shippped in my name . . . Permit me to ask you in the simple language of truth whether in Havana or anywhere else there has ever been a deal of this nature—that is, a merchant lending you his name as a cover . . ."
   Also mixed up in all this was a shipment of blacks. The affair was so scandalous that Arango, despite his irascible character, replied courteously and paid up. The whole development of these deals can be studied in: Fondo Pérez Beato, leg. 15, Biblioteca Nacional.

96. *Acuerdo de la Junta de Gobierno del Real Consulado* (1796).

97. This is one case of the already mentioned duplication of activities, for it was also undertaken by the Real Consulado. See: *Espediente sobre traducir al castellano las obras francesas de Dutrone de la Couture y Corbeaux acerca del cultivo de la caña*, Real Consulado, leg. 92, no. 3925.

98. "Unhappily there are only vestigial remains of this Junta. For some time it has lacked the firm prop of a permanent executive officer and a chairman who would also be a permanent spokesman—men honored by the Sovereign and authorized by him to put an energetic case on issues arising." (Arango, *Obras*, vol. II, p. 620.)

99. O'Gavan, *Observaciones sobre la suerte de los negros del Africa* (1821).

100. As with the rest of Cuba sugar history, all the activity of the Sociedad Económica was chronicled by the *hacendados* themselves. Undoubtedly it was an outstanding institution as a center of conformity and diffusion of producer-ideology—which is to say, the ideology of the period's dominant class. It had lofty virtues but its panegyrists have raised it to a category it never occupied, since its activity was strictly limited to the interests of one social class. Its history, as usual, has been written without any mention of sugar, which was its basic motive power. Raimundo Cabrera wrote of it: "Since the Sociedad Económica's foundation, the face of Cuba has changed: the poor and uncultured colony, reduced to an appendage of a military trading agency, charted the course of the peoples who owe their growth and development to popular education, intelligent work, and improved methods." (Cited in Ortiz, *La Hija Cubana del iluminismo*, 1943.)
   Cabrera's words are true provided one interprets them backward. That is, the foundation and creative work of the Sociedad Económica were possible because the face of Cuba had changed. For another idyllic interpretation of the Sociedad see: *Homenaje a la benemérita Sociedad Económica de Amigos del País de La Habana* (1936).

101. *Libro diario del ingenio La Purísima Concepción. Año 1799*, Miscelánea de Libros, no. 12588, Archivo Nacional.

102. Topographical map of the island of Cuba, 1835. Vives' map thus identifies El Cangre and San José mills.

103. Espada y Landa, *Memoria reservada sobre diezmos*, Papeles de Vidal Morales y Morales, Miscelánea, vol. V, Biblioteca Nacional.

104. The Tinguaro mill was founded in 1839 by Francisco Diago, son of the big Galician merchant-*hacendado* Pedro Diago. Francisco was a relative of the Aldamas and a typical representative of Cuba's liberal bourgeoisie.

105. *Carta de Juan Maldonado Barnuevo a S.M. acerca del traslado de la Catedral de Santiago de Cuba a La Habana, los azúcares, diezmos y otros particulares. Enero 10 de 1602.* Published in: *Papeles existentes en el Archivo General de Indias relativos a Cuba y muy particularmente a La Habana* (1931).

106. *Espediente instructivo para suavizar la suerte de los negros esclavos*, Real Consulado, leg. 150, no. 7405.

107. Barrera y Domingo, *Reflexiones histórico físico . . .* , p. 173.

108. *Informe firmado por José Ricardo O'Farrill, Juan José*

Paunón y Gabriel Raymundo de Azcárate en 5 de julio de 1799, Real Consulado, leg. 93, no. 3938.

109. *Espediente sobre eximir del pago de Diezmos a los primeros ingenios que se establezcan según el método extranjero y a todos los frutos de esta Isla*, Real Consulado, leg. 101, no. 4330.

110. Duque de Estrada, *Explicación de la Doctrina Cristiana acomodada a la capacidad de los negros bozales* (1823). There was an edition in 1797. The original manuscript is in the Biblioteca Nacional manuscript section.

111. For complete information on the uprising in the Count de Casa Bayona's mill, see: *Representación extendida por Don Diego Miguel de Moya y firmada por casi todos los dueños de ingenios de la jurisdicción, en enero 19 de 1790*, Real Consulado, leg. 150, no. 7405.

112. Delmonte, *Lista cronológica de los libros inéditos e impresos que se han escrito sobre la Isla de Cuba* (1882).

113. "Religion must be taught and the sanctity of Sunday preserved. When letting the people out on Sundays the overseer reads one of the three mysteries and two pages of the Christian Doctrine Catechism. The three mysteries are the Trinity, the Incarnation, and the Eucharist. At evening prayers some parts of the Mass, in which the Christian must participate as a just tribute to his Maker for the daily blessings he receives, are recited. The parts of the Mass are: making the sign of the cross, the Our Father and Ave María, the Credo, the Commandments, the Sacraments, the Articles of Faith, the Corporal Works of Mercy, Mortal Sins, general Confession and Act of Contrition with the 'Blessed and Praised Be.' The best method of teaching and worship is to say two of these every night together with the Ave Maria and Our Father and Bendito. In this way managements will fulfill their obligation of conscience and responsibility. Reading a chapter of the Saints of the Gospel, and a brief explanation of the Mass, would be highly gratifying to the Supreme Being, since He desires in His vineyard many laborers for whom He promises a rich reward in the other life." (Montalvo y Castillo, *Tratado general*, pp. 33–34; see also: *Punto 13 Trata sobre la religión*, pp. 47–48.)

114. *Informe del Síndico del Real Consulado en 22 de abril de 1835. Espediente sobre los perjuicios que ocasionan las tabernas situadas a inmediaciones de las fincas de Campo*, Real Consulado, leg. 78, no. 3135.

The Junta de Información propounded the same thesis but without the smallest reservation, speaking of the "indispensable necessity to infuse the religious spirit not only in the slave but in the free man; for it is the sole means of making the former bear his plight with resignation and be humble, industrious, and respectful . . ."

Nicolás Azcárate opposed this concept of religion, insisting that if the gospel were preached according to the principles of Jesus Christ, it would be against slavery and would waken aspirations to freedom. Pastor supported him, arriving at the conclusion that Christianity was opposed to slavery and hence should not be taught in the sugarmills. San Martín took the contrary view, that there was no conflict between slavery and Christianity. He said: "Render unto Caesar the things that are Caesar's. Knowledge of Christianity makes the slaves more submissive." (Sédano y Cruzat, *Cuba desde 1850 a 1873* [1873].)

115. Perpiñá, *El Camagüey* (1889), p. 355.

116. Machado y Gómez, *Cuba y la emancipación de sus esclavos* (1864), p. 45.

117. *Informe del Marqués de Cárdenas de Montehermoso*, Real Consulado, leg. 93, no. 3938.

118. Arango, *Obras*, vol. II, p. 172.

119. Real Consulado, leg. 93, no. 3938.

120. ". . . to give a lone man the [corpse] of a woman to carry along sometimes remote trails is to expose him to the commission of excesses." (Ibid.)

121. "In the harvest season the standstill day becomes Sunday since, as has been said before, sugar production is not subject to natural weeks . . . In the case of several contiguous or nearby mills, their managements could suitably come to an agreement that each slave crew should take Sunday on a different day of the week . . ." (*Cartilla práctica del manejo de ingenios o fincas destinadas a producir azúcar, escrita por un Montuño* [1862], p. 70.)

122. Real Consulado, leg. 93, no. 3938.

123. Ibid.

124. *Espediente sobre disminuir los días festivos en nuestros campos*, Real Consulado, leg. 94, no. 3960.

125. Intendencia General de Hacienda, leg. 7, no. 14.

126. Real Consulado, leg. 101, no. 4330.

127. Ibid.

128. Espada y Landa, *Memoria reservada sobre diezmos*, Papeles de Vidal y Morales, Miscelánea, vol. V, Biblioteca Nacional.

129. Calvo y O'Farrill, *Memoria sobre los medios que convendría adoptar para que tuviese La Habana los caminos necesarios* (1795).

130. All the correspondence between the Bishop and the Real Consulado is in the voluminous cited file of the Real Consulado, leg. 101, no. 4330.

131. When he ousted the producers from the Junta de Diezmos, Bishop Espada accused the Real Consulado of "overstepping its prerogatives," invading those of the tithe system. Although we conclude our narration with

the Real Orden of August 2, 1806, the Real Consulado file with further details of the church-sugarmill imbroglio does not end till 1832. See: Real Consulado, leg. 101, no. 4330.

132. O'Gavan, *Observaciones sobre la suerte de los negros de Africa*. As an example of other publications of this type appearing from this date, see: *Reglas para los hacendados que aspiren a proporcionar a sus esclavos la instrucción religiosa* (1855).

133. Caballero described himself as "an echo" of Nicolás Calvo; and Calvo, as we have seen, was the period's most important sugar ideologist after Arango. See: Caballero, *Escritos Varios*, vol. I, p. 187.

134. Groethuysen, *Formation of Bourgeois Consciousness in France During the 18th Century* (1943), p. 431 (Spanish edition). For the Marxist analysis of the same phenomenon see Engels, *Socialism: Utopian and Scientific*.

135. Ibid., p. 57.

136. Ibid., pp. 414 and 413.

137. Arango, *Obras*, vol. II, p. 6.

138. Scorn for purchased nobility grew along with bourgeois consciousness. In Arango and Calvo, the sugarocracy's first two ideologists, the sentiment was equally strong. Arango wrote: ". . . honors should only be conferred in recognition of talent and virtue, not for lineage." (Notes to *Discurso sobre fomento de la agricultura*.) Arango was the only noble whose title was not bought but was conferred by the King. The title of Marquis de la Gratitud was given him in his last years when the French bourgeoisie was likewise ennobling itself. Calvo declined titles; and it is symptomatic that Caballero should have written the article *Nobleza mal entendida*. (See: *Papel Periódico de La Habana*, March 17, 1791.) Statements against the purchase of nobility were continuous through the nineteenth century; the first long article on the subject appeared in *El Censor Universal* (Havana), Sunday, June 30, 1811.

139. See innumerable references to this in: *Correspondencia reservada del General Don Miguel Tacón con el Gobierno de Madrid, 1834–1836* in the Biblioteca Nacional manuscript collection. This remarkable documentation, to be published with a preface by Juan Pérez de la Riva, provides the first opportunity to study the true significance of this period from the historical literature.

140. Delmonte, *Centón epistolario de Domingo Delmonte, 1923–1926*.

141. Marx, *Capital*, vol. I, p. 605.

142. Arango, *Obras*, vol. I, p. 110.

143. Ibid., vol. II, pp. 145–187.

144. Ibid., p. 172.

145. Heineccio, *Elementos de derecho Romano* (1826). The concluding words of Saco's translator's preface are signed "The Translator."

146. Real Consulado, leg. 94, no. 3954.

147. The bourgeois concept of property in the means of production was applied to the slave because he formed a part of fixed capital. This is one of the sugarocracy's typical ideological contradictions, resulting from production of merchandise with slave labor. Thus Arango could write, referring to slaves: "Can a finger be placed on the sanctuary of property acquired in conformity with law; of property whose inviolability is one of the great objects of any political association, and one of the first articles of any constitution?" (Arango, *Obras*, vol. 88, p. 151.)

148. See Marx, *Capital*, vol. I.

149. Arango, *Obras*, vol. II, p. 499.

150. Rafael Cowley described José Estévez y Cantal as "the unhappy Estévez," and Valdés Rodríguez wrote of the great afflictions he suffered. Luis Felipe Le Roy has noted these two references without explaining them. Estévez was a man who studied seriously but could not offer chemical miracles to the *hacendados*. We have seen how Calvo, Arango, and others on the Sociedad Patriótica's commission to establish a chair of chemistry agreed that chemistry was the science of making sugar. When Estévez returned from his studies with a broad range of knowledge which did not, however, at once raise production, the Real Consulado felt frustrated. The general belittlement of the Cuban scientist's activity from that moment on embittered his life. In 1828 Casaseca took the opposite line, dedicating himself almost exclusively to sugar and becoming the producers' scientific darling. They wanted not a chemist but a sugar technician. For a remarkable study of Estévez, see Le Roy's documented introduction to Estévez, *Trabajos científicos* (1951).

151. *Espediente formado en virtud de oficio del presidente de la Sección de Educación de la Real Sociedad Patriótica, participando el proyecto de establecer una Cátedra de Economía Política en esta ciudad, y solicita para ello la cooperación de este Cuerpo*, Real Consulado, leg. 97, no. 4085; *Espediente sobre el proyecto del Ldo. Pedro José Rodríguez de establecer una Cátedra de Economía Política en la Real Universidad de esta ciudad*, Real Consulado, leg. 99, no. 4187.

152. On this point we may repeat what we wrote in our study of Saco: "Annexationism, the Siboney [inhabitants before the Spanish arrival] cult, adoration of foreign heroes—three manifestations of the same spiritual hollowness, if not the same sordid interests. They correspond with the moment when, the old Creole hierarchies having been obliterated, Cuba's sugarocracy placed its economic

security above the spiritual structure of the nation. The contradictions of the sugar regime, the slave-owning liberalism of the *hacendado*, formed a nucleus of negative ideas based not on what should be but on what he did not want to be. Hence there was a constant flight from reality. And hence the economically motivated annexationists—the ones who gave the movement its power—were joined by a large group of idealists who were frustrated by the semi-plantation reality and the absence of positive values." (Manuel Moreno Fraginals, *José Antonio Saco*, pp. 63–64.)

153. The distribution of the Havana mills in 1776 may be seen on the map of the Havana jurisdiction, now in the Archivo de Indias and partially published in: *Planos de ciudades iberoamericanas y Filipinas existentes en el Archivo de Indias* (1951), no. 69.

154. Estimate based on tithe books in the Archivo Nacional. See Part 4 of this book.

155. *Libro para la cuenta y razón de los valores y gastos del Diezmo del ramo de azúcares del Partido de Río Blanco correspondiente al año de 1817, puesto en Administración al cargo de Don Bernardino San Martín. Por el quatrenio de 1817 a 1820*, Miscelánea de Libros, no. 3233, Archivo Nacional.

156. *Libro para la cuenta y razón de los valores y gastos del ramo de azúcares del Partido de Guanajay correspondiente al año de 1817, puesto en administración al cargo de Don Bernardino San Martín*, Miscelánea de Libros, no. 2158, Archivo Nacional.

157. Martín, *Esquema elemental de temas sobre la caña de azúcar como factor topoclimático de la geografía social de Cuba* (1944), pp. 24–27.

158. *Espediente promovido por el Ayuntamiento de Matanzas sobre los medios que pueden conducir al fomento de la población y comercio- Representación a S.M.*, Real Consulado, leg. 2, no. 106.

159. In 1827 the Matanzas jurisdiction had 111 mills producing a total of 1,733,000 arrobas of purged sugar; in 1829 it had 141, and two years later, 203. See: *Cuadro estadístico de la siempre fiel isla de Cuba, correspondiente al año de 1827, precedido de una descripción histórica, física, geográfica y acompañada de cuantas notas son conducentes para la ilustración del cuadro* (1829).

160. Matanzas developed so fast that in 1846 there were 373 sugarmills within the boundaries of the present province. This enormous growth dislocated the territory's political divisons and required the creation of Cárdenas Tenencia, carved from the former Matanzas jurisdiction. In the big development in the center toward Palmillas, Nueva Bermeja (Colón) was founded. We should add that of the mills recorded in the 1846 census as belonging to the Güines jurisdiction, thirty-three were Matanzas mills of the Güines-Bemba line of expansion. See: *Cuadro*

estadístico de la siempre fiel isla de Cuba correspondiente al año de 1846.

161. Data from *Anuario Azucarero de Cuba* (1960).

162. Arozarena, *Informe presentado a la Junta de Gobierno del Real Consulado de la siempre fiel isla de Cuba* (1828).

163. *Espediente formado para pedir noticias estadísticas a las diputaciones de lo interior con objeto de conceder habilitación a algunos puertos menores de esta Isla*, Real Consulado, leg. 71, no. 2751. See also: Real Consulado, leg. 93, no. 3953.

164. *Informe de la Diputación de la ciudad de Trinidad de la Isla de Cuba a la Junta de Gobierno del Real Consulado. Trinidad, 1⁰ de diciembre de 1795*, Real Consulado, leg. 71, no. 2751.

165. Echegoyen, *Fabricación de azúcar*, p. 42.

166. Ely, *Comerciantes cubanos del siglo XIX* (1960).

167. Topographical map of the island of Cuba (1835).

168. *Informe de Francisco Rodríguez en julio 3 de 1807*, Real Consulado, leg. 93, no. 3953.

169. *Informe de Tomás Padilla, en junio 21 de 1807*, Real Consulado, leg. 93, no. 3953.

170. *Contra Don Juan de Echeverría por fraude de Alcavala en la venta de un trapiche a Don Juan Muñoz. Octubre de 1776*, Intendencia General de Hacienda, leg. 618, no. 11.

171. *Informe del Teniente Gobernador de Santa Clara en agosto 31 de 1807*, Real Consulado, leg. 93, no. 3953.

172. Betancourt, *Historia de Puerto Príncipe* (1845?); Torres Lasqueti, *Colección de datos históricos-geográficos y estadísticos de Puerto Príncipe y su jurisdicción* (1888). We note Lasqueti's work because it adds some interesting data to Betancourt's writings. Except for these small portions, his book is a barefaced plagiarism of Betancourt.

173. *Respuesta dada por el Diputado de la Villa de Puerto Príncipe arreglada a las 27 preguntas que le hace el Real Consulado de La Habana en 31 de octubre de 1795*, Real Consulado, leg. 71, no. 2751. See also: Real Consulado, leg. 93, no. 3953.

174. *Informe de Ignacio Zarragoitía y Jáuregui fechado en Puerto Príncipe, a marzo 5 de 1805*, Real Consulado, leg. 93, no. 3953.

175. *Espediente sobre fomentar la agricultura y comercio de Puerto Príncipe*, Real Consulado, leg. 2, no. 103.

176. On January 21, 1843, Joaquín de Agüero y Agüero freed his slaves Gregorio, Victoria, Juan de la Cruz, Josefa, Felipe, and Tomás. The slave traders' reaction was so heated that they induced the Governor to make an exhaustive probe of the motives behind this abolitionist move. "El Lugareño" wrote to Domingo Delmonte in 1843: "The young man's position is most dubious. The

General had them brought in for interrogation . . . He not only has the government, but many of his countrymen, against him." (Delmonte, *Centón epistolario.* . . .)

177. Concha, *Memoria dirigida al Exmo. Sr. D. Francisco Serrano y Domínguez, Capitán General de la isla de Cuba* (1861).

178. *Informe de Miguel de Aguilera fechado en Holguín a 30 de junio de 1807*, Real Consulado, leg. 93, no. 3953; *Espediente sobre habilitación del puerto de Gibara*, Real Consulado, leg. 74, no. 2823.

179. Calvo y O'Farrill, *Memoria sobre los medios . . .*

180. Jáuregui, *Memoria sobre proporcionar arbitrios para la construcción de caminos en esta jurisdicción* (1795). The other published memorandum is Calvo's, cited in the previous note. These two bibliographical rarities, and the unpublished ones by Alonso Benigno Muñoz de Campos, the Marquis de Arcos, Juan Antonio Morejón, and La Faye, can be seen in: *Espediente sobre los medios que convendrá adoptar para la construcción de los caminos necesarios*, Real Consulado, leg. 115, no. 4844.

181. *Espediente sobre composición de la calzada de Guadalupe comenzada por el Ayuntamiento de esta Ciudad (La Habana)*; *Espediente sobre composición de la calzada del Horcón*, Real Consulado, leg. 115, no. 4846.

182. *Espediente instruído á excitación del Sr. Síndico Don Francisco de Arango con el fin de que se efectúe el antiguo proyecto del Sr. Conde Macuriges de abrir un canal que reuniese los ríos de los Güines y de la Prensa*, Real Consulado, leg. 11, no. 4844. See also: Thrasher, *Nota adicional sobre el canal de los Güines;* Von Humboldt, *Ensayo político sobre la isla de Cuba.* Güines being for a long time Cuba's basic sugar zone, the greatest road-building efforts were logically made there—among them the enormous movement of earth across the Candela hills. See: *Espediente sobre la composición del mal paso de las lomas de La Candela en el camino de Güines*, Real Consulado, leg. 116, no. 4868.

183. Saco, *Memorias sobre caminos en la isla de Cuba* (1830).

184. Saco, *La supresión del tráfico de esclavos africanos en la isla de Cuba, examinada con relación a su agricultura y a su seguridad* (1845), p. 29.

185. Carrera y Heredia, *Plano general de los ferrocarriles construidos, en construcción y proyectados desde La Habana hasta El Júcaro* (1846); Cuba, Dirección de Obras Públicas, *Isla de Cuba. Con el estado de los ferrocarriles, telégrafos y faros* (1859).

186. Sugar was also the mother of the Puerto Príncipe railroad. Its promoter, Gaspar Betancourt Cisneros, wrote to Delmonte on September 18, 1836: "Havana is the declared enemy of all progress in our province, because those idiots think our sugar will strangle Havana's. But just the opposite is true: the only way to avoid the collapse of all is that all should produce, and that Cuban sugar be so plentiful and cheap that our rivals will be forced to leave the field to us." (Delmonte, *Centón epistolario.* . . .)

187. *El Sr. Ignacio de Cárdenas y Cárdenas propone costear la construcción de una casilla telegráfica en el punto de Santa Quiteria que es el intermedio de las estaciones de la Macagua y Sierra Morena*, Real Consulado, leg. 36, no. 1591; *Espediente sobre rematar en pública subasta la contrata de suministro de los efectos y artículos necesarios para el consumo de las estaciones telegráficas*, Real Consulado, leg. 36, no. 1599; *Espediente relativo a la propuesta del Administrador del Camino de hierro de esta ciudad para hacerse cargo de la conservación y entretenimiento de la línea telegráfica*, Real Consulado, leg. 36, no. 1583; *Carta telegráfica de la siempre fiel isla de Cuba* (1865).

188. *Espediente sobre edificaciones del empedrado de esta ciudad y conservación de un piso provisional promovidos por este cuerpo con motivo de consulta hecha por la ciudad sobre estinción o limitación de carreteras*, Real Consulado, leg. 77, no. 3016.

189. *Espediente promovido por Don Blas Morán para la introducción de carretas que, con solo el tiro de un caballo cargan cuatro cajas de azúcar*, Real Consulado, leg. 101, no. 4281; *Espediente sobre el proyecto de sustituir carretas de un buey a los carretones que se usan para el tráfico interior y esterior de esta ciudad*, Real Consulado, leg. 78, no. 3103; *Espediente promovido por varios hacendados sobre la prohibición acordada por el Ayuntamiento para que las carretas conductoras de frutos entren en esta ciudad*, Real Consulado, leg. 77, no. 3038; *Espediente promovido por varios hacendados, solicitando permiso para que las carretas que traen frutos entren en la ciudad*, Real Consulado, leg. 77, no. 3023.

190. *Espediente relativo a varias composiciones ejecutadas en el muelle de este puerto en año próximo pasado*, Real Consulado, leg. 85, no. 3459.

191. In 1842 the number of trips that sugar, alcohol, and molasses carts had to make within the Havana area was estimated at 700,000. Cantero wrote of them: "Apart from the unbearable noise and confusion they caused in the streets, they did considerable damage to the paving . . . they churned up quantities of mud as they moved . . ."
   In 1843 the "Regla warehouses" began to be built, the first being 135 x 80 yards and completed in 1844. It had a 50,000-box capacity. Two more were built, one of the same size and one of 135 x 100 yards, and a fourth (171 x 100) was put up in 1851. The final capacity of all these was 180,000 boxes. From 1851 on, more than a million boxes a year were moved, in addition to muscovado hogsheads and barrels of molasses. In 1855 construction of the San José warehouses in the Havana area was initiated. Similar expansion occurred in the ports of Matanzas, Cienfuegos,

Trinidad, and Sagua. (See: Cantero, *Los ingenios*, 1857.)

192. Rodríguez Ferrer, *Naturaleza y civilización de la grandiosa isla de Cuba*, 1876–77, vol. I, pp. 681–765.

193. Zayas, *Ingenios de fabricar azúcar*, p. 33. In *Memorias de la Sociedad Patriótica de La Habana*, May 1837.

194. Sagra, *Cuba en 1860* (1861), p. 69.

195. *Espediente instruido con los antecedentes del recurso dirigido a las Cortes generales y extraordinarias sobre las reservas hechas en la Junta de Maderas del 22 de junio de 1812 por el Ingeniero Don Diego de la Parra contra el decreto que restituye a los particulares el dominio de los arbolados,* Real Consulado, leg. 94, no. 3955.

196. *Espediente sobre cumplimiento de la Real Orden de 5 de octubre último que previene el fomento del cultivo de la cera en esta Isla,* Real Consulado, leg. 92, no. 3927.

197. Sagra, *Cuba en 1860*, p. 67.

198. Study of Cuban toponymy initiated by the Instituto de Geografía de la Academia de Ciencias (in preparation, data supplied by Professor Juan Pérez de la Riva).

199. O'Farrill, *Memoria sobre bosques, Anales de la Real Junta de Fomento y Sociedad Económica de La Habana*, vol. IV, (1851), p. 236; Mopox y Jaruco, *Ruina de nuestros preciosos montes, necesidad de reponerlos, Memorias de la Sociedad Económica de Amigos del País*, (1843), p. 232.

200. Pizarro y Gardín, *Reposición de los bosques que se consumen anualmente en el combustible de los ingenios, Memorias de la Sociedad Económica de Amigos del País* (1846), p. 373.

201. *Gaceta de La Habana*, March 2, 1848, and March 10, 1848.

202. Sagra, *Cuba en 1860*, Chapter 1.

203. *The State of the Sugar-Trade* (1747).

204. Marx, *Capital*, vol. III.

205. José de Arango, *Jozo, Discurso dirigido al Excmo. Sr. Gobernador y Capitán General, Memorias de la Sociedad Económica de Amigos del País* (1817), pp. 264–273.

206. *Espediente formado para contratar la leña necesaria de las máquinas del camino de hierro,* Real Consulado, leg. 38, no. 1664.

207. These are the final words in Sagra's chapter on forests in *Cuba en 1860*.

208. This is a traditional folksong, transmitted orally, collected by Professor José Sainz Triana of the Universidad Central de Las Villas.

209. After the late-eighteenth-century awakening of Havana's sugarocracy came a period of economic and political subjection which left its mark on historical literature. With the ruin of the slave-owning producers, Cuba was an economic and then a cultural colony until 1959. This explains why after more than a century of pride in being "the world's sugarbowl," not one sugar history has been written by a Cuban. Furthermore, all the so-called historians have worked from data offered by and copied from four foreigners—von Humboldt, Pezuela, Sagra, and Queipo. None of these was a specialist in sugar problems —all went into this field as a sideline to much more general studies. The ignorance displayed in sugar studies throughout this century suggests the extent of bad faith and intellectual incapacity. A class holding to the political slogan "Without sugar, no country" knew very well that without sugar Cuban history could not be written. Excepted from this judgment are Ramiro Guerra, Julio Le Riverend, and Raúl Cepero Bonilla, but even these three accepted the false statistics of Pezuela and von Humboldt, partly invalidating their intellectual efforts. The generally used sources for sugar studies were: von Humboldt, *Ensayo político sobre la isla de Cuba*; Pezuela, *Diccionario geográfico, estadístico, histórico de la isla de Cuba* (1863); Sagra, *Cuba en 1860*; Vázquez Queipo, *Informe fiscal sobre fomento de la población blanca en la isla de Cuba y emancipación progresiva de la esclava* (1845). As secondary sources for specific aspects, most historians have used: Cantero, *Los ingenios*; Rebello, *Estados relativos a la producción azucarera de la isla de Cuba* (1860); García de Arboleya, *Manual de la isla de Cuba* (1859). With the exception of Rebello, these are all secondhand.

210. Referring to the source used in it, Arango writes this note on von Humboldt's work: "That estimate (which was not made by the man who signed it) cannot apply today; and with this in mind I must put on record what I previously omitted." The document to which Arango refers is: *Demostración de Don José Ignacio Echegoyen sobre Diezmos. Espediente sobre ecsimir de pago de diezmos a los primeros ingenios que se establezcan según el método extranjero y a todos los frutos de esta Isla,* Real Consulado, leg. 101, no. 4330. Echegoyen was sugarmaster of La Ninfa mill and a man much in the confidence of Arango. See: Echegoyen, *Fabricación de azúcar*.

211. Average production capacities are calculated on the basis of the following sources: For 1760, see Miscelánea de Libros, no. 2646, Archivo Nacional. For 1792, see Intendencia General de Hacienda, leg. 7, no. 14. For 1804, see *Libro para la cuenta y razón de los valores y gastos del Diezmo del Partido de Río Blanco, etc.,* Miscelánea de Libros, no. 3233; for Cano district, M.L. 3275; for Managua district, M.L. 3022; for Guanabacoa district, M.L. 1921; for Güines district, M.L. 1470; for Guanajay district, M.L. 2158; for Matanzas district, M.L. 1894; for Segunda Casa district, excepting Tapate district, M.L. 3226; for Segunda Casa, excepting Juanelo district, M.L. 12992; for Segunda Casa, excepting Santiago district, M.L. 3573; for Segunda Casa,

excepting Güira district, M.L. 3272. For 1827: *Cuadro estadístico de la siempre fiel isla de Cuba* (1829). For 1860: Rebello, *Estados relativos a la producción azucarera*. . . .

212. Villa-Urrutia, *Informe presentado a la Real Junta de Fomento de Agricultura y de Comercio de esta isla* (1843).

213. Characteristics of the different cane varieties have been taken from these works: Agete y Piñero, *Apuntes sobre la evolución de las variedades de caña en Cuba (1796–1940)*, *Memoria de la décimocuarta conferencia anual de la Asociación de Técnicos Azucareros de Cuba* (1940), pp. 11–261; Agete y Piñero, *La caña de azúcar en Cuba* (1945); Artschwager, *Sugar Cane* (1958); Deerr, *Cane Sugar* (1911); Delteil, *La canne à sucre* (1884); Evans, *Manual del hacendado azucarero* (1849); Kerr, *A Practical Treatise on the Cultivation of the Sugar Cane* (1851); Reynoso, *Ensayo sobre el cultivo de la caña de azúcar* (1864); Richardson Porter, *Naturaleza y propiedades de la caña de azúcar con reglas prácticas para la mejora de su cultivo y la elaboración de sus productos* (1832); Wray, *The Practical Sugar Planter* (1848).

214. Landa, *El administrador de ingenio* (1866).

215. Dau, *Ingenios sin esclavos* (1837).

216. Deerr, *Cane Sugar*; Artschwager, *Sugar Cane*.

217. Sicard, *Monographie de la canne à sucre de la Chine dite sorgho à sucre* (1861); Stewart, *Sorghum and Its Products* (1857); Stansbury, *Chinese Sugar Cane and Sugar Making* (1857). Concern about sorghum also reached Cuba. See: Lovering, *Observaciones y experimentos sobre el sorghum saccharatum o azúcar de caña china*, *Memorias de la Sociedad Económica de Amigos del País* (1858), p. 49.

218. *Espediente promovido por el Sr. Conde de Saguins Vasieur, solicitando la cooperación de la Junta para efectuar el proyecto de traer a esta Isla nueva semilla de la caña de Otahití*, Real Consulado, leg. 95, no. 3994; *Espediente promovido por el Sr. Teniente de Síndico para que haga traer de los EE.UU. alguna semilla de la caña de Otahití, por haber degenerado la existente en el País*, Real Consulado, leg. 95, no. 3993. The only successful expedition was that of Tomás de Juara y Soler, who ordered Otaheite cane from the Pacific Islands. The seed arrived in fifteen boxes via Tahiti–California–Panama–Colón–New Orleans–Havana. The voyage took four months. Much of the seed was planted in his Conchita mill, producing white cane similar to what he already had. See: *Carta de Tomás de Juara y Soler a Alvaro Reynoso, desde La Habana, 23 de noviembre de 1862, Cartas de Alvaro Reynoso*, vol. I, Biblioteca Nacional.

219. Reynoso, *Ensayo sobre el cultivo de la caña de azúcar*, pp. 24 and 26.

220. Ibid., p. 39.

221. The data for the end of the eighteenth century are from: *Exposición que D. Joseph Ricardo O'Farrill hace a la Sociedad del método observado en la Isla de Cuba, en el cultivo de la caña dulce y la elaboración de su zugo*. For the 1850s, see: Reynoso, *Ensayo sobre el cultivo de la caña de azúcar*; Landa, *El administrador de ingenio*.

222. *Espediente relativo a la communicación del Sr. Teniente de Gobernador de Cárdenas sobre la adopción de medidas para evitar los frecuentes incendios que ocurren en los campos de aquella jurisdicción*, Real Consulado, leg. 80, no. 3266.

223. Reynoso, *Ensayo sobre el cultivo de la caña de azúcar*, p. 45. The mill to which Reynoso refers is Las Cañas, as is clear from his travel notebook (which remains among the documents of the Sociedad Económica).

224. O'Farrill, *Exposición*, p. 128.

225. Reynoso, *Ensayo sobre el cultivo de la caña de azúcar*.

226. Prejudice against the plough continued up to the time of Reynoso. The Sociedad Económica was obliged to publish a series of studies showing the advantages of this kind of planting. See: Bella, *Labores profundas y arados de subsuelo*, *Memorias de la Sociedad Económica de Amigos del País*, (1863), p. 45; Cagigas, *Utilidades comprobadas del uso del arado en los ingenios*, Informe a la Diputación de la Sociedad Económica en la Villa de Güines, (1842), p. 341; Reynoso, *Sembradora de nueva invención* (1862), p. 354.

227. Reynoso, *Ensayo sobre el cultivo de la caña de azúcar*, p. 519.

228. Reynoso, *Verhandeling over de cultuur van suikerriet* (1865).

229. Montes de Oca, *Tratado de agricultura especial sobre la preparación de terrenos y las labores de los mismos concernientes a la siembra de caña* (1903).

230. Dumont, *Guía de ingenios que trata de la caña de azúcar desde su origen, de su cultivo y de la manera de elaborar sus jugos* (1832).

231. Casaseca, *Memoria sobre el rendimiento en caña y azúcar de los ingenios de esta isla y sobre el estado actual de la elaboración*, *Espediente sobre tareas del Instituto de Investigaciones Químicas*, Real Consulado, leg. 95, no. 4027. This memorandum was published in the records of the Real Junta de Fomento and the Sociedad Patriótica, but we have preferred to work from the original manuscript since the printed edition shows several differences in the figures. Converting to tons per hectare, these figures are:

San Narciso	95
Urumea	90
Santa Elena	89
Alava	84
Ponina	70
Belfast	30

232. Both the Macagua and Las Cañas mill figures appear in: Pimienta, *Los dos primeros libros del manual práctico de la*

fabricación del azúcar de caña (1881). Converting to tons per hectare, the figures are:

Yield in tons per hectare	Number of canefields	Percent
Less than 40	7	4.4
41 to 50	9	5.7
51 to 60	38	23.8
61 to 70	38	23.8
71 to 80	17	10.7
81 to 90	16	10.0
91 to 100	12	7.5
101 to 110	13	8.2
111 to 120	7	4.4
Over 121	2	1.5

233. Converting to tons per hectare:

Plantings in cleared forests	103 to 120
Good lands	77 to 102
Average lands	60 to 76
Ordinary lands	47 to 59

234. Sánchez de Arregui, *Proyecto de sociedad para refaccionar ingenios y anticipar fondos a los Sres. Hacendados* (1876); *Anuario azucarero de Cuba.* (1957).

235. *Cartilla práctica del manejo de ingenios o fincas destinadas a producir azúcar.*

236. According to Andres de Zayas, a robust Negro should cut 800 to 1,000 arrobas of cane a day, a less capable one 700 to 800 arrobas, and the average for men and women cutters should be 500 to 600. Zayas, *Observaciones sobre los ingenios, Memorias de la Sociedad Económica de Amigos del País,* (1835), pp. 174–175.

237. ". . . and one or two *macuencos* to pick up the stray cane." (*Cartilla práctica*). ". . . so that except for two or three blacks cleaning the trains, and the *macuencos* and sick who beat and stir the sugar in the driers . . ." (Suárez y Romero, *Ingenios,* published in *Cuadros de Costumbres* [1856]).

238. Oliván, *Informe a la Junta de Gobierno del Real Consulado y Agricultura y Comercio de la siempre fiel isla de Cuba* (1831); Dau, "Bueyes en los ingenios," *Diario de La Habana,* April 13, 1832. See also: Dau, *Ingenios sin esclavos,* pp. 10–11.

239. Ibid.

240. The camel-importing project was approved by Real Orden of May 24, 1833, which conceded their duty-free entry for ten years. The curious, unpublished report on the benefits camels would bring the sugar industry is in the Archivo General de Indias, Seville, Sección Ultramar, leg. 148. Patrico de la Guardia was one of the first to introduce camels into Cuba. The Real Consulado's high hopes for this novelty may be found in: *Espediente sobre la solicitud de*

Don Patricio de la Guardia para que se liberte del pago de derechos algunos camellos que trata de introducir en Canarias, Real Consulado, leg. 107, no. 4461. In 1841 the San Ignacio mill in Matanzas' Yumuri district had thirty-one camels. See: *Cuadro estadístico de la siempre fiel isla de Cuba* (1846).

241. *Voto de Ramón de La Sagra sobre el trabajo esclavo en la Junta de Información,* Ministerio de Ultramar, *Extracto de las contestaciones dadas a interrogatorio sobre reglamento de trabajo de la población de color y asiática.* In: Ministerio de Ultramar, *Cuba desde 1850 a 1873* (1873), Conferencias de la Junta Informativa de Ultramar celebradas en esta capital en los años de 1866 y 1867.

242. Echegoyen, *Fabricación de azúcar,* p. 43.

243. Villa-Urrutia, *Informe presentado a la Real Junta de Fomento . . . , p.* 14.

244. Various articles were written and handbooks and conversion tables published concerning Cuban measurements, and arithmetic books of the period define and give the equivalents of measures used. Differences are frequently found in publications of the same period, however. For this reason the present work takes as its standard the equivalents appearing in internal sugarmill documents or in auctions of materials. In fixing equivalents we have used the following sources: Herrera, *Medidas Cubanas,* in *Boletín de Artes,* no. 7, 1844; Reynoso, *Ensayo sobre el cultivo de la caña de azúcar,* pp. 4–5; *Pliego de condiciones con que la Real Junta de Fomento contrata el abasto de leña para las atenciones del armamento de limpia del puerto,* Información de Antonio Escobedo al Real Consulado en 16 de mayo de 1839. See also: *Espediente formado para contratar la leña necesaria de las maquinas del camino de hierro,* Real Consulado, leg. 38, no. 1664; *Espediente formado para verificar la contrata de leña que han de consumir las máquinas del camino de hierro en el término de un año,* Real Consulado, leg. 38, no. 1688; *Espediente sobre celebrar una contrata de 2,000 cuerdas de leña para el camino de hierro,* Real Consulado, leg. 40, no. 1795.

245. Reynoso, *Ensayo sobre el cultivo de la caña de azúcar,* p. 5.

246. Dau, "Añil silvestre," *Gaceta de La Habana,* March 2, 1848, p. 2.

247. Echegoyen, *Fabricación de azúcar,* p. 42, n. 13.

248. The Guáimaro mill used fourteen furnaces. It and the Palmarito were the largest in the Trinidad area. See: Arozarena, *Informe presentado a la Junta de Gobierno del Real Consulado. . . .* For the data on La Ninfa, see: *Estado de la zafra de 1827,* Fondo Pérez Beato, leg. 16, Biblioteca Nacional.

249. *The Art of Making Sugar.*

250. *Cartilla práctica del manejo de ingenios o fincas destinadas*

a producir azúcar, p. 46; Montalvo y Castillo, *Tratado general*, p. 9.

251. Frías, *Ensayo sobre la cría de ganado en la isla de Cuba, Memorias de la Sociedad Patriótica* (1845); Bachiller y Morales, *Número y valor de los ganados de la isla de Cuba, Memorias de la Sociedad Patriótica* (1849); Sagra, *Cuba en 1860,* chapter on haciendas and cattle ranches.

252. These commercial transactions with slaves are often mentioned in harvest registers. See: *Estados de zafra del ingenio Río Abajo (1841–1856),* Archivo del Palacio Valle, Sancti-Spíritus.

253. *Espediente relativo a la comunicación del Sr. Teniente de Gobernador de Cárdenas sobre la adopción de medidas para evitar los frecuentes incendios que ocurren en los campos de aquella jurisdicción,* Real Consulado, leg. 80, no. 3266.

254. For a detailed description of the vertical grinding mills used in Cuba, see: *Exposición que D. Joseph Ricardo O'Farrill hace a la Sociedad del método observado en la Isla de Cuba, en el cultivo de la caña dulce y la elaboración de su zugo* (1793), pp. 141–143.

255. Deerr, *History of Sugar*, vol. II, P. 537. Smeaton (1724–1792) was famous for the Eddystone Light, built in 1759. For an interesting biographical note on this great transformer of the sugar industry, see: Kip Finch, *The Story of Engineering* (1960).

256. *Espediente sobre la invención por Don Esteban Boris de un trapiche de moler caña,* Real Consulado, leg. 101, no. 4279.

257. What produced the Industrial Revolution was the change from manual skill to machinery. The claim that the steam engine in the sugarmills produced an industrial revolution is false: it was a simple substitution of energy, leaving the work machine itself untouched: "The machine, which is the starting-point of the industrial revolution, supersedes the workman, who handles a single tool, by a mechanism operating with a number of similar tools, and set in motion by a single motive power, whatever the form of that power may be. Here we have the machine, but only as an elementary factor in production by machinery." (Marx, *Capital*, vol. I, p. 376.)

258. *Diario de La Habana,* June 11, 1817.

259. Oliván, *Informe a la Junta de Gobierno. . . .* For a detailed description of Oliván's horizontal grinding mill, bought from Derosne-Cail, see: *Espediente sobre la cuenta presentada por Don Martín Inchuste del importe de su trabajo impendido en la colocacion del tren del Sr. Oliván en el Ingenio San José,* Real Consulado, leg. 32, no. 1534.

260. Villa-Urrutia, *Informe presentado a la Real Junta de Fomento . . . ,* pp. 9–10.

261. Kerr, *A Practical Treatise on the Cultivation of the Sugar Cane.* Some efforts were, however, made to improve the grinding mill's yield. José Pizarro y Gardín bought from John L. Constable a four-roller, double-effect grinding mill with which he obtained a 69 percent yield in weight of juice. See: *Trapiches de cuatro cilindros de doble efecto, Memorias de la Sociedad Patriótica* (1845), p. 205. From the description, the four-roller trapiche seems to have been of the De Mornay type. See, Deerr, *History of Sugar*, vol. II, p. 545.

262. Rosillo y Alquier, *Noticia de dos ingenios y datos sobre la producción azucarera de la isla de Cuba* (1873).

263. *Espediente promovido por el Pbro. Don Joaquín de Zaya solicitando que de los fondos de esta corporación se le auxilie con 4.000 pesos para poner en ejecución su descubrimiento del movimiento perpetuo,* Real Consulado, leg. 101, no. 4285; *Espediente relativo al invento de una máquina para moler caña y aserrar madera hecho por D. Antonio Quesada,* Real Consulado, leg. 101, no. 4322.

264. *Espediente promovido por el Sr. Don José Montalvo y Castillo solicitando auxilio para la mejora de una máquina de su invención destinada a la presión de la caña de azúcar,* Real Consulado, leg. 101, no. 4313.

265. The six-roller Derosne grinding mill was in every way the same as the patent 8731 of 1840 obtained by James Robinson. For details of it see: Deerr, *History of Sugar*, vol. II, p. 544.

266. Details of the *Equipages du Père Labat*, with drawings, are in: Labat, *Nouveau voyage aux îles de l'Amérique*, vol. I, p. 224. See also drawings under "Sucre" in *La Grande Encyclopédie* (2nd edition).

267. For technical data on clarifiers at La Nueva Holanda and in Antonio Morejón's sugarmill, see Agustín Ibarra's report of July 30, 1798, in: *Espediente promovido por varios dueños de ingenios situados en tierras de Guanabacoa para que este Cuerpo manifieste a S. M. los perjuicios que les causaría el cumplimiento de la provisión del Real y Supremo Consejo de las Indias que dispone se restituyan las tierras a los naturales de Guanabacoa,* Real Consulado, leg. 92, no. 3933.

268. Richardson Porter, *Naturaleza y propiedades de la caña de azúcar. . . .*

269. "Clarifiers have already been abandoned almost universally and we have returned to our traditional kettles." (Note by Arango on p. 324 of von Humboldt's *Ensayo político*.)

270. French technicians of the period themselves recognized that their whole system of kettles was copied from the English: "We owe to the English the expeditious method of making sugar. It consists of a single reverberatory furnace which brings all the kettles to the boil." (Le Breton, *Traité sur les propriétés et les effets du sucre* [1789].)

In Casaseca, the two basic problems are brought out—technique and work. On the first, science says to the Jamaica train: " . . . you are bad servants who ruin your masters, causing them to lose a large part of the riches of their fields; because long and arduous studies, enlisting physics, chemistry, and mechanics, have made possible the construction of better trains, incomparably more profitable than yours." (Casaseca, *Diálogo de un tren jamaiquino con la ciencia, Memorias de la Sociedad Económica de Amigos del País* [1854], p. 107.)

271. *Anales de Ciencias, Agricultura, Comercio y Artes, 1828–1831.* Sagra's articles on sugar technification appear constantly through the three years of publication.

272. Cuban historians have overlooked this process, which had a decisive influence on Cuban history. For a remarkably accurate summary of the conflict between colonial sugar and native sugar, see: Lavesse, *Histoire de France contemporaine depuis la Révolution jusqu'à la paix de 1919* (1921), pp. 182 ff.

273. Casaseca, *De la necesidad de mejorar la elaboración del azúcar en la isla de Cuba y de las mejoras de que es susceptible esta fabricación* (1842). For a description of these apparatuses written in the second half of the nineteenth century, with contemporary drawings, see: Soames, *Treatise on the Manufacture of Sugar from the Sugar Cane* (1872). For a description in modern terms of the whole technological process of the nineteenth century, see Chapter 33, "Invention and Research," of Deerr's *History of Sugar.*

274. Oliván, *Informe a la Junta de Gobierno.* . . .

275. The real truth about Oliván's experiment is revealed in the anonymous pamphlet, *Algo sobre cierto discurso que cierto señor diputado a Cortes pronunció en Madrid, en la sesión del día 19 de diciembre de 1837,* by Trino Usauna. The author was undoubtedly someone well acquainted with the Real Consulado from the inside, since we have been able to confirm everything he says. See: *Espediente formado con el objeto de enagenar el tren de fabricar azúcar y el alambique traídos de Francia por el Sr. Alejandro Oliván,* Real Consulado, leg. 32, no. 1539.

276. For the results obtained by Villa-Urrutia, see his *Informe presentado a la Real Junta de Fomento, de Agricultura y Comercio de esta isla.* Economic data in: *Espediente promovido por el Sr. D. Wenceslao de Villa-Urrutia solicitando 9.000 ps. en calidad de préstamo de los fondos de la Junta para completar el tren de fabricar azúcar inventado por Sr. Derosne, que ha establecido en su ingenio Bolumbre. Trata también del informe presentado por dicho Sr. Villa-Urrutia sobre los resultados de zafra elaborada en el tren Derosne en 1843.* Technical data in: *Espediente promovido por el Dr. Don Mariano Vieta para que la Junta le compre su secreto de elaborar el azúcar con un 30% en el producto común,* Real Consulado, leg. 95, no. 4007. This file is one of the many

in the Real Consulado whose title bears no relation to its content.

277. Among other works Casaseca translated Derosne, *De la elaboración del azúcar en las colonias y de los nuevos aparatos destinados a mejorarla* (1844). For an account of Casaseca's official activity in Paris, see: *Espediente sobre comisión al Sr. Don José Luis Casaseca para acsaminar en los paises extrangeros los progresos en la elaboración del azúcar. Trata del abono de sueldo al expresado Casaseca como catedrático de Química; y sobre la traducción e impresión de la obra de Derosne y Cail,* Real Consulado, leg. 95, no. 4004.

278. Casaseca, *De la necesidad de mejorar la elaboración del azúcar.*

279. Scoffern, *The Manufacture of Sugar in the Colonies and at Home* (1849). The whole lead-acetate rumpus may be found in: *Espediente formado a consecuencia de moción del Exmo. Sr. Síndico para que se demuestre la falsedad de la noticia que han publicado los periódicos ingleses de que en los ingenios de esta Isla se emplea para la fabricación de azúcar el acetato de plomo,* Real Consulado, leg. 96, no. 4039.

In the United States, lead acetate was banned for sugar refining, and Cuba of course had to follow suit. The sole firm using it in Havana was the big Havana refinery, which belonged to a United States firm. See also: *Espediente sobre los perjuicios que se originan del uso y ejercicio en esta Isla del privilegio que se concedido para el refino del azúcar con el empleo del acetato de plomo,* Real Consulado, leg. 96, no. 4040.

280. *Espediente Arcanum del Dr. Stolle para la clarificación del guarapo de la caña de azúcar,* Real Consulado, leg. 97, no. 4067. This was published in the Havana *Gaceta* under the title: *Informe dirigido a la Real Junta de Fomento de Agricultura y Comercio de esta Isla sobre los ensayos practicados en el Ingenio San Francisco en Guanajay, con el Arcanum del Dr. Stolle de Berlin, en los trenes communes llamados jamaiquinos, por D. José Luis Casaseca, viernes 23 de septiembre de 1853.*

281. *Espediente relativo al descubrimiento hecho por el Ldo. Ramón María de Hita para la purificación de guarapo,* Real Consulado, leg. 96, no. 4037.

282. All the documentation on Melsens is in: *Espediente sobre adquisición de datos relativos al proceder de Sr. Melsens para la elaboración del azúcar,* Real Consulado, leg. 96, no. 4036. See also: Melsens, *Nuevo sistema para estracción del azúcar de la caña y de la remolacha* (1849). Despite Casaseca's pessimism, bisulphite of lime was a major step forward in sugar technology. Its initial failure in Cuba was solely due to the obsolete Jamaica trains, which permitted no technical progress. Lime bisulphite began to play the same role in mills of the period as the old *guásima* or *maguey* sap. It had remarkable molasses-whitening properties, but it did not work out in Jamaica-train boilings

because of their very high temperatures, which generally caused it to burn, though it was effective with vacuum apparatuses operating at low temperatures. A few years after this first failure it was successfully tried out at Las Cañas mill. Subsequently, this sulfitization system was used to obtain a practically white sugar without refining and with a pol. 97. The San Antonio mill, located on the Camajuaní highway near Santa Clara, became famous for its sulfitized centrifugal sugar. For a contemporary account of the correct method, see: Aenille, *Algunas ideas acerca del empleo del ácido sulfuroso y del bi-sulfito de cal en la elaboración del azúcar* (1867).

283. Dau, *Manual para la elaboración del azúcar de cañas.*

284. Arritola, *Tren de elaborar azúcar* (1871).

285. "Nor have we seen here the making of sugar without lye: our sugarmasters have not succeeded in clarifying the syrup with the perfection observable in the French train we are recommending." *Informe del Marqués de Casa Peñalver, julio 5 de 1797;* see also: *Informe de José Ricardo O'Farrill de 8 de agosto de 1798.* Both documents are in Real Consulado, leg. 92, no. 3933.

286. Pizarro y Gardín, *Folleto a los maestros de azúcar sobre la cal en el proceso de descachamiento* (n.d.); *Instrucción para el uso y administración de la cal en la elaboración del azúcar* (1847).

287. Dumont, *Guía de ingenios que trata de la caña de azúcar desde su origen. . . .*

288. Belot's calimeter was a very simple apparatus consisting of a burette or glass tube with two scales: one graduated in pounds and fractions thereof, the other in the equivalent in grams; a test tube similarly graduated in hectolitres and gallons; a centigrade thermometer, a hydrometer, and various measures for the lime. With this apparatus a sample of the juice was taken and alkalized with correctly weighed quantities of lime. The reaction was tested with blue litmus paper until the desired degree of alkalization was obtained. Since the containers used had correct scales, once the required quantity of lime was determined in this pilot test the quantity needed for all the juice was figured by a simple rule of three. Since the burette and test tube had comparative, not real, scales, once the number of gallons of juice to be limed was known this was marked on the test tube. The lime measuring apparatus also gave the total necessary equivalent of lime. Thus Belot's famous calimeter was no more than a simplified form of the old litmus-paper method. See Betancourt, *Método teórico-práctico de elaboración de azúcar de caña* (1893), pp. 36–37. The "calometer" of Allonis y Sanabría, similar to Belot's, was also used at the end of the period under study, and a little later Campi's "reactometer" came on the market. Campi was a Catalan technician, a good businessman with a sugarmill implement store on the Calle Mercaderes which he made famous and which survived until 1926.

289. *Expediente relativo al descubrimiento hecho por Don Alejandro Bauzan de una sustancia que llama cal nativa aplicable a la elaboración del azúcar,* Real Consulado, leg. 96, no. 4042; *Expediente sobre la escención de derechos de introducción a la cal de mármol,* Real Consulado, leg. 105, no. 4500.

290. The use of Brix degrees, as of many other United States measures, is clear evidence of technical penetration into our mills. The first reference to them is in: Pimienta, *Los dos primeros libros del manual práctico de la fabricación del azúcar de caña.*

291. The first mention of Baumé's hydrometer in sugar is in: Dutrone de la Couture, *Précis sur la canne et sur les moyens d'en extraire le sel essentiel . . .* (1790). Other interesting references are in: Le Breton, *Traite sur les propriétés et les effets du sucre* (1789). First Cuban mention is in Arango's report on his voyage to Jamaica with the Count de Casa-Montalvo. According to the priest Caballero, Calvo y O'Farrill had hydrometers in his chemical lab at the end of the eighteenth century. For fascinating data on the hydrometer from days of classical antiquity see: Deerr, *History of Sugar.*

292. Note by Luis Felipe LeRoy in: Estévez, *Trabajos científicos,* p. 105.

293. According to Deerr, the polarimeter's first use in the sugar industry was due to Ventzke, and its first use in the United States to McCullogh (Deerr, *History of Sugar,* vol. II, p. 588). The first reference we can find to the industrial use of Biot's polarimeter is in: Baudeimont, *Du Sucre et sa fabrication* (1841), p. 12. Despite many attempts, however, industrial use of Biot's polarimeter met with great problems since it was only designed for the special conditions of a research lab. Thanks to successive modifications, especially Mitscherlich's and Ventzke's, a much more usable instrument was obtained. Later Soleil made a more easily handled apparatus which revolutionized sugar analysis: being designed solely for this, it was called a saccharimeter. In the 1840s Duboscq perfected Soleil's saccharimeter, which from then on was sold under the name of the Soleil-Duboscq saccharimeter. This was the one brought to Cuba in 1849 by Eduardo Finlay. See: *Expediente sobre la publicación e introducción del nuevo sacarímetro de Sr. Soleil.* For a detailed study of the evolution of polarimeters and saccharimeters see: Browne, *Physical and Chemical Methods of Sugar Analysis* (1941). The first sugar enterprise to use the poliarimeter was the Grar factory in 1849–1850; it installed a special lab under M. Pesier. See Dubrunfaut, *Le Sucre dans ses rapports avec la science, l'agriculture, l'industrie, le commerce, l'économie publique et administrative* (1873), vol. II, p. 171.

294. The purged molasses was extremely rich in crystallizable sugar. In the 1850s Dubrunfaut analyzed Cuban molasses exported to France to be made into alcohol, and found this composition:

Crystallizable sugar	51.16
Non-crystallizable sugar	13.75
Salts	2.52
Water	26.00
Various organic substances	6.57
	100.00

Before distillation this molasses was filtered and clarified and yielded up to 28 percent muscovado. The sale of molasses very rich in sucrose was another gimmick by sugarmen to avoid high European duties on sugar. See Dubrunfaut, *Le Sucre dans ses rapports. . . .*

295. The re-boiling process in Jamaica trains meant submitting molasses several times to high temperatures; thus the sugar obtained was of very low quality. To differentiate the first sugar from the re-boiled, the former was called "juice" sugar and the latter "molasses" (or *conchuela*) sugar.

296. Casaseca, *Memoria sobre el rendimiento en caña y azúcar.* In: *Espediente sobre temas del Instituto de Investigación Química*, Real Consulado, leg. 95, no. 4027.

297. Ibid.

298. *Espediente sobre los auxilios que solicita el Dr. D. Eduardo Finlay para plantificar una máquina de purgar azúcar por medio del vacío*, Real Consulado, leg. 39, no. 1717.

299. The nineteenth-century sugar story in Cuba is a mournful parallel of eighteenth-century developments in the English and French Antilles. What we see in Cuba in 1860 had been thus described by Le Breton in Santo Domingo in 1789: "It's amazing how most colonists in America send muscovado to Europe, where it is refined. This spares them expensive buildings, leaves more blacks free for field jobs, and permits two or three months of uninterrupted harvesting." (Le Breton, *Traité sur les propriétés et les effets du sucre* [1789].)

300. These classifications may be seen in any issue of *La Gaceta* or *La Aurora de Matanzas*, in which quotations were published almost daily.

301. Credit & debit book, note 1, Miscelánea de Libros, no. 2646.

302. La Ninfa mill harvest register, Fondo Pérez Beato, leg. 15, Biblioteca Nacional.

303. For data on the importation and characteristics of sugar containers, see: *Espediente promovido por varios dueños de ingenios sobre la necesidad de importar envases de los Estados Unidos para los azúcares de la Isla*, Real Consulado, leg. 72, no. 2785; *Espediente sobre remediar la escasez de envases para azúcares en esta plaza, introduciendo los de Nueva Orleans*, Real Consulado, leg. 71, no. 2762.

304. *Espediente relativo a la solicitud de los Sres. Conde de Jaruco y José Guerrero para que se fije el abono de 40 libras de tara por cada envase de cedro o jobo para el azúcar*, Real Consulado, leg. 76, no. 2987.

305. The whole involved business of fixing sugar-container measurements and tares, together with its international repercussions, is in: *Espediente relativo a evitar el abuso que se está introduciendo en la Isla de usar pesas y romanas estranjeras*, Real Consulado, leg. 76, no. 3001; *Espediente relativo a las quejas del Comercio de Cádiz por el aumento de tara y valor de los envases de azúcar*, Real Consulado, leg. 75, no. 2940; *Espediente sobre establecer una marca que asegure la cabida de 10 frascos en los barriles de miel de purga y aguardiente*, Real Consulado, leg. 71, no. 2750; *Espediente sobre establecer una marca que asegure la cabida de 10 francos en los barriles de miel de purga y aguardiente*, Real Consulado, leg. 76, no. 2951; *Espediente relativo a la queja de los comerciantes de esta ciudad, los de Málaga y Santander por los perjuicios que les infiere la diferencia de la tara marcada en los envases de azúcar y el peso que realmente tienen*, Real Consulado, leg. 76, no. 2956.

What was never discussed in the Real Consulado, however, was the real defrauding of the treasury by merchants and *hacendados*. The boxes they claimed to weigh 17 arrobas net in fact weighed 22 to 25. Thus, by payments on weight considerably below the reality, the excise was bilked of at least 25 to 30 percent of the payment due it.

306. Molasses was the most valuable article imported by the thirteen colonies. We have quoted Woodrow Wilson's words: "Out of the cheap molasses of the French Islands, she [New England] made the rum which was the chief source of her wealth." After the second half of the seventeenth century, big distilleries in Massachusetts, Rhode Island, and Connecticut were turning molasses into alcohol; a small part was consumed locally and the rest went to England and Africa as currency for the slave trade. The molasses trade became so important that John Adams observed: "I know not why we should blush to confess that molasses was an essential ingredient in American independence." Long before the famous Boston Tea Party there was a violent rebellion against the Molasses Act of 1733, which Charles Beard considered a basic antecedent of independence. Especially after 1764, the colonists openly defied the English navy when it tried to stop the sugar trade with the West Indies. In 1772, 40 percent of all imports at the port of New York came from the British sugar islands. By 1785 Cuba had taken the place of the old English colonies. This also shows that free trade was a reality for Cuba many years before it was approved. For a

short, interesting study of these matters see: Taussig, *Some Notes on Sugar and Molasses.*

307. Real Consulado, leg. 76, no. 2951.

308. *Espediente sobre nombramiento de colegas en la Diputación de Matanzas. Trátase del Fomento de la Agricultura y Comercio en aquella comarca,* Real Consulado, leg. 5, no. 289.

309. *Espediente promovido por el Sr. D. José Luis Casaseca, en solicitud de alguna recompensa por el proceder que ha inventado para quitar a los aguardientes el olor a mosto,* Real Consulado, leg. 95, no. 3995.

310. Villa-Urrutia, *Informe presentado a la Real Junta de Fomento,* p. 9.

311. Sagra, *Cuba en 1860.* Converting to tons of sugar per hectare and pounds per acre, these figures read:

	Tons per hectare	Pounds per acre
All Cuban mills	1.9	1,666
Western area	1.8	1,600
Eastern area	2.4	2,090
With Jamaica trains	1.7	1,525
With vacuum pans	2.4	2,122
With Derosne vacuum pans	2.4	2,111
With Rillieux vacuum pans	2.4	2,142
With ox-powered grinding mills	2.0	1,789

The twenty-one mills with the highest yields are:

		Tons per hectare	Pounds per acre
1.	San Martín	4.6	4,071
2.	Las Cañas	4.5	3,996
3.	San Joaquín	4.2	3,707
4.	Flor de Cuba	3.8	3,370
5.	Belén	3.6	3,206
6.	Porvenir	3.5	3,038
7.	Aguica	3.3	2,871
8.	Arco Iris	3.2	2,854
9.	Vizcaya	3.1	2,731
10.	Santa Rita	3.0	2,615
11.	Luisa	3.0	2,605
12.	Jesús Nazareno	2.9	2,588
13.	Habana	2.9	2,566
14.	Santa Elena	2.9	2,535
15.	Concepción	2.9	2,515
16.	Petrona	2.8	2,492
17.	Santa Susana	2.8	2,456
18.	Asunción	2.8	2,453
19.	Santa Gertrudis	2.7	2,403
20.	Andrea	2.7	2,359
21.	Santa Lutgarda	2.6	2,319

312. Casaseca, *Memoria sobre el rendimiento en caña y azúcar.*

313. Sagra, *Cuba en 1860.*

314. Rosillo y Alquier, *Noticias de dos ingenios . . . ;* Pimienta, *Los dos primeros libros del manual práctico de la fabricación del azúcar de caña.*

315. Clerget, *Analyse des substances sacchariferes au moyen des propriétés optiques de leurs dissolutions, evaluation du rendement industriel* (1849).

316. Dubrunfaut, *Le Sucre dans ses rapports avec la science. . . .* For the normative process, see: Dureau, *De la fabrication du sucre de betterave.*

317. Sidersky, *Traité d'analyse des matières sucrées* (1890).

318. The first analysis of Cuban sugar—without industrial interest—was made by: Peligot, *Recherches sur la nature et les propriétés chimiques des sucres* (1838).

319. Delteil, *La Canne à sucre.*

320. Browne, *Physical and Chemical Methods of Sugar Analysis.*

321. Note by Arango to: von Humboldt, *Ensayo político sobre la isla de Cuba,* p. 308.

322. *Comparecencia de John Harbottle, ante el Select Committee, presidido por Lord Bentinck, en 3 de abril de 1848.* In *Seventh Report from the Select Committee on Sugar and Coffee Planting* (1848).

323. Valle family archives, Palacio del Valle, Sancti Spíritus.

324. We have descriptions of Las Cañas mill in : Sagra, *Cuba en 1860;* Rosillo y Alquier, *Noticia de dos ingenios . . . ;* Cantero, *Los ingenios.* There are also important handwritten, unpublished notes by Reynoso in his travel diary, now in the Biblioteca de la Antigua Sociedad Económica de Amigos del País.

325. Harvest and grinding records of some of these mills have been preserved in the Archivos de Julio Lobo, now part of the Biblioteca Nacional collection.

326. Re-boilings yielded 1 to 1.5 percent more sugar. Initially the centrifugal was used only for this re-boiled sugar, obtaining what was then called "molasses muscovado."

327. These prices appeared almost daily in *La Gaceta* and the *Aurora de Matanzas.*

328. *Bando de gobernación y policía de la isla de Cuba expedido por el Exmo. Sr. Gerónimo Valdés, Presidente, Gobernador y Capitán General* (1842); and appendix.

329. Wakefield, *England and America* (1834).

330. Arrate, *Llave del nuevo mundo* (1949).

331. Real Consulado, leg. 150, no. 7405.

332. Real Consulado, leg. 93, no. 3943.

333. Engels, *The Condition of the Working Class in England.*

334. Real Consulado, leg. 150, no. 7405.

335. O'Gavan, *Observaciones sobre la suerte de los negros.*

336. Letter from Anastasio Orozco y Arango to Domingo Delmonte in: Delmonte, *Centón epistolario, 1923–1926.*

337. Marx, *Capital,* vol. I., pp. 766ff.

338. *Carta de Richard Tunno a Arango y Parreño desde Baltimore en 9 de diciembre de 1805,* Fondo Pérez Beato, leg. 15, Biblioteca Nacional.

339. *Informe de Don Francisco Hernández y Don Magín Tarafa sobre el comercio de negros. La Habana, 7 de febrero de 1810.* In: *Espediente sobre prórroga de término concedida por S.M. en Real Orden de 22 de abril de 1804 para traer negros de la costa de Africa,* Real Consulado, leg. 74, no. 2836.

340. Ely, *La economía cubana entre las dos Isabeles* (1960), pp. 115ff.

341. Marx, *Capital,* vol. III, p. 569.

342. The Morillas file is one of many on this subject. See: *Espediente sobre la moción del Sr. Morillas en la Sociedad Patriótica para que el azúcar y café se elaboren por brazos libres,* Real Consulado, leg. 186, no. 8777.

343. Arango, *Obras,* vol. II, p. 333.

344. This proposal was among those discussed in the first year of the Real Consulado's life. See: *Acuerdo de la Junta de Fomento del Real Consulado de Agricultura y Comercio, en la celebrada el día miércoles 21 de diciembre* (1796). Arango repeats it in 1832; see: Arango, *Obras,* vol. II, p. 535.

345. *Ideas sobre los medios de establecer el libre comercio de Cuba y de realizar un empréstito de 20 millones de pesos.* In: Arango, *Obras,* vol. II, pp. 292–308.

346. Saco, *Carta de un cubano a un amigo suyo,* pp. 39–40.

347. Marx, *Capital,* vol. I, p. 196 n. See also the authors cited by Marx: Cairnes, *The Slave Power* (1862), p. 46; Olmsted, *A Journey in the Seaboard Slave States, with Remarks on Their Economy* (1861), p. 146.

348. Sagra, *Estudios coloniales con aplicación a la isla de Cuba,* p. 12.

349. Madán, *Llamamiento de la isla de Cuba y la nación española* (1854), p. 178.

350. *Espediente sobre querer Don Juan Agustín Ferrety y José María de la Torre introducir en esta Isla dos mil colonos,* Real Consulado, leg. 185, no. 8341.

351. Paula y Serrano, *Memoria presentada a la Real Sociedad Patriótica en el concurso de 1839.*

352. Delmonte, *Escritos de Domingo Delmonte* (1929), vol. I, p. 147.

353. *Espediente sobre la solicitud de Doña Juana Benita Ramona para que se le entregue a su hijo D. Francisco Rufino, contratado para el camino de hierro,* Real Consulado, leg. 8, no. 542.

354. Ibid.

355. *Espediente sobre la queja que al Sr. Alcalde de Bejucal dieron 23 Isleños del Camino de Hierro, sobre el mal alimento que se les da,* Real Consulado, leg. 8, no. 550; *Espediente sobre renovación de la contrata de raciones para blancos y para negros empleados en el Camino de Hierro,* Real Consulado, leg. 37, no. 1647.

356. *Espediente promovido por el Cura del Cerro cobrando los derechos de entierro de los negros que han fallecido en la obra del Camino de Hierro,* Real Consulado, leg. 39, no. 1745..

357. *Espediente sobre presentación de once isleños de los contratados para el Camino de Hierro, solicitando pasaporte para venir a esta ciudad a quejarse de los capataces a cuyo cuidado están,* Real Consulado, leg. 8, no. 528; *Espediente sobre la queja hecha por maltrato, por el Isleño Agustín Santana, trabajador del Camino de Hierro,* Real Consulado, leg. 8, no. 537; *Espediente relativo a la falta de asistencia a los enfermos del Camino de Hierro,* Real Consulado, leg. 8, no. 538; *Espediente sobre el desamparo en que se hallan los irlandeses despedidos del Camino de Hierro,* Real Consulado, leg. 8, no. 540; *Espediente sobre la inutilidad del Isleño Don Lorenzo González Matos para los trabajos del Camino de Hierro para que fue contratado en su país,* Real Consulado, leg. 8, no. 543.

358. Resolution of the Real Junta de Fomento de Agricultura y Comercio, August 30, 1844. In *Memorias de la Sociedad Económica de La Habana* (1844).

359. Luz y Caballero, *De la vida íntima* (1949), p. 192.

360. Estorch, *Apuntes para la historia sobre la administración del Marqués de la Pezuela en la Isla de Cuba* (1856).

361. Saco, *Introducción de colonos africanos en Cuba y sus inconvenientes* (1861). In: Saco, *Colección póstuma* (1881).

362. Marx, *Capital,* vol. I, p. 766.

363. *Carta de Miguel Aldama a Domingo Delmonte, desde La Habana a 9 de febrero de 1844.* In: Delmonte, *Centón epistolario. . . .*

364. Feijóo Sotomayor, *Isla de Cuba* (1853).

365. Ibid., pp. 12–18.

366. These prices prevailed throughout the 1850s, as sugarmill account books show. For example, the Dos Mercedes mill paid 16 to 20 pesos a month to free blacks and 20 to 28 to hired ones. See: *Cuentas corrientes del ingenio Dos Mercedes,* Miscelánea de Libros, no. 11341, Archivo Nacional.

367. *Circular de 7 de octubre de 1854.* In: *Gaceta de La Habana,* October 9, 1854.

368. For instance, the Galicians Manuel Romero and Pablo Vérez who were contracted for 16 pesos a month—somewhat less than the average free black's pay in the same mill. See: Miscelánea de Libros, no. 11341, Archivo Nacional.

369. Conrado y Asprer, *Cartas sobre emigración y colonias*, (1881), pp. 33 and 129.

370. Figuera, *Estudios sobre la Isla de Cuba* (1866).

371. *Bases bajo las cuales se establece en La Habana una Compañía en Comandita* (1878).

372. Saco, *La esclavitud en Cuba y la revolución de España* (1868).

373. Valiente, *Reformes dans les îles de Cuba et de Porto Rico* (1869), Chapter 24.

374. Saco, *Algunas reformas en la isla de Cuba.*

375. *Anales de la Real Junta de Fomento y de la Sociedad Patriótica* (1854), p. 383.

376. Poey, *Informe presentado al excmo. Sr. Capitán General, sobre el proyecto de colonización africana* (1862), p. 12.

377. ". . . more than half of the tobacco planters left their lands and sought jobs in sugar as overseers, administrators, etc." (Guerra y Sánchez, *Manual de historia de Cuba*, p. 196); ". . . and in view of the need for white men to elaborate sugar and for overseers to direct and manage big haciendas, young persons of this background who own no land regularly take up such positions . . ." (Acosta, *Memoria sobre la ciudad de San Felipe y Santiago de Bejucal* [1830]; in: *Los tres primeros historiadores de Cuba* [1876], vol. I, pp. 517–585.)

378. *Acuerdo del Cabildo Habanero en 8 de agosto de 1816. Espediente sobre establecer arbitrios con que costear cuatro cuadrillas destinadas a perseguir por los campos los salteadores y mal entretenidos*, Real Consulado, leg. 77, no. 3040. See also: *Espediente sobre estrañamiento de esta Ysla a los estranjeros vagos y sin ocupación conocida*, Real Consulado, leg. 77, no. 3020; *Espediente instruido para acordar medidas que eviten la inseguridad en los caminos de esta jurisdicción por los malhechores que asaltan y roban a los caminantes*, Real Consulado, leg. 78, no. 3125.

379. Saco, *Memoria sobre la vagancia en la isla de Cuba*. In: *Revista Bimestre Cubana*, March–April 1832, pp. 19–65; Reyes, *Memoria, en actas de las juntas generales de la Real Sociedad de Amigos del País* (1831).

380. Suárez Argudín, *Memoria general, o sea, resumen de las razones justificativas del proyecto de inmigración de brazos libres africanos que para la sustentación de la riqueza agrícola . . .* (1861).

381. Madán, *Llamamiento de la isla de Cuba a la nación española* (1854).

382. Machado y Gómez, *Cuba y la emancipación de sus esclavos.*

383. *Nuevo reglamento y arancel que debe gobernar en la captura de esclavos cimarrones* (1796). For later editions, with their variations, see: *Reglamento de cimarrones* (1824, 1829).

384. Arango, *Obras*, vol. I., p. 258.

385. Archivo General de Indias, section II (Cuba), leg. 2221.

386. *Espediente relativo al reclamo que hace la Junta de Sanidad de los partes mensuales de las defunciones en el Depósito de Cimarrones*, Real Consulado, leg. 79, no. 3216; *Espediente sobre subarriendo de los negros del Depósito judicial inútiles para las calzadas*, Real Consulado, leg. 42, no. 1878.

387. Zorrilla, *Recuerdos del tiempo viejo* (1880).

388. *Espediente sobre abono al contratista de colonos asiáticos del saldo de los 315 recibidos por la fragata Duke of Argile; y acerca del examen de los libros y cuentas de la contaduría*, Real Consulado, leg. 50, no. 2165.

389. *Informe sobre la importación de asiáticos para los trabajos de la agricultura de esta isla* (1851), p. 262.

390. Feijóo y Sotomayor, *Isla de Cuba.*

391. *Colección de Reales Ordenes y Disposiciones de las Autoridades Superiores de la Isla de Cuba, publicada en la Gaceta de La Habana desde el 21 de septiembre de 1854* (1857).

392. Poey, *Informe presentado al excmo. Sr. Capitán General . . . , p. 39.*

393. *Informe del Ayuntamiento de Matanzas* (1865). In *Memorias de la Sociedad Económica de Amigos del País* (1882).

394. Sagra, *Cartas de Banaguises*. In *Diario de la Marina*, June 12, 1860; republished in: Argudín y Otros, *Proyecto de Inmigración Africana* (1860), p. 144.

395. Real Consulado, leg. 150, no. 7405.

396. Delmonte, *Obras*, vol. I. pp. 133 ff.

397. Caballero, *Matrimonio entre esclavos* (1796). In: Caballero, *Escritos varios* (1956), vol. II, p. 7.

398. Suárez y Romero, *Los domingos en los ingenios*. In: *Colección de artículos de Anselmo Suárez y Romero* (1859).

399. A description of Trinidad mill is in: Cantero, *Los ingenios.*

400. Barrera y Domingo, *Reflexiones histórico físico naturales médico quirúrgicas.*

401. Chateausalins, *El Vademecum de los hacendados cubanos* (1831), p. 46.

402. Data from the notable historian-physician Dr. Jorge

Beato. For Dr. Finlay's battle against tetanus in the newly born, see: Finlay, *Carlos Finlay y la fiebre amarilla* (1942). See also: Aróstegui, *Tétanos de los recién nacidos en La Habana: Memoria presentada al III Congreso Médico Panamericano de 1901.*

403. Poey, *Informe presentado al excmo. Sr. Capitán General . . .*, p. 56.

404. The first mention of sugarmill work rhythm measured with a watch is that of Governor Luis de Las Casas at the test of La Faye's horizontal grinding mill. Later this kind of control became routine. See: *Fondo de la Real Sociedad Económica de Amigos del País*, leg. 57, no. 10, Biblioteca Nacional.

405. *Discurso del redactor sobre agricultura aplicado a la división de trabajo en los ingenios de azúcar.* In: *Memorias de la Sociedad Económica de La Habana*, no. 44, August 1, 1823.

406. The prescribed holidays, on which it was obligatory to hear mass and not to work, were popularly known as "two cross" days because of the way they were marked on calendars. They were: January 1, Circumcision of Our Lord; January 6, Epiphany, or Festival of the Three Kings; February 2, Purification, or Candlemas; March 25, Incarnation of Our Lord Jesus Christ; June 24, Nativity of Saint John Baptist; June 29, Saint Peter and Saint Paul; July 25, Apostle Santiago; August 15, Assumption of Our Lady; September 8, Nativity of the Blessed Virgin Mary; November 1, All Saints Day; December 8, Immaculate Conception of the Blessed Virgin Mary; December 25, Nativity of Our Lord Jesus Christ; December 26, Second Day of Christmas. In addition to these fixed days, there were the movable feasts: Easter Monday, Ascension, Whit Monday, Corpus Christi Thursday, Holy Thursday, Good Friday, and the local patron saint's day. The movable feasts were also "two cross" days. Arango, however, described the attitude of the vicar of San Julián de los Güines as "an abusive, unauthorized, corrupt notion that in rural communities the feast of the patron saint of the place . . . should be considered as a holiday . . ." With regard to the statutory church holidays, see: Arboleya, *Manual de la isla de Cuba* (1859), pp. 294–295. Arango's report is in: *Expediente formado para que los días de los Patronos no sean considerados en el campo como días feriados*, Real Consulado, leg. 77, no. 3028. For the *hacendados'* reaction to the observance of religious holidays, see: *Representación extendida por Don Diego Miguel de Moya y firmada por casi todos los dueños de ingenios de la jurisdicción en enero 19 de 1790*, Real Consulado, leg. 150, no. 7405.

407. Landa, *El administrador de ingenio* (1866), Chapter 7.

408. Montalvo y Castillo, *Tratado general de escuela teórico-práctica . . .*, p. 9.

409. *Bando de Gobernación y Policia de la Isla de Cuba expedido por el excmo. Sr. Don Gerónimo Valdés, Presidente, Gobernador y Capitán General* (1842); and appendix.

410. Suárez y Romero, *Ingenios*. In: *Colección de artículos de Anselmo Suárez y Romero* (1859).

411. Suárez y Romero, *El corte de caña*. In ibid.

412. *Cartilla práctica del manejo de ingenios o fincas destinadas a producir azúcar.*

413. The system is described in detail by Landa, who however explains that to get such results (blacks sleeping more than five or six hours) it was necessary "to increase the wherewithal for grinding and elaboration—machinery and trains, if need be, and hands . . ." Landa, *El administrador de ingenio*, Chapter 8.

414. *Gaceta de La Habana*, Tuesday, January 7, 1862; reprinted in *Aurora de Matanzas*.

415. Suárez y Romero, *Bohíos al atardecer*. In: *Colección de artículos de Anselmo Suárez y Romero*.

416. *Cartilla práctica del manejo de ingenios o fincas destinadas a producir azúcar.*

417. Caballero, *Escritos varios*, vol. II.

418. Jovas, *El aprendiz de Tacho de Antaño*. In: *El Ingenio*, October 1900, p. 248.

INDEX

Abolition, 60, 61, 70, 91, 106, 115, 133, 134, 138

Administration, 23, 61

Africa, 132, 140

Africans, 13, 31, 61

Agricultural implements. *See* Implements

Agriculture (*see also* Farming), 26, 89, 90

Allwood, Philip, 19, 30, 35

Animal power, 15, 25, 29, 35, 40, 82, 83, 84, 85, 99, 103, 111, 125, 192

Antilles, 15, 16, 17, 26, 27, 30, 31, 38, 69, 86, 89, 98, 100, 101, 106, 111

Arango y Parreño, Francisco de, 13, 15, 16, 19, 20, 21, 22, 23, 24, 26, 27, 28, 30, 31, 32, 33, 35, 40, 43, 44, 47, 48, 49, 50, 51, 52, 55, 57, 58, 59, 60, 61, 62, 68, 69, 71, 74, 75, 76, 81, 82, 94, 109, 119, 120, 121, 127, 131, 132, 133, 134, 138, 139–40, 142, 144, 148

Artisan(s), 16, 131, 153

Barbados, 26, 32, 82, 109

Beef (*see also* Cattle), 16, 28, 69

Blacks (*see also* Slaves), 16, 17, 19, 60, 100, 133; free city, 139; hired, 137

Bourgeois, 18, 30, 31, 40, 60

Bribery, 23, 43, 140

British. *See* English.

British Guiana, 117

Canary Islands, 52, 85

Cane, 65; Batavia, 86; Creole, 20, 30, 33, 35, 85, 86, 125; importation, 84; Otaheite, 30, 35, 39, 49, 75, 85, 86, 87, 93, 125; Sorghum, 87; -yield, 91, 93, 106

Capital, 18, 21, 25, 41, 49, 60, 61, 67, 113, 131, 132, 149; accumulated, 20, 25, 29, 69, 133; development of, 17; investment and loan, 27, 28, 113, 127, 131; lack of, 52

Capitalism, 17, 18, 23, 24, 27, 30, 33, 48, 61

Catholicism. *See* Church

Cattle (*see also* Beef), 16, 20, 24, 65; -raising, 16, 69, 100

Charles III. *See* Crown

Chemistry, 31, 32, 33, 50, 62, 112

China, 87, 125

Chinese, 112, 113, 141, 152

Christianity (*see also* Church), 140

Church (*see also* Priests), 16, 27–28, 41, 51, 52, 53, 54, 55, 56, 57, 58, 59, 60

City, 16, 59, 72, 73, 139, 140

Class, 22, 33, 48, 49, 58, 59, 60, 70; peasant, 22; producing, 27, 50; -struggle, 133

Clergymen. *See* Church

Colony, 18, 21

Colonial, -laws, *see* Law(s); society, 18; versus commercial interests, 50

Colonization, 135, 136, 137, 138

Competition, 20

Cost(s), production, 15, 29, 122, 143; transport, 73; -curve, 20

Credit(s), 27; -opened by English, 17; minimal, 26

Creole(s), 15, 17, 31, 48; -capital, 69; -children, 94; -manufacturer, 48, 50, 120; -oligarchy, 16, 17, 30; -plough, 33, 89, 91

Crown, 16, 17, 19, 22, 24, 26, 47, 49, 57, 58, 59, 60, 75

Cuban Revolution, 9–10, 11, 94

Currency, 26, 27

Danes, 19

Data, 81, 82, 124

Decree(s). *See* Laws

Deforestation. *See* Forests

Depression, 27

Development, 20, 134

Diago, Pedro, 35, 36, 40, 81, 102, 104, 124, 132

Diet. *See* Food

Dutch Treaty, 119

Dutrone de la Couture, 32, 38, 50, 61, 82, 85, 144

Echegoyen, José Ignacio, 32, 38, 74, 81, 86, 96, 127
Economic, -complex, 17, 26; -determinants, 142
Economy, plantation, 15, 98; political, 62; sugar, 9, 57, 71
Education, Jesuit College, 69; religious, 53, 54; technical, 61, 62
Engels, Frederick, 132
England, 17, 31, 32, 42, 59, 86, 101, 113
English, 15, 16, 17, 19, 25, 27, 29, 76, 91, 94, 102, 110, 132, 137
Erosion. See Soil
Europe, 21, 31, 72, 94, 106, 111; beet-sugar factories in, 109, 111; workers from, 134
Exploitation, agricultural, 25; of Negro, 18
Export(ation), 15, 16, 21, 25–26, 28, 49

Factoría, 15, 21, 22, 23, 24
Factory, 20, 30; big, 26; European, 109, 111; French, 111, 125; sugar-beet, 125, 134; -personnel, 135
Factory Act, 148
Family, 16
Farmer(s), 139; small (see also Peasantry), 131
Farming (see also Agriculture); habits, 89; planting system, 89; rational, 135; scientific, 91
Ferdinand VII (see also Crown), 60, 62
Fire(s) 53 (see also Rebellion), bagasse-shed, 39, 96, 100; canefield, 100
Firewood. See Fuel
Food, 43, 44, 100; and profit, 136; -shortages, 100; and slaves, 25, 55, 56, 69, 87, 100; and workers, 141
Forest(s), 16, 17, 20, 21, 26, 38, 41, 61, 65, 66, 67, 71, 73, 74, 75, 82, 87, 89, 93, 96, 119; reforestation, 98; reserves proposed, 76
France, 17, 28, 59, 62, 86
French, 76, 88, 101, 108, 109, 119, 123; -Revolution, 17; -sugarmasters, 31
Freemen, 140
Fuel, 96; availability of, 38–39, 49; bagasse, 32, 38, 39, 75, 85, 86, 96, 97, 98, 99, 101, 102, 125; brush, 96, 97; -consumption, 83; -problem, 98

Galicians, 137
Government, 30, 121
Grinding mill(s), 16, 23, 24, 34, 35, 36, 37, 38, 50, 71, 72, 99, 100, 101, 102, 103, 104, 106, 112, 114, 123, 125, 144, 148
Güines, 22, 23; land in, 35, 66, 71

Haiti, 16, 27, 28, 29, 31, 32, 41, 69
Haitian, Revolution, 101; -sugar, 22, 23
Havana, 15, 16, 65, 67
History, 23, 59, 76, 106, 135; Cuban, 11, 15, 23, 59, 60, 67, 69–70; economic, 81

Historians, 15, 16, 39, 81, 109, 115
Historical process, 17
Histories, 50

Ideology, 50, 60
Implements, 25, 88–89, 91, 134
Import(ation), 68, 84, 86
Industrial Revolution, 30, 31, 48, 67, 72, 101, 112; Cuba's, 83, 113
Industrialization, 134
Industry, big, 66, 141–42; distilling, 27, 122; Havana, 26; subsidiary, 119; sugar, 21, 28
Inflation, 26, 27, 41
Instruments of production, 56
Interest (loans), 29
Inventions (see also Technology), 59–60
Investment, 30; long-term, 143–44
Irish, 135, 136, 137
Italy, 28

Jamaica, 16; sugarman, 101, 103; -train, 32, 39, 98–99, 67, 74, 83, 94, 97, 106, 109, 110, 111, 113, 114, 115, 116, 117, 124, 126, 142, 144, 148, 153
Junta de Fomento, 35, 48, 49, 90, 98, 106, 111, 114, 116, 121, 122, 136, 139, 141

Labor (see also Slave and Worker), availability of, 49; cheap, 139; -code, 141; -conditions, 131; -economization, 103; -force, 17, 18, 31, 55, 88, 94, 124, 132; forced, 139; -hierarchy, 144; -market, 131, 134, 135; -shortage, 20, 60, 83, 89, 119, 133, 141; slave, 15, 16, 31, 33, 39, 40, 41, 48, 49, 60, 62, 67, 89, 91, 109, 111, 118, 123, 131, 134, 141, 144, 148, 149; surplus, 149; -system, 112, 134; wage, 111, 131, 138, 141
La Faye, 23, 32, 36, 50, 71, 101
Land, contour, 87; division of, 24; impoverishment of, 94; -occupied by sugarmill, 21; pasture, 100; price of, 25, 41; -shortage, 88; -speculation, 25; tobacco, 139 (see also Tobacco); virgin, 111, 137
Landlord class, 21, 22, 24, 25
La Ninfa, 20, 23, 36, 94, 97, 100, 111, 134, 142, 144
Las Casas, Luis de, 23, 36, 40, 43, 47, 48, 50, 52, 75, 122, 139
Latifundio, 21, 25, 95, 137
Law(s), 16, 19, 49, 60; colonial, 15, 20, 49; Factory Act, 131; fugitive slave, 52; historical, 52; land ownership, 21; military, 137; police, 139; Roman, 61; Spanish, 27, 61; sugar, 127
Laws of the Indies, 21, 27, 30, 52, 69, 74
Legal, interest rate, 49; literature, 23, 24; slave trade, 133; system, 21, 42; victory, 74
Legislation, 61, 75
Livestock (see also Cattle), 49
Loans (see also Interest), 30, 49

Lumber (*see also* Forest(s)), 22, 76

Lumpenproletariat, 82, 135, 138, 139

Luxury, 60

Machine(s) (*see also* Technology), 25, 31, 36, 95, 103, 106, 111, 113, 120, 134, 144

Machinery, 15, 100, 124–25

Machinists, 152

Manufacture(rs), 27, 59, 66

Market(s) 27, 59, 111, 126; Cuban, 117; European, 111; U.S., 26; world, 18, 31, 47, 61, 131

Marx, Karl, 18, 21, 60, 76, 79, 132, 137

Meat. *See* Beef *and* Cattle

Mechanization (*see also* Machines), 72, 83, 84, 89, 90, 96, 97, 99, 103, 107, 117, 120, 124, 127, 136, 144, 148

Medical care, 26, 152

Merchant(s), 15, 16, 26, 28–29, 47, 48, 49, 50, 73, 133; -attacked, 69, 70; -control over *hacendado,* 121; economic power of, 48; moneylending, 27, 29, 30; replaced producers, 50; Spanish, 30, 43, 44, 48, 69, 133

Mexican government, 140

Mill, John Stuart, 62

Modernization, 106, 113

Molasses, 27, 29, 32, 34, 65, 71, 73, 117, 118, 119, 121–22, 124, 125, 126

Money. *See* Currency

Montesquieu, 48

Mulatto(es), 16, 41, 59, 114, 134, 141

Muscovado, 32, 70, 82, 97, 113, 115, 117, 118, 119, 121, 122, 123, 124, 125, 126, 127

Nationalism, 48, 70

Negro (*see also* Black *and* Slave), 18, 24, 25, 27, 35, 44, 70, 142; free, 41

New York, 68, 106, 107

Oligarch(s), 17, 19, 21

Oligarchy, Cuban, 15, 16, 21, 22, 23, 24, 25, 29, 40, 42, 43, 44, 47, 48, 50, 62, 67 (*see also* Creole)

Overseer, 152

Overwork, 18

Peasant(s), 21, 22, 41, 50, 67, 131, 138, 139

Peasantry, small, 19, 22, 24, 74

Platt Amendment, 51

Political invention, 59

Population, rural, 82; slave, 27, 43

Ports. *See* Seaports

Portugal, 31

Price, curve, 27; of food, 44; of land, 25; of slaves, 16, 41–42; of sugar, 17, 27, 28, 29, 82, 127

Priest(s) (*see also* Church), 42, 52, 53, 54

Producer, 18, 48, 49, 50

Production, 15, 17, 18, 23, 25, 31, 38, 41, 67, 68, 69, 71, 73, 84, 123, 132; -capacity, 19, 20, 25; forms of, 18; -instruments, 31, 134; large-scale, 30, 40; means of, 21; methods, 18, 90; volume of, 15

Product quality, 81

Productivity, agricultural, 123

Profit, 19, 24, 28, 99, 133, 136, 139

Proletariat, 134, 135

Property, 21, 25, 74, 76, 139; of Negro, 100; -rights, 22, 61, 131

Puerto Príncipe, 68, 69, 70, 100, 122, 136–37

Railroad, 72, 73, 95, 97, 122, 135, 136, 140 (*see also* Transport); Havana, 59; influence of, 72

Raspadura, 26, 82, 118

Real Consulado, 19, 23, 27, 35, 42, 44, 47, 48, 49, 50, 51, 55, 56, 57, 62, 69, 71, 75, 87, 100, 101, 111, 117, 121, 122, 132, 135, 136, 140, 143, 148

Rebellion (*see also* Slave escapes), 137; slave, 53–54, 60, 87, 100, 106, 134, 135, 136; sugarocrat, 57; wage-worker, 136

Recession, 27

Refined sugar, 82

Refineries, 41

Refining sugar, 32

Religion, 42, 49; ineffectiveness of, 58–59; rise of structures, 69; role of, 55

Religious instruction (*see also* Education), 53, 54

Revolt (*see also* Rebellion *and* Fires), slave, 53–54

Reynoso, 91, 94, 95, 100, 113

Riccardo, 62

Road(s) (*see also* Transport), 20, 21, 40, 47, 65, 70, 71, 72; -construction, 49, 71; Havana-Güines, 22; and sugar development, 67

Rum, 27, 122

Sagra, Ramón de la, 76, 77, 89, 91, 94, 95, 100, 109, 111, 124, 125, 129, 135, 141

Science (*see also* Technology), and manufacture of sugar, 61, 125

Seaport(s), 16, 17, 20, 21, 28, 65, 73

Secularization (*see also* Church), 53

Shipyard(s), 16, 19, 74

Slave(s), 19, 20, 25, 26, 28, 31, 41, 49, 52, 53, 60, 62, 68, 70, 72, 87, 88, 89, 94, 98, 106, 120, 125, 134, 138; -accidents, 26, 101–102; -children, 143; -deaths, 55, 140, 142, 143, 148; domestic, 73; -escapes, 39, 74; -exploitation, 142; fugitive, 49, 54, 139, 140; introduced by English, 16–17; -life, 148; -prices, 16, 41, 118, 132, 134, 142, 149; as property, 101; and religion (*see also* Church), 52, 54; replaced by free workers, 74, 106; -system, 40, 68, 87, 99, 113, 123, 132; treatment of, 99, 100–101, 142; -women, 142, 143, 152

Slave dealer(s). *See* Slave traders
Slaver. *See* Slave trade
Slavery, 16, 18, 29, 31, 32, 40, 43, 60, 61, 62, 74, 91, 127, 131, 132, 134, 139, 144; anti-slavery tradition in Church, 53; Church cooperation with, 49; crisis of, 83; influence of on mill, 62; justification of, 53; sugarocrat formula for, 61; wages, 134, 135, 140; work ethic of, 56
Slave trade, 15, 16, 19, 29, 41–42, 47, 49, 50, 53, 67, 131, 132–33, 134, 136, 140; concerns created, 19; ideologists, 50; national, 19
Slave traders, 19, 27, 68, 73, 91, 114, 132, 141
Smith, Adam, 21, 62, 71
Sociedad Patriótica, 35, 47, 48, 50, 51, 61, 139
Social relations, 79
Soil (*see also* Land), 20, 22, 24, 33, 66, 67, 89; erosion, 77, 93–94; red earth, 86
Spain, 17, 30, 33, 47, 52, 59, 62, 70, 100, 132, 133, 136; and timber rights, 75
Spanish, feudal past, 33; farming habits, 89; train, 97; worker, 137
Specialization, 144
Speculation, 27, 121
Standardization, 121, 122, 125
Steam, 103, 104, 106, 111; engine, 11, 31, 32, 53, 82, 88, 97, 102, 103, 105, 107, 114, 134; applied to trapiche, 38, 72; -plough, 90, 91
Storage, 29, 73
Sugar, 24, 41, 109, 111; -boom, 16, 41, 67, 68; development of, 9, 15, 17, 20; -expansion, 20, 21, 27, 30, 47, 65, 67; internal struggle of, 115
Sugar Islands. *See* Antilles
Sugarmaster, 10, 31, 40, 61–62, 81, 85, 93, 97, 99, 114, 115, 116, 118, 125, 153
Sugarmill(s), absorbs worker 19–20; average, 71; capacity, 28, 83; growth, 66; hierarchical structure of, 149–52; internal data, 81; names, 51; owner, 152; types, 82–83
Sugarocracy, 19, 22, 23, 24, 27, 28, 30, 31, 33, 50, 51, 58, 59, 60, 62, 71, 74, 76, 114, 115, 122, 131, 134, 148
Sugarocrat, 31, 36, 39, 52, 57, 58, 59, 60, 62, 67, 68, 70, 75, 76, 87, 143, 148
Surplus value, 18, 21

Tahiti, 87
Tax(es) (*see also* Tithes), 26, 49, 122; -exemption, 83, 132
Taylorism, 41, (not mentioned by name) 144
Technical, bibliography, 32; control, 35; innovations, 39; personnel, 135; resources, 111; stagnation, 41

Technician(s), 23, 31, 32, 36, 61, 73, 88, 91, 101, 118, 123, 125, 148
Technification, 42
Technique, modern industrial, 127; production, 25, 35, 102, 109, 142
Technology, 40, 79, 82, 85, 116; character of, 18; Cuban contribution to, 108; eighteenth-century method, 38, 39; innovations in, 39, 101; as motor of capitalism, 30–31
Tithes, 56, 57, 58
Tobacco, 19, 20, 21, 23, 33, 47, 67; -growers, 24, 61, 131, 139
Trade, 17, 27, 41, 42, 67; contraband, 16
Transport, 35, 65, 122; extortion in, 121
Transportation, carts, 94, 95, 96; costs, 72; railroad, 59; sea and river, 71; streets, 72, 73; sugar, 26, 29
Travel, sugarocrat, 31, 32, 94, 106
Trapiche, 20, 22, 25, 26, 28, 36, 37, 38, 56, 65, 68, 82, 84, 86, 101

Unemployment, 122
United States, 26, 27, 28, 31, 33, 35, 61, 70, 86, 87, 91, 94, 99, 101, 115, 122, 126, 127; and Hawaii, 86; influence, 27; laborers from, 152; lumber, 76; priests from, 52; and slave trade, 133; Spanish ambassador to, 43–44; and sugar trade, 67
Usury, 29, 133

Valiente, José, 20, 23, 42, 43, 44, 52
Values, political, 60, 73

Wage, 41
War, 27; Anglo-Spanish, 16, 26; with France, 42; for Independence, 70, 76; Ten Years, 70, 85
Wood (*see also* Forests *and* Fuel), 20, 34, 49, 97, 99, 119, 120
Work, as commodity, 18; conditions, 136; process, 18; regime, 16, 18, 20, 55, 56 (*see also* Slave), 62, 148; seasonal, 25; -speed-up, 26; -stoppage, 148; -system, 135; -time, 88
Worker (*see also* Labor), as capital, 136; exploitation, 142; free, 135; -protest, 136; wage, 18, 19, 20, 21, 25, 26, 40, 41, 61, 62, 73, 91, 100, 106, 111, 112, 131, 132, 134, 135, 138, 141; women, 94, 134
Yield(s), 20, 76, 93, 112, 113, 123, 126, 127; of women slaves, 142